S P O R T S
SPEED

SECOND EDITION

George Blough Dint...
Virginia Commonwealth University
Co-Founder of National Association for Speed and Explosion

Robert D. Ward, PED
Former Strength and Conditioning Coach
of the Dallas Cowboys

Tom Tellez, MEd
Head Men's and Women's Track and Field Coach
University of Houston

With Contributions by
Dr. Barry Sears
Author of the *New York Times* Best-Seller, *The Zone*

Human Kinetics

Library of Congress Cataloging-in-Publication Data

Dintiman, George B.
     Sports speed / George Dintiman, Bob Ward, Tom Tellez. -- 2nd ed.
     p.   cm.
     Rev. ed. of: Sport speed. c1988
     Includes bibliographical references and index.
     ISBN 0-88011-607-2
     1. Physical education and training.   2. Sprinting.   3. Speed.
     I. Ward, Robert D., 1933-   . II. Tellez, Tom, 1933-   .
     III. Dintiman, George B.   Sport speed.   IV. Title.
     GV711.5.D56   1997
     613.7'07--dc21   96-47831
                                                                              CIP

ISBN: 0-88011-607-2

Copyright © 1997 by George B. Dintiman, Robert D. Ward, and Thomas Tellez
Copyright © 1998 by George B. Dintiman and Robert D. Ward

This book is a revised edition of *SportSpeed*, published in 1988 by Leisure Press.

Acquisitions Editor: Martin Barnard; **Developmental Editor:** Julie Rhoda; **Assistant Editor:** Sandra Merz Bott; **Editorial Assistant:** Jennifer Jeanne Hemphill; **Copyeditor:** Heather Stith; **Proofreader:** Sarah Wiseman; **Indexer:** Sheila Ary; **Graphic Designer and Graphic Artist:** Robert Reuther; **Photo Editor:** Boyd LaFoon; **Cover Designer:** Jack Davis; **Photographer (cover):** D. Graham/H. Armstrong Roberts; **Printer:** Versa Press

Human Kinetics books are available at special discounts for bulk purchase. Special editions or book excerpts can also be created to specification. For details, contact the Special Sales Manager at Human Kinetics.

Printed in the United States of America   10   9   8   7   6   5   4   3   2

Human Kinetics
Web site: http://www.humankinetics.com/

United States: Human Kinetics, P.O. Box 5076, Champaign, IL 61825-5076
1-800-747-4457
e-mail: humank@hkusa.com

Canada: Human Kinetics, Box 24040, Windsor, ON N8Y 4Y9
1-800-465-7301 (in Canada only)
e-mail: humank@hkcanada.com

Europe: Human Kinetics, P.O. Box IW14, Leeds LS16 6TR, United Kingdom
(44) 1132 781708
e-mail: humank@hkeurope.com

Australia: Human Kinetics, 57A Price Avenue, Lower Mitcham, South Australia 5062
(08) 277 1555
e-mail: humank@hkaustralia.com

New Zealand: Human Kinetics, P.O. Box 105-231, Auckland 1
(09) 523 3462
e-mail: humank@hknewz.com

CONTENTS

Introduction   **viii**

    Speed Versus Quickness   viii

    Speed Improvement Research   ix

    Summary   xii

Chapter 1   **ASSESSING YOUR SPEED**   **1**

    Basic Testing Program   2

    Advanced Testing Program   32

    Building Your Program   35

    Sport-Specific Speed   42

Chapter 2   **SEVEN STEPS TO IMPROVING PLAYING SPEED**   **45**

    The Seven-Step Model   45

    Training With the Seven Steps   53

    Moving on to the Next Step   54

Chapter 3   **STEP 1: BASIC TRAINING**   **55**

    General Preparation   56

    Basic Training Sports Check   57

    Organizing Your Basic Training   74

    Flexibility Principles   78

    The Cool-Down Period   83

    Summary   83

Chapter 4   **STEP 2: STRENGTH AND POWER TRAINING**   **85**

    The Purpose of the Functional Strength Program   86

    Work and Power   87

Acceleration or Mass? 88
Work Fast to Be Fast 89
Inertial Impulse 90
Olympic Lifts 91
Sample Power Output Program 97
Functional Strength Program for the Serious
    Athlete 98
Strengthening the Hamstring Muscle Group 112
Shoulder and Arm Exercises for Throwers 115
Strengthening the Knee 115

Chapter 5   **STEP 3: BALLISTICS   116**
Maintaining Equilibrium: Flow 117
Noting Performance and Skills 118
Ballistics Training 118
Escaping and Avoiding Tight Spots 120

Chapter 6   **STEP 4: PLYOMETRICS   122**
How Plyometric Training Works 122
Frequency, Volume, Intensity, Recovery,
    and Progression 128
Plyometric Exercises and Drills 131

Chapter 7   **STEP 5: SPORT LOADING   157**
Weighted Body Suits 160
Weighted Vests 160
Harnesses 164
Parachutes 165
Uphill Sprinting 167
Stadium Stairs 168
Sand Runs 168
Weighted Sleds 168
When to Use Sport Loading 169

Chapter 8 **STEP 6: SPRINTING FORM AND SPEED ENDURANCE 171**

Sprinting Speed: Stride Length × Stride Frequency 172
The Stride Cycle 174
Arm Action 175
Sharpening Your 40-Yard Dash 176
Key Sprinting Form Drills 181
Speed Endurance Training 188

Chapter 9 **STEP 7: OVERSPEED TRAINING 191**

Neuromuscular Training 191
Guidelines for Overspeed Training 192
Types of Overspeed Training 193

Chapter 10 **DESIGNING YOUR PERSONAL PROGRAM 205**

The Attack Plan for Your Sport 205
Preseason Speed Improvement 205
In-Season Speed Improvement 208

Chapter 11 **SPORTS SPEED NUTRITION 221**
—by Barry Sears

The Macronutrients 222
The Dietary Balancing Act 223
Keeping Insulin and Glucagon in the Right Zone 228
Proper Hydration for Speed Training 230
Losing and Gaining Weight 231

Appendix A *Designing Your Own Playing Speed Improvement Program* **233**

Appendix B *Your Speed Profile* **235**

Bibliography **237**

Index **241**

About the Authors **243**

This book is dedicated to the memory of Richard C. Conner (1931-1995) who walked in greatness as one of God's children. He will always be remembered as a dedicated father, husband, athlete, coach, and friend.

FOREWORD

So you want to get faster—congratulations! Speed training is one of the best things you can do to better your performance as an athlete. I've been able to improve my speed at every level—high school, college, the national and world championships, and even the Olympics. No matter what your starting point, you can always get faster with the right combination of training, determination, and hard work.

Back in high school, my fastest time in the 100 meters was 10.43. In college I started working on my strength and explosive power with Coach Tellez at the University of Houston—and my times have been dropping ever since.

In my senior year at Houston I won the U.S. 55-Meter Indoor Championships (6.15), finished second in the NCAA Indoor 55-Meter (6.17) and won the Indoor Long Jump (26 feet, 6-1/4 inches). I capped the season with a personal record (PR) in the 100 meters, winning the U.S. Championships in 9.94.

Since leaving college I've continued to train with Coach Tellez, alongside such teammates on the Santa Monica Track Club as Carl Lewis, Mike Marsh, and Michelle Finn. During this time I've lowered the 100-meter world record twice (to 9.90 in 1991 and 9.85 in 1994).

The bottom line is that the techniques outlined in this book can make you faster. Speed and quickness can give you an edge over your competition—just look at the best players in your sport! All the exercises, drills, and workouts you'll need are outlined by the experts • in *Sports Speed*, Second Edition. Good luck and good training!

Leroy Burrell
100-meter world-record holder (9.85, 1994; 9.90, 1991)
U.S. record holder, 100 meter (9.85)

ACKNOWLEDGMENTS

No individual has sufficient experience, education, native ability, and knowledge to insure the accumulation of a great fortune without the cooperation of other people. —Napoleon Hill, *Think and Grow Rich*

The authors are indebted to several individuals for their valuable assistance with the second edition of *Sports Speed*. We would like to thank Matt Williams, Dawn Crow, Carrie Proost, and Darcie Shaw from Virginia Commonwealth University, and world-class sprinters, Leroy and Michelle Burrell, Frank Rutherford and Floyd Heard who volunteered their time and energy to be photo subjects for this book.

George wishes to thank his colleagues at the Outer Banks of North Carolina—Buzz Bisset, John Harper, Gay Hopkins, Clay Richardson, and John Summers—for helping him maintain his sanity during difficult times.

Bob wishes to thank Dan Inosanto—brilliant martial artist, educator, movie actor, and friend—who laid the foundation for the application of martial arts to other sports; Dr. Reg McDaniel of Mannatech, Inc., for scientific support; Larry McBryde of Southwest Ergonomics for biomechanical consultation; Tom Weth of Polar Electro, Inc.; CIC for the equipment and materials that are moving science to the athletic field; Randy White for his unparalleled commitment to being a master in his art; Tom Landry and Tex Schramm who supported a coaching environment at the Dallas Cowboys and encouraged creative thinking; Dr. Ralph Mann for his insight and tenacity in taking sport into the 21st century; Dr. John Cooper, peerless educator and friend, for launching him on a lifelong journey toward sport analysis with practical observations and science as companions; Dr. Jim Counsilman, great sport scientist and swim coach from Indiana University, for his creative application of the sciences to sport; Bert Hill, friend and conditioning coach, for his knowledge and support over the years; and the many others who contributed to my understanding of "how to play faster" in any sport. And to Joyce Ward, he gives thanks beyond words.

In addition we owe a debt of gratitude to many people at Human Kinetics who committed themselves to the careful review, editing, and production of this book. In particular we wish to thank Martin Barnard, Julie Rhoda, Sandra Merz Bott, Jennifer Hemphill, and Bob Reuther. They provided us with valuable insight and guidance in all phases of the creation of this book, from the first written word to the last details of organization, design, illustration, and production.

Our families amply provided us with the support that all authors need. Although we have come to expect family support, we nevertheless want to take this opportunity to thank them for being there.

INTRODUCTION

To be what we are, and to become what we
are capable of becoming is the only end of life.
—Robert Louis Stevenson

The greatest concern among today's athletes in soccer, football, basketball, baseball, rugby, lacrosse, field hockey, and most other sports is how to improve playing speed—the speed of all movements, including starting, stopping, accelerating, changing the direction of the body, delivering or avoiding a blow, sprinting, and split-second decision making during sports competition. Improving your playing speed depends on a complete approach to conditioning including strength training, plyometric drills, and improving technique and form. Without adequate speed and quickness, stardom in most sports is nearly impossible.

SPEED VERSUS QUICKNESS

Speed is the measure of how fast an athlete can sprint short distances. A high maximum speed by itself does not guarantee athletic success, however. Coaches and athletes in all sports are quite aware that an individual may be capable of sprinting at 27 or more miles per hour and still lack the explosive power to accelerate rapidly, change direction rapidly, or get the entire body or a body part moving rapidly. Quickness refers to the ability of an athlete to perform specific movements in the shortest possible time. It also involves the ability of the nervous system to process and produce rapid contractions and relaxations of the muscle fibers. Fast, explosive movements of the entire body, which occur in the starting and acceleration phases of sprinting or of adjusting a body part to start a new movement or rapidly change direction, demonstrate an athlete's quickness.

Few athletes are as quick as the Dallas Cowboys' all-pro running back Emmitt Smith at reaching the line of scrimmage, accelerating downfield, and reacting to defenders with rapid, explosive changes of direction. Although Smith is very quick, he does not possess the overall speed of numerous other NFL players. During his college years, Herschel Walker of the Dallas Cowboys was a world-class sprinter. Although Walker is faster than Emmitt, he lacks quickness in reacting to defenders, changing total body and body part direction, and accelerating. Detroit Lions' running back Barry Sanders and former Dallas Cowboys' Hall of Famer Tony Dorsett are both quick and fast—a combination that is certain to result in these athletes taking their place in history as two of the greatest running backs of all time.

Although the seven-step speed training model presented in this book is designed to improve both the speed and quickness of athletes in all sports with the exact training emphasis based on the required skills in the sport or activity, this book is about more than speed and quickness. It doesn't stop at helping athletes accelerate faster and sprint faster in a vacuum or a straight line. Seldom will they ever have the luxury of doing so during competition. This book provides a complete program to improve playing speed for a specific sport. It is designed to train athletes for the specific movements and skills that must be performed at high speed in their sport. It covers all aspects of training to make athletes perform every skill and movement required during competition faster and quicker.

SPEED IMPROVEMENT RESEARCH

Through the years, coaches and athletes recognized the importance of speed and quickness but were convinced that they were "God-given" genetic qualities that no one could do anything about. As a result, speed training did not exist among team sport coaches but was relegated entirely to the track coach and those interested in sprinting events. Even among sprint coaches, emphasis was placed on the improvement of form and conditioning (wind sprint and other interval sprint training programs). The idea was to produce an athlete with upper- and lower-body movement in tune with the kinesiological principles of sprinting and then condition that athlete through the use of repeated sprints both longer and shorter than the distance of the sprinting event. At the university and professional levels, coaches recruited fast, quick athletes, rather than attempting to improve speed and quickness in athletes with superior playing skills.

As long as the United States continued to win the 100-, 200-, and 400-meter dash in the Olympic games, American training techniques went unquestioned, and the use of the old methods continued. When

Valeri Borzov won the 100-meter dash in the 1972 Olympics Games and American sprint supremacy was dethroned, the United States began to realize that there was more to speed improvement than genetics and conditioning. As early as 1963, however, we began to challenge and test (within our own fields) both the genetic theory and the two-prong approach to speed improvement involving form and muscular endurance training. We recognized that sprinting speed was increased not only by improving form (the start and mechanics of sprinting), holding maximum speed longer, and reducing the slowing effect at the end of a sprint (interval sprint training) but also by improving acceleration and taking faster and longer steps. None of the training programs in use during the 1960s had much impact on the latter two target areas, yet these were the most important.

Although the use of weight training and weightlifting seeped into organized sports programs in the United States from various hot spots around the country, Bob Hoffman, the world's foremost weight lifting coach, probably had the greatest influence on our respective work in speed improvement and in today's conditioning programs. As early as the 1960s we and others were independently testing our own conditioning and speed improvement theories. Our work during this time began to focus on analyzing the effectiveness of training the neuromuscular system. If the muscles involved in sprinting were forced to move at faster rates than ever before through methods such as overspeed training, could we permanently increase the number of steps an athlete takes per second and also improve the length of her stride? During his speed camps in the 1960s, Dr. George Dintiman towed athletes behind a motor scooter and automobile to force faster and longer steps. Dr. Dintiman began publishing his work on improving speed (Dintiman 1970; 1980; 1984), and with Bob Ward in 1988, published the first edition of *Sports Speed*.

During the late 1960s and early 1970s, Tom Tellez, then assistant track coach at UCLA, was training UCLA football players under head coach Dick Vermeil. This taking speed training to the football field was one of the early attempts to improve the speed of athletes in sports other than track and field. Since that time, Coach Tellez has become one of the world's greatest sprint coaches, training the great Carl Lewis, Leroy Burrell, Mike Marsh, Michelle Finn, and many other world-class sprinters.

In the NFL in the mid-1970s, Dr. Bob Ward joined the Dallas Cowboys program to become the first NFL strength and conditioning coach with full coaching status. Dr. Ward revolutionized the way football players were evaluated and selected and the way they concentrated on strength training, speed training, and general conditioning. Many of his special training techniques, synthesized in the seven-step model, are still followed by the majority of NFL teams.

The rest is history. Together, in this book we've refined the original seven-step model devised by Dr. Ward to provide you with a "can't miss" approach to improving your playing speed in any sport. The new seven-step model developed from the findings of researchers (highlighted in boxes throughout the text) and our experiences with thousands of athletes in different age groups, including high school, university, professional, and Olympic athletes. This model includes basic training (to improve muscle strength and endurance), functional strength and power (to improve quickness and explosive power), ballistics (to improve quickness and explosive power in specific body parts), plyometrics (to improve total body explosive power and quickness), sport loading (to improve high-speed muscular contraction), sporting speed and speed endurance (to improve sports-specific form and endurance), and overspeed training (to improve maximum sprinting speed).

The literature indicates that quickness is trained throughout the entire sprinting act when training exercises and programs are similar to the trained event in terms of range of motion, force, and pace. The drills presented in this book to improve speed of muscle contraction (initial firing to maximum firing of muscles) and acceleration, such as high knee lift drills, sprinting in-place drills, arm pumping drills, plyometrics, and overspeed training, all develop quickness for sprinting and competitive movements in most sports. The programs presented in steps 3 (ballistics), 4 (plyometrics), 5 (sport loading), 6 (form and speed endurance), and 7 (overspeed training) of the seven-step speed training model are all designed to improve both speed in covering a short distance, such as a 100-meter sprint, and quickness of muscle movements of the entire body or body parts.

Today, genetics is considered only one factor in determining one's maximum speed potential. It is also now widely accepted that athletes do not reach their potential unless they use a complete approach to playing speed improvement. Athletes and coaches in practically all sports now follow the seven-step speed training model or a variation of this approach. Speed coaches have been hired at all levels of competition, and the sports world is aware that, with the proper training, athletes can dramatically improve both speed and quickness.

SUMMARY

Speed improvement is complicated and involves an individualized approach that identifies your specific strengths and weaknesses through careful testing, identifies the factors that are critical to your sport and position, and identifies the training programs needed to improve your speed and quickness in short distances. The seven-step model takes this individualized approach in helping you reach your speed potential.

Before diving into the seven-step speed training model, this book covers some basic tests (chapter 1) to give you an idea of where you are now, so you can plan your speed improvement program. Remember, the future belongs to those who prepare. Go for it!

ASSESSING YOUR SPEED

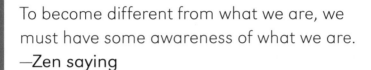

To become different from what we are, we
must have some awareness of what we are.
—Zen saying

Your first step toward getting faster is to work with a friend
or coach and test yourself in the six general areas of the Basic Testing
Program:

- Sprinting speed
- Strength
- Stride length
- Flexibility
- Explosive power and quickness
- Body composition

The test battery evaluates all phases of speed in short distances,
including quickness and explosive power (rapid, explosive movement from a stationary position and the change of direction at high
speed), acceleration, and maximum speed. Evaluating these six areas
gives you all the information needed to identify your key strengths
and weaknesses associated with speed improvement. Later in your
program you can return to this chapter and complete the Advanced
Testing Program for a more detailed analysis.

Test scores mean nothing unless you put forth your best effort on
every trial. Giving your maximum effort at all times will provide you
with meaningful scores that will be used to prepare an effecti.ve
speed improvement program based on your individual needs. The
more accurate the test scores, the easier it is to identify the key factors
that are limiting your speed. "Loafing" or "loading" (providing only
partial effort knowing you will then show more improvement on a
later test) only hurts you. The end result could be a program that

emphasizes areas where you have already reached optimum performance. Focusing on these areas, while neglecting your weaknesses, may not improve your sprinting speed. Remember, this testing program is designed solely to help you. It is your chance to receive a comprehensive, accurate assessment to help you design your personalized speed improvement program.

BASIC TESTING PROGRAM

The following sections provide a thorough explanation of the purpose, procedure, and interpretation of results for each of the six test areas.

Sprinting Speed Tests

Stationary 40-, 80-, and 120-Yard Dash

Purpose: The 120-yard dash provides information on practically all phases of sprinting speed and quickness including the start, acceleration, maximum speed (miles per hour, and feet per second), and speed endurance (sustained speed) with just one sprint.

© Ted Sonnier

Procedure: Assume a three-point football or a track stance. One timer starts the watch on your first muscular movement and stops the watch when you trip the flag draped over the finish tape at the 40-yard mark. The second timer starts the watch at the 40-yard mark and stops it when you trip the flag at the 80-yard mark. The third timer starts the watch at the 80-yard mark and stops it when you trip the flag at the 120-yard mark. It is important for you to sprint full speed for the entire 120 yards, running through each tape without slowing or changing form at the 40-, 80-, and 120-yard marks. Continue sprinting 10-yards beyond the last tape. Your coach may have an electronic timing system that allows you to test yourself.

Record the 40-yard time on the test score sheet (table 1.1) to the right of Stationary 40. Record the time elapsed from the 40-yard mark to the 80-yard mark next to Flying 40, and record the time elapsed from the 80-yard mark to the 120-yard mark to the right of 80- to 120-yard time.

What Your Stationary 120-Yard Dash Scores Mean: With only one 120-yard sprint, you already know a lot about yourself. You can now evaluate your 40-yard dash time and your speed endurance. Additional information from this 120-yard sprint will be used later to determine acceleration time and steps per second (stride rate).

• *Stationary 40-Yard Dash:* Keep in mind that everyone can improve their 40-yard dash time so, no matter what your time was, it will get better with training. The importance of this test also varies for athletes in different sports.

• *Speed Endurance:* This score compares your flying 40-yard time (40- to 80-yard dash time) to your 80- to 120-yard dash time. If both scores are the same, or almost the same, you are in excellent physical condition to sprint a short distance, such as 40 yards, repeatedly during a soccer, football, basketball, rugby, lacrosse, or field hockey game without slowing down due to fatigue. If your flying 40 time and the time elapsed from the 80-yard to the 120-yard mark (also a flying 40) differ by more than two-tenths of a second, check sporting speed/speed endurance on your test score sheet. These programs will improve your speed endurance.

TABLE 1.1

Test Score Sheet			
Test area	Score	Standard	
SPRINTING SPEED			
120-yard dash:	_____	Everyone can improve their 40-yard dash time. Specific test scores below help to identify areas of weakness and the specific training programs needed to improve these limiting factors.	
Stationary 40:	_____		
Flying 40:	_____		
80- to 120-yard time:	_____		
SPEED ENDURANCE (Difference between flying 40 and 80- to 120-yard time)	_____	No more than 0.2 second between flying 40 and 80- to 120-yard time.	
NASE repeated 40s:	__ __ __ __ __ __ __ __ __ __	No more than 0.2 second difference among the ten trials.	
STRENGTH Leg press:	_____	Multiply your body weight by 2.5. Your leg press score should be higher.	
Leg curl (right/left):	___/___	Hamstrings strength (leg curl) should be at least 80% of quadriceps strength (leg extension). Do each leg separately.	
Leg extension (right/left):	___/___		
Hamstring/quadriceps strength (leg curl divided by leg extension [right/left]):	___/___		

Weakness*	Programs in the seven-step model
___ Yes ___ No	Basic training Functional strength/power training Sporting speed/speed endurance Sport loading
___ Yes ___ No	Basic training Functional strength/power training Sporting speed/speed endurance
___ Yes ___ No	Basic training Functional strength/power training Sporting speed/speed endurance Sport loading
___ Yes ___ No	Basic training Functional strength/power training Sprint loading

*If a weakness is found, check the training programs to the right that are designed to remove the weakness. These training programs are described in detail in chapter 3.

(continued)

Test area	Score	Standard	
MUSCLE BALANCE **Hamstrings** (right/left): **Quadriceps** (right/left): **Arm curl** (right/left): **One-arm military press** (right/left): **Single leg press** (right/left):	___/___ ___/___ ___/___ ___/___ ___/___	Find your 1RM for each arm and leg for each exercise. Right and left leg scores should not differ by more than 10%.	
STRIDE Stride length:	_____	Find your range from the stride length matrix in table 1.2.	
FLEXIBILITY Sit-and-reach:	_____	Above the 75 percentile on table 1.3.	
Practical ROM tests:	_____	Successfully complete each test.	
EXPLOSIVE POWER AND QUICKNESS **Standing triple jump:**	_____	Males: Jr. H.S.: 20'+ ; Sr. H.S.: 25'+; college and older: 28'+. Females: Jr. H.S.:15'+; Sr. H.S.: 20'+; college and older: 23'+.	
Quick hands test:	_____	Males: Jr. H.S.: 47; Sr. H.S.: 60; college: 80. Females: Jr. H.S.: 33; Sr. H.S.: 42; college: 57.	
Quick feet test:	_____	Males: Jr. H.S.: 3.8 or faster; Sr. H.S.: 3.3 or faster; college: 2.8 or faster. Females: Jr. H.S.: 4.2 or faster; Sr. H.S.: 3.8 or faster; college: 3.4 or faster.	

Weakness	Programs in the seven-step model
____ Yes ____ No	Speed strength training with emphasis on the muscle group for the weaker limb
____ Yes ____ No	Plyometrics Sporting speed Overspeed training
____ Yes ____ No	Flexibility training for the hamstring muscle group
____ Yes ____ No	Increase your flexibility training with emphasis in the failed areas.
____ Yes ____ No	Plyometrics Weight training
____ Yes ____ No	Ballistics Weight training Upper body plyometrics
____ Yes ____ No	Plyometrics Weight training

(continued)

Test area	Score	Standard	
Right and left leg hops:	R: ____ L: ____ Diff: ____	2.5 and below is excellent, 2.6 to 3.0 is good; if you scored above 3.0 and/or a difference of more than 0.2 second between legs, check programs at right.	
BODY COMPOSITION Biceps: Triceps: Subscapula: Suprailiac: Total:	____ ____ ____ ____ ____	Find your percent of body fat from table 1.4. If you exceed 15% (males) or 20% (females) consult your coach or physician and follow his or her advice before beginning any weight loss attempts.	
OTHER TESTS Stride rate:	____	Use table 1.5 to find your ideal stride rate.	
Acceleration time (Stationary 40 minus flying 40):	____	No more than 0.7 second difference.	
NASE future 40:	____	This score provides an estimate of your potential for improvement. Add 0.3 second. This is approximately how fast you should eventually complete a 40-yard dash.	

Weakness	Programs in the seven-step model
___ Yes ___ No	Plyometrics Weight training
___ Yes ___ No	Consult your coach or physician; fat loss may or may not be needed depending upon your age, sport, or position.
___ Yes ___ No	Overspeed training
___ Yes ___ No	Ballistics Sprint loading Sporting speed Plyometrics

NASE Repeated 40s

The NASE (National Association of Speed and Explosion) Repeated 40s is a more sport-specific test to evaluate speed endurance for sports that require repetitions of short sprints. Your first step is to estimate the time lapse between the sprints typically required in your sport. In football, for example, there is a 25- to 30-second lapse between plays (the huddle); soccer, rugby, lacrosse; and field hockey have lapses that last 5 to 15 seconds, and basketball has lapses that last 15 to 25 seconds. The NASE test requires ten 40-yard dashes at 15-second intervals for soccer, rugby, lacrosse, and field hockey; 25 seconds for football; and 20 seconds for basketball.

Your task is to complete ten 40-yard dashes at the appropriate interval and record each score in the order they are completed on your test score sheet (table 1.1). Ideally, the best and worst time should not differ by more than 0.3 second. If a greater difference is uncovered, check the sporting speed/speed endurance program on your score sheet. These two training programs are designed to correct your speed endurance deficiency.

Strength Tests

Leg Press/Body Weight Ratio

Purpose: The object of this test is to find the maximum amount of weight you can press for one repetition. Record this amount to the right of leg press on your test score sheet.

Procedure: Adjust the seat on a Universal, Nautilus, or similar leg press station or free weight stand (squat) until knees are bent at right angles. The object is to locate your 1RM (one repetition maximum or maximum lift for one repetition) and record that lift in pounds. Divide your body weight into the total pounds lifted to find your leg strength/body weight ratio.

© Joe Cambioso

What Your Leg Strength Score Means: Your leg strength/body weight ratio indicates how easily you can get and keep your body moving at high speeds. This ratio is extremely important to speed improvement in short distances. A good ratio is 2.5:1, or a leg press score two and one-half times your body weight. If you weigh 150 pounds, for example, your leg press score should be at least 375 pounds (150 × 2.5 = 375). At college and professional levels of competition, ratios of 3:1 and 4:1 (three or four times body weight) are desirable. If your score is less than two and one-half times your body weight, check the functional strength/power training program on your test score sheet; you need to increase your leg strength.

Hamstring/Quadriceps Strength

Training for speed improvement traditionally causes a greater strength increase in the quadriceps than in the hamstring group.

Purpose: The strength of the hamstring muscle group is the weak link in sprinting and often needs to be increased. Unfortunately, the majority of athletic movements and exercises (leg press, leg extension, high knee lifts, jogging, sprinting, and numerous calisthenics) strengthen the quadriceps muscles while very few (leg curl) strengthen the hamstring muscle group. This imbalance is an important factor in limiting sprinting speed in athletes. Ideally, your leg extension (quadriceps muscle group) and leg curl (hamstring muscle group) scores should be the same. In almost every athlete at all ages, however, the quadriceps muscles (leg extension test) are much stronger than the hamstring muscles (leg curl test). The average leg curl score in 1,625 middle school and high school football players tested was less than 50 percent of the leg extension score. Such an imbalance in one or both legs is associated with injury (hamstring muscle pulls) and reduced performance in sprinting short distances.

Leg extension.

Leg curl.

A speed-strength imbalance between two opposing muscle groups such as the quadriceps (agonists) and the hamstrings (antagonists) may be a limiting factor in the development of speed. Experts also feel that the speed-strength of the hamstring muscle group is the weakest link in most athletes and should be improved to 80 to 100 percent of the speed strength of the quadriceps group. A minimum of 75 to 80 percent is recommended for the prevention of injury.

Procedure: Complete the leg extension test by sitting with your back straight while grasping both sides of a Universal Gym or Nautilus bench. Test each leg separately. Connect your right foot under the leg press pad and extend your leg. Your task is to find your 1RM (amount of weight you can extend for just one repetition). To complete the leg curl test, lie on your stomach and connect your right heel to the leg curl pad, grasp the sides of the seat or the handles with both hands, and flex your leg to your buttocks. Repeat the test with your left foot. Record the scores for both legs on your test score sheet.

What Your Hamstring and Quadriceps Strength Scores Mean:
Divide your leg extension score, in pounds, into your leg curl scores
to find the ratio for each leg separately. Example: If your right
extension score is 50 pounds and your right leg curl score is 30
pounds, your ratio is 30 divided by 50, which is 60 percent. If your left
leg extension score is 40 and your leg curl score is 20, your ratio is 20
divided by 40, which is 50 percent.

If your right and left leg curl scores are not at least 80 percent of
your leg extension scores, check the functional strength/power
training and sprint loading programs on your test score sheet. These
programs contain a wide variety of hamstring strengthening exercises specific to sprinting and will improve your hamstring strength.

Now compare the scores of your right and left legs. In the preceding example, the right leg was considerably stronger than the left in
both the quadriceps and hamstring muscle groups. To eliminate this
imbalance, you need to devote more training attention to the left leg.
Check the speed-strength training program, which is designed to
correct the imbalance, on your score sheet to the right of the test
measuring muscle balance.

Stride Length Test

Stride Length

Purpose: Finding your ideal stride length is an important part of
achieving maximum speed potential. Understriding or overstriding
may adversely affect your overall speed in short distances.

Speed can be improved by increasing stride length and
maintaining the same stride rate (steps per second).

Procedure: Place two markers 25 yards apart on a smooth dirt
surface approximately 50 yards from the starting line. (The soft dirt
surface will allow the runner's foot print to be seen. Runners reach
maximum speed prior to arriving at the 25-yard area. Stride length
is measured from the tip of the rear toe to the tip of the front toe and
recorded to the nearest inch. Record the average of two strides to the
nearest inch to the right of Stride length on your test score sheet.

What Your Stride Length Score Means: Find your ideal stride length from table 1.2 for your age group. Locate your height in inches on the vertical column. Your ideal stride length appears to the right under your age group. If your measured stride length is less than this range, check plyometrics, sporting speed, and overspeed training on your test score sheet. These training programs will increase your stride length. If your stride length is greater than this range and you are sprinting without overstriding, do not change your stride. If your score indicates that you are overstriding, the form drills in step 6 will help you achieve your most efficient stride length.

Flexibility Tests

To achieve your maximum speed potential, you must possess an adequate range of motion in the shoulders, hips, and ankles. Flexibility in these areas is affected by joint structure. Ball-and-socket joints (hip and shoulder) have the highest range of motion (ROM); the wrist is one of the least flexible joints with a ROM of 80 degrees, which is less than the 130 degrees of the knee joint. Excess muscle bulk (decreases ROM); age (decreases flexibility); gender (females are more flexible than males); connective tissue (restricts movement) such as tendons, ligaments, fascial sheaths and joint capsules; injuries; and existing scar tissue (decreases ROM) are additional factors affecting ROM.

Flexibility testing is essential to the preparation of individualized speed improvement programs based on weaknesses. Flexibility tests also reveal excessive range of motion or joint laxity that may predispose athletes to injury. Once an optimum level of flexibility is developed, athletes should focus on other training areas while maintaining this flexibility.

Because flexibility is joint-specific, a single test does not provide an accurate assessment of range of motion. It is also impractical to measure the ROM of every joint. In addition, the flexibility of some joints is not critical to sprinting speed. The tests described in the following sections can be completed easily with little equipment and provide important information on ankle flexion and extension, shoulder flexibility, and hamstring flexibility.

TABLE 1.2

Estimate of Ideal Stride Length by Age*

	STRIDE LENGTH (inches)		
Height	Males 9-16	Males 17 and older	All females
50	53-61	59-67	54-62
51	54-62	61-69	55-63
52	55-63	62-70	56-64
53	56-64	63-71	57-65
54	58-66	64-72	58-66
55	59-67	66-74	59-67
56	60-68	67-75	60-68
57	61-69	68-76	62-70
58	62-70	69-77	63-71
59	63-71	71-79	64-72
60	64-72	72-80	65-73
61	66-74	73-81	66-74
62	67-75	74-82	67-75
63	68-76	76-84	68-76
64	69-77	77-85	70-78
65	70-78	78-86	71-79
66	71-79	79-87	72-80
67	72-80	81-89	73-81
68	74-82	82-90	74-82
69	75-83	83-91	75-83
70	76-84	85-93	76-84
71	77-85	86-94	78-86
72	78-86	87-95	79-87
73	79-87	88-96	80-88
74	80-88	89-97	81-89
75	82-90	91-99	82-90
76	83-91	92-100	83-91
77	84-92	93-101	85-93
78	85-93	95-103	86-94
79	86-94	96-104	87-95
80	87-95	97-105	—
81	88-96	98-106	—
82	90-98	100-108	—
83	91-99	101-109	—
84	92-100	102-110	—

*Information from elite male and female sprinters can also help you determine your ideal stride length. Average maximum stride lengths of top male sprinters are reported as 1.14 × height (± 4 inches), 1.240 × height, and 1.265 × height. Younger male athletes (16 and under) should use the lower value of 1.14 and older athletes the 1.265 value. The average stride length of 23 female champion sprinters was 1.15 × height and 2.16 × leg length. Since exact height is easier to measure than leg length (measured from the inside of the groin to the bottom of the heel), the 1.15 measure is more commonly used. It is also important to keep in mind that stride length varies among champion sprinters and may be as long as 9 1/2 feet or more.

Sit-and-Reach

Purpose: The sit-and-reach test measures the flexibility of the lower back and the hamstring muscle group (the large group of muscles located on the back of the upper leg). An optimal level of flexibility in both areas is important in the improvement of playing speed.

© Mary T. Hall

Procedure: After warming up to elevate your body temperature (as indicated by perspiration), remove your shoes, and sit on the floor with hips, back, and head against a wall, legs fully extended, and feet contacting a sit-and-reach box. Place one hand on top of the other so the middle fingers are together. Lean forward slowly as far as possible; without bouncing, slide your hands along the measuring scale on top of the box. Your hands should reach at least slightly beyond your toes. Complete four trials and record your best score to the nearest one-fourth inch. If a sit-and-reach box is not available, you can build one by nailing a yardstick on top of a 12-inch by 12-inch square box. The yardstick extends exactly 9 inches from the front of the box where the feet are placed.

What Your Sit-and-Reach Score Means: The sit-and-reach test provides an indication of hamstring flexibility. If your score falls below the 50th percentile for your age (table 1.3), check the flexibility training programs to improve ROM on your test score sheet.

Practical ROM Tests

Purpose: You can quickly assess the range of motion in the ankle, neck, elbow and wrist, groin, trunk, hip, and shoulder in less than five minutes by self-administering the practical tests described below.

Procedure: Perform the following tests. When you have completed them, mark the space next to Practical test on the test score sheet.

- *Ankle.* Lie on your back with both legs extended and the backs of your heels flat on the floor. Point your toes downward away from shins attempting to reach a minimum of 45 degrees (halfway to the floor). Now point toes toward shins to a minimum of right angles. Compare the flexion and extension of the right and left ankles.
- *Elbow and wrist.* You should be able to hold your arms straight with palms up and little fingers higher than your thumbs.
- *Groin.* While standing on one leg, raise the other leg to the side as high as possible. You should be able to achieve a 90-degree angle between your legs.
- *Hips.* While standing, hold a yardstick or broom handle with your hands shoulder-width apart. Without losing your grasp, bend down and step over the stick (with both feet, one at a time) and then back again.
- *Neck.* Normal neck flexibility allows you to use your chin to sandwich your flattened hand against your chest.
- *Shoulders.* In a standing position, attempt to clasp your hands behind your back by reaching over the shoulder with one arm and upward from behind with the other. Repeat this procedure, reversing the arm positions.

What Your Practical ROM Test Results Mean: If you failed any of the practical tests, include stretching exercises in your warm-up routine that are designed to improve the ROM in these areas.

TABLE 1.3

Norms in Inches for Sit-and-Reach Test for Ages Five Through College

Percentile	AGE													
	5	6	7	8	9	10	11	12	13	14	15	16	17+	College
MALES														
95	12.50	13.50	13.00	13.50	13.50	13.00	13.50	13.75	14.25	15.50	16.25	16.50	17.75	17.75
75	11.50	11.50	11.00	11.50	11.50	11.00	11.50	11.50	12.00	13.00	13.50	14.25	15.75	15.50
50	10.00	10.25	10.00	10.00	10.00	10.00	10.00	10.25	10.25	11.00	12.00	12.00	13.50	13.50
25	8.75	8.75	8.75	8.75	8.75	8.00	8.25	8.25	8.00	9.00	9.50	10.00	11.00	11.50
5	6.75	6.25	6.25	6.25	4.75	4.75	5.25	4.75	4.75	6.00	5.25	4.50	6.00	7.50
FEMALES														
95	13.50	13.50	13.50	13.75	13.75	13.75	14.50	15.75	17.00	17.50	18.25	18.25	18.50	18.50
75	12.00	12.00	12.25	12.25	12.25	12.25	12.50	13.50	14.25	15.00	16.25	15.50	15.75	16.25
50	10.75	10.75	10.75	11.00	11.00	11.00	11.50	12.00	12.25	13.00	14.25	13.50	13.75	14.50
25	9.00	9.00	9.50	9.00	9.00	9.50	9.50	10.00	9.50	11.00	12.25	12.00	12.25	12.50
5	7.00	7.00	6.25	6.75	6.75	6.25	6.25	6.00	6.75	7.00	7.50	5.50	8.75	9.50

Adapted, by permission, from American Association for Health, Physical Education, Recreation, and Dance, 1980, *Health Related Physical Test Manual* (Reston, VA: AAHPERD) and R.R. Pate, 1985, *Norms for College Students: Health Related Physical Fitness Test* (Reston, VA: AAHPERD).

Explosive Power and Quickness Tests

Standing Triple Jump

Complete several standing triple jumps at slow speed until perfect form and technique are mastered. Then complete your final maximum effort jump.

© Mary T. Hall

© Mary T. Hall

Purpose: The standing triple jump provides a non-invasive technique (without resorting to muscle biopsy) to estimate your percent of fast-twitch muscle fiber in key areas. High scores are also associated with both starting acceleration in sprinting, explosive power, quickness, and speed in short distances.

Procedure: In the standing long jump position, jump forward as far as possible using a two-foot take-off, landing on only one foot before immediately jumping to the opposite foot, taking one final jump, and landing on both feet. Practice the standing triple jump test at low speeds until the technique is mastered. The movement is identical to the triple jump in track and field, except for the use of a two-foot take-off (standing broad jump). You must jump off both feet to initiate the test for successful completion. Record the best of five trials on your test score sheet.

What Your Standing Triple Jump Score Means: The standing triple jump provides an indication of your genetic potential to become a fast sprinter. Don't be discouraged if you have a low score; low scores can be improved. If you do not meet the standards on the score sheet, check plyometrics and speed strength training, the two programs designed to improve your explosive power and quickness. Some athletes may score high in this test and still not record excellent times in the sprinting tests, such as the 40-yard dash. These individuals may be very explosive and quick to change direction and accelerate to full speed without possessing the maximum speed of faster athletes.

Quick Hands

Purpose: The quick hands test provides information on the presence or absence of fast-twitch muscle fiber in the muscles involved in moving the arms and hands rapidly. The potential ability you have to use your upper extremities is indicated by this test. Even though heredity plays a major role in your ability to move quickly, proper training can improve the speed and accuracy of your upper extremity performance.

Procedure: Find a padded surface that can be hit such as a boxing bag, football dummy, martial arts or boxing focus gloves. Standing with your palms flat against the equipment and arms extended, step an inch or so closer so the length of your reach will emphasize speed and not your hitting force. Have someone time you for 20 seconds as you strike the object of the target with the palm of your hand as many times as you can. Focus on executing a firm and quick hit. The timer should count the number of strikes as well as tell you when to start and stop. Do the test twice and record the best of these two trials on the score sheet.

What Your Quick Hands Score Means: The quick hands test provides an indication of your genetic potential to become a fast player. Remember, this test shows how quickly you are able to strike your opponent. If your score is below the standard, you can improve by performing the test daily in practice.

Muscle Fiber Types

All athletes possess three types of muscle fiber in various parts of their bodies:

- **slow-twitch red (type I):** This type of muscle fiber develops force slowly, has a long twitch time, has a low power output, is fatigue-resistant (high endurance), has high aerobic capacity for energy supply, but has limited potential for rapid force development and anaerobic power.

- **fast-twitch red (type IIa):** This intermediate fiber type can contribute to both anaerobic and aerobic activity. It develops force moderately fast and has moderate twitch time, power output, fatigability, aerobic power, force development, and anaerobic power.

- **fast-twitch white (type IIb):** This fiber type develops force rapidly and has a short twitch time, a high power output, fatigability (low endurance), low aerobic power, and high anaerobic power.

Although slow-twitch fibers cannot be changed into fast-twitch fibers with training, high amounts of aerobic training may convert some fast-twitch white (type IIb) fibers to fast-twitch red (type IIa) fibers. This conversion results in more fibers being available than can contribute to aerobic performance and may hinder sprinting speed. Sprint training techniques may convert some fast-twitch red fibers to fast-twitch white fibers; this conversion aids explosive movements, such as sprinting.

Quick Feet

Purpose: The quick feet test also provides information on the presence or absence of fast-twitch muscle fiber in the muscles involved in sprinting and indicates your potential to execute fast steps (stride rate) and quick movements. Although hereditary factors such as limb length, muscle attachments, and proportion of fast-twitch fibers do place a limit on one's maximum potential, everyone can improve their speed and quickness with proper training.

Procedure: Place 20 two-foot long sticks or a 20-rung stride rope on a grass or artificial turf field. (A football field with each yard marked can also be used.) Space sticks exactly 18 inches apart for a total distance of 10 yards. Athletes should pump their arms vigorously in a sprint-arm motion and use very little knee lift while running the ten yards without touching the sticks. The timer starts the stopwatch when the athlete's foot first touches the ground between the first and

© Mary T. Hall

second stick and stops the watch when contact is first made with the ground beyond the last stick. Record the best of two trials on the score sheet.

What Your Quick Feet Time Means: Like the standing triple jump and quick hands test, the quick feet test provides an indication of your genetic potential to become a fast sprinter. Keep in mind that low scores can be improved. If you do not meet the standards on the score sheet, check plyometrics and weight training, the two programs designed to improve your explosive power and quickness.

> Speed of arm and leg movements are specific to the limb as are the type and direction of movements with the limb. Training programs to improve speed therefore must involve the muscles and specific movements of sprinting.

Right and Left Leg Hops

Purpose: Right and left leg hops provide an excellent assessment of your speed strength in each leg. They also allow you to compare the explosive power of your dominant leg and your non-dominant leg.

High scores are also associated with a higher stride length during the sprinting action.

Procedure: With a 15-yard flying start, subjects begin a one-legged hop at the starting tape and continue hopping 20 yards to the finish tape. Flags are used on start and finish tapes as in the flying 120-yard dash described previously. The test involves an all-out effort first on your dominant leg, and then on your non-dominant leg.

What Your Right and Left Leg Hops Score Means: Right and left leg hops provide an excellent assessment of your explosive power in each leg. They also allow you to compare the explosive power of your dominant and non-dominant leg so that you can focus on the less explosive limb, if necessary, to correct the imbalance. If your score fails to meet the standards shown on your test score sheet, check the plyometrics and weight training programs listed, which are designed to bring about improvement.

Comparing the speed-strength of left limbs to right limbs, agonist to antagonist, upper body to lower body, and strength to total body weight provides valuable information to the athlete who wants to improve speed by focusing upon his or her weakness areas or limiting factors.

Body Composition

Skinfold Measures

Purpose: The purpose of body composition tests is to determine whether your percent of body fat falls within an acceptable range. Excess fat and pounds restrict your speed and movement.

For optimum sprinting speed in sports competition, body fat should not exceed 10 percent for men and 15 percent for women. Useless fat weight is an added burden to be moved at high speed that slows down the athlete.

Procedure: Unless underwater weighing equipment is available in your school or setting, the most accurate and practical method of determining your percent of body fat is through the skinfold technique. Because a major portion of fat storage lies just under the skin, measurements in millimeters can be used to predict total body fat.

Body fat can be measured by determining the thickness of four skinfolds. The procedure is to grasp a fold of skin and subcutaneous fat (just under the skin) firmly with your thumb and forefinger, pulling it away and up from the underlying muscle tissue. Attach the jaws of the calipers one centimeter below the thumb and forefinger. All measurements should be taken on the right side of the body while the athlete is in a standing position. Working with a partner, practice taking each other's measurements in the four areas described until you consistently get a similar score on each attempt.

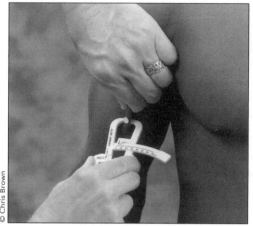

© Chris Brown

- *Triceps.* With the arm resting comfortably at the side, take a vertical fold parallel to the long axis of the arm midway between the tip of the shoulder and the tip of the elbow.

- *Biceps.* With the arm in the same position, take a vertical fold halfway between the elbow and top of the shoulder on the front of the upper arm.

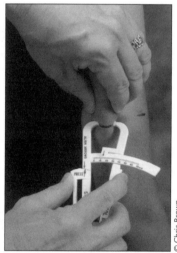

© Chris Brown

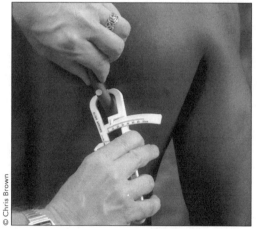

© Chris Brown

- *Subscapula.* Take a diagonal fold across the back, just below the shoulder blade.

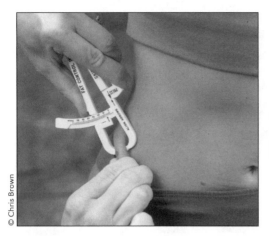

© Chris Brown

• *Suprailiac*. Take a diagonal fold following the natural line of the iliac crest, just above the hip bone.

Record the information on your score sheet to complete your evaluation. For example, Ted is a 17-year-old who weighs 185 pounds. His four skinfold measurements were 3, 4, 9, and 9 millimeters. Follow his evaluation to help you understand the procedure:

1. Total the four skinfold measures in millimeters. Ted's total would be 25 millimeters (3 + 4 + 9 + 9). Record this total on the test score sheet.

2. Find the percent of body fat based on this total from table 1.4. In this example, move down the first vertical column to 25 and over to the 17 to 29 age group for males in column two. Ted has about 10.5 percent fat. Record the percentage on the test score sheet.

3. Determine the amount of weight that the athlete should lose, if any, to improve sprinting speed. Although the ideal percent of body fat may be somewhat lower for optimum sprinting speed, reasonable values fall between 10 and 15 percent for males and 15 and 20 percent for females. Growing athletes falling within these ranges do not need to diet. Ted is already at his ideal percent of body fat.

What Your Body Composition Score Means: Ideal body fat for athletes depends upon age, sport, and position. For optimum sprinting speed, athletes should strive for the 10 to 15 percent (males) and 15 to 20 percent (females) range or lower. Although some body fat is essential to life (3 to 4 percent for men, and 10 to 12 percent for women), athletic performance (including speed and quickness) and health can be adversely affected by excess body fat.

TABLE 1.4

Fat as a Percentage of Body Weight Based on the Sum of Four Skinfolds, Age, and Sex

Skinfolds (mm)	PERCENT OF FAT, MALES (Age in years)				PERCENT OF FAT, FEMALES (Age in years)			
	17-29	30-39	40-49	50+	16-29	30-39	40-49	50+
15	4.8	—	—	—	10.5	—	—	—
20	8.1	12.2	12.2	12.6	14.1	17.0	19.8	21.4
25	10.5	14.2	15.0	15.6	16.8	19.4	22.2	24.0
30	12.9	16.2	17.7	18.6	19.5	21.8	24.5	26.6
35	14.7	17.7	19.6	20.8	21.5	23.7	26.4	28.5
40	16.4	19.2	21.4	22.9	23.4	25.5	28.2	30.3
45	17.7	20.4	23.0	24.7	25.0	26.9	29.6	31.9
50	19.0	21.5	24.6	26.5	26.5	28.2	31.0	33.4
55	20.1	22.5	25.9	27.9	27.8	29.4	32.1	34.6
60	21.2	23.5	27.1	29.2	29.1	30.6	33.2	35.7
65	22.2	24.3	28.2	30.4	30.2	31.6	34.1	36.7
70	23.1	25.1	29.3	31.6	31.2	32.5	35.0	37.7
75	24.0	25.9	30.3	32.7	32.2	33.4	35.9	38.7
80	24.8	26.6	31.2	33.8	33.1	34.3	36.7	39.6
85	25.5	27.2	32.1	34.8	34.0	35.1	37.5	40.4
90	26.2	27.8	33.0	35.8	34.8	35.8	38.3	41.2
95	26.9	28.4	33.7	36.6	35.6	36.5	39.0	41.9
100	27.6	29.0	34.4	37.4	36.4	37.2	39.7	42.6
105	28.2	29.6	35.1	38.2	37.1	37.9	40.4	43.3
110	28.8	30.1	35.8	39.0	37.8	38.6	41.0	43.9
115	29.4	30.6	36.4	39.7	38.4	39.1	41.5	44.5
120	30.0	31.1	37.0	40.4	39.0	39.6	42.0	45.1
125	30.5	31.5	37.6	41.1	39.6	40.1	42.5	45.7
130	31.0	31.9	38.2	41.8	40.2	40.6	43.0	46.2
135	31.5	32.3	38.7	42.4	40.8	41.1	43.5	46.7
140	32.0	32.7	39.2	43.0	41.3	41.6	44.0	47.2
145	32.5	33.1	39.7	43.6	41.8	42.1	44.5	47.7
150	32.9	33.5	40.2	44.1	42.3	42.6	45.0	48.2
155	33.3	33.9	40.7	44.6	42.8	43.1	45.4	48.7
160	33.7	34.3	41.2	45.1	43.3	43.6	45.8	49.2
165	34.1	34.6	41.6	45.6	43.7	44.0	46.2	49.6
170	34.5	34.8	42.0	46.1	44.1	44.4	46.6	50.0
175	34.9	—	—	—	—	44.8	47.0	50.4
180	35.3	—	—	—	—	45.2	47.4	50.8
185	35.6	—	—	—	—	45.6	47.8	51.2
190	35.9	—	—	—	—	45.9	48.2	51.6
195	—	—	—	—	—	46.2	48.5	52.0
200	—	—	—	—	—	46.5	48.8	52.4
205	—	—	—	—	—	—	49.1	52.7
210	—	—	—	—	—	—	49.4	53.0

In two-thirds of the instances, the error was within ± 3.5% of the body weight as fat for the women and ±5% for the men.

Reprinted, by permission, from J.V.G.A. Durnin and J. Womersley, 1974, "Body Fat Assessed from Total Body Density and Its Estimation from Skinfold Thickness." *British Journal of Nutrition* (Cambridge: Cambridge University Press), 32.

Dieting to lose body fat is very dangerous and is not recommended for growing athletes or anyone without careful supervision. The maximum rate of weight loss for athletes is 1 percent of body weight per week (1 to 2 pounds for those weighing 200 pounds or less). This rate requires a calorie deficit of 500 to 1,000 calories each day. Faster rates of weight loss, losing more than 5 percent of total weight, or weight loss programs exceeding four weeks may result in loss of lean muscle mass, dehydration, and overtraining and may cause changes in vitamin and mineral status that could hinder performance. A sound weight loss program requires careful supervision and a combination of caloric restriction, slow weight loss, and regular exercise, including strength training to avoid loss of lean muscle mass and add muscle weight while losing fat weight. Make sure you consult your coach and physician (and parents, if you are under 18) before beginning any weight loss program.

Information You Learn Without Testing

You now have enough information to find out two more important things about yourself: how many steps you take per second and how well you accelerate from a stationary position to full speed.

Figuring Your Stride Rate

Purpose: Figuring out your stride rate allows you to compare the number of steps you take per second with faster sprinters, even Olympic-caliber sprinters such as Michael Johnson and others who take between 4.5 and 5 steps per second. It also determines whether stride rate is an area of weakness for you that requires special attention in your training program.

Procedure: To determine how many steps you take per second while sprinting, use the Stride Rate Matrix in table 1.5. Find your stride length in inches on the vertical column. Now move your pencil to the right until you locate your flying 40-yard dash time on the horizontal column. Circle the point where these two scores intersect. This is your stride rate. Record the score on your test score sheet. You can also calculate your stride rate with some simple math from your flying 40-yard dash time and stride length: 1440 inches (40 yards) divided by stride length (in inches), divided by your flying 40-yard dash time equals stride rate (steps per second).

What Your Stride Rate Score Means: The stride rate of champion male sprinters approaches five steps per second; champion female sprinters average 4.48 steps per second. Because everyone can

TABLE 1.5

Stride Rate Matrix

FLYING 40-YARD DASH TIME

Stride length (in.)	3.6	3.7	3.8	3.9	4.0	4.1	4.2	4.3	4.4	4.5	4.6	4.7	4.8	4.9	5.0	5.1	5.2	5.3	5.4	5.5	5.6
50	8.0	7.7	7.5	7.3	7.2	7.0	6.8	6.7	6.5	6.4	6.2	6.1	6.0	5.9	5.7	5.6	5.5	5.4	5.3	5.2	5.1
51	7.8	7.6	7.4	7.2	7.0	6.8	6.7	6.5	6.4	6.2	6.1	6.0	5.8	5.7	5.6	5.5	5.4	5.3	5.2	5.1	5.0
52	7.6	7.4	7.2	7.1	6.9	6.7	6.5	6.4	6.3	6.1	6.0	5.8	5.7	5.6	5.5	5.4	5.3	5.2	5.1	5.0	4.9
53	7.5	7.3	7.1	6.9	6.7	6.6	6.4	6.3	6.1	6.0	5.9	5.7	5.6	5.5	5.4	5.3	5.2	5.1	5.0	4.9	4.8
54	7.4	7.2	7.0	6.8	6.6	6.5	6.3	6.2	6.0	5.8	5.8	5.7	5.5	5.4	5.3	5.2	5.1	5.0	4.9	4.8	4.7
55	7.2	7.0	6.9	6.7	6.6	6.4	6.2	6.0	5.9	5.7	5.7	5.6	5.5	5.3	5.2	5.1	5.0	4.9	4.8	4.7	4.6
56	7.1	6.9	6.7	6.6	6.4	6.3	6.1	6.0	5.8	5.6	5.5	5.4	5.3	5.2	5.1	5.0	4.9	4.8	4.7	4.6	4.6
57	7.0	6.8	6.6	6.5	6.3	6.1	6.0	5.9	5.7	5.5	5.4	5.3	5.2	5.1	5.1	5.0	4.9	4.8	4.7	4.6	4.5
58	6.9	6.7	6.6	6.4	6.2	6.0	5.9	5.8	5.6	5.4	5.3	5.2	5.1	5.0	5.0	4.9	4.8	4.7	4.6	4.5	4.4
59	6.8	6.7	6.5	6.3	6.1	6.0	5.8	5.7	5.6	5.4	5.3	5.2	5.1	5.0	4.9	4.8	4.7	4.6	4.5	4.4	4.4
60	6.7	6.6	6.4	6.2	6.0	5.9	5.7	5.6	5.4	5.2	5.1	5.0	4.9	4.8	4.7	4.6	4.5	4.4	4.3	4.2	4.1
61	6.6	6.5	6.3	6.1	5.9	5.7	5.6	5.5	5.3	5.3	5.1	5.0	4.9	4.8	4.7	4.6	4.5	4.4	4.3	4.2	4.1
62	6.4	6.4	6.2	6.0	5.9	5.7	5.6	5.4	5.3	5.2	5.0	4.9	4.8	4.7	4.6	4.5	4.4	4.3	4.3	4.2	4.1
63	6.3	6.3	6.2	6.0	5.9	5.7	5.5	5.3	5.2	5.1	5.0	4.9	4.8	4.7	4.6	4.5	4.4	4.3	4.2	4.1	4.0
64	6.2	6.1	6.0	5.8	5.7	5.6	5.4	5.2	5.1	5.0	4.9	4.8	4.7	4.6	4.5	4.4	4.3	4.2	4.1	4.0	4.0
65	6.2	6.1	5.9	5.8	5.6	5.5	5.3	5.2	5.0	49.	4.8	4.7	4.6	4.5	4.4	4.3	4.2	4.1	4.0	4.0	3.9
66	6.1	6.0	5.8	5.7	5.6	5.4	5.2	5.2	5.0	4.9	4.8	4.7	4.6	4.5	4.4	4.3	4.2	4.1	4.0	4.0	3.9
67	6.0	5.9	5.7	5.6	5.4	5.3	5.1	5.0	5.0	4.8	4.7	4.6	4.5	4.4	4.3	4.2	4.2	4.1	4.0	3.9	3.8
68	5.9	5.8	5.6	5.5	5.3	5.2	5.0	4.9	4.7	4.6	4.5	4.4	4.3	4.3	4.2	4.1	4.0	4.0	3.9	3.7	3.8
69	5.8	5.7	5.5	5.4	5.3	5.1	5.0	4.9	4.8	4.6	4.5	4.4	4.3	4.3	4.2	4.1	4.0	3.9	3.9	3.8	3.7
70	5.7	5.6	5.4	5.3	5.1	5.0	4.9	4.8	4.7	4.6	4.5	4.3	4.3	4.2	4.1	4.0	4.0	3.9	3.8	3.7	3.7
71	5.6	5.5	5.3	5.2	5.1	5.0	4.8	4.7	4.6	4.5	4.4	4.3	4.2	4.1	4.1	4.0	3.9	3.8	3.8	3.7	3.6
72	5.6	5.4	5.3	5.1	5.0	4.9	4.8	4.7	4.6	4.4	4.3	4.3	4.2	4.1	4.0	3.9	3.8	3.8	3.7	3.6	3.5
73	5.5	5.3	5.2	5.1	4.9	4.8	4.7	4.6	4.5	4.4	4.3	4.2	4.1	4.0	4.0	3.9	3.8	3.7	3.6	3.6	3.5
74	5.4	5.3	5.1	5.0	4.9	4.8	4.6	4.5	4.4	4.3	4.2	4.1	4.0	4.0	3.9	3.8	3.7	3.6	3.5	3.5	3.4
75	5.3	5.2	5.1	4.9	4.8	4.7	4.6	4.5	4.4	4.3	4.2	4.1	4.0	3.9	3.8	3.8	3.7	3.6	3.5	3.4	3.4

76	5.3	5.1	5.0	4.9	4.7	4.6	4.5	4.4	4.3	4.2	4.1	4.0	3.9	3.8	3.8	3.7	3.6	3.6	3.5	3.4	3.3
77	5.2	5.0	4.9	4.8	4.7	4.6	4.5	4.4	4.3	4.2	4.1	4.0	3.9	3.8	3.8	3.7	3.6	3.5	3.4	3.4	3.3
78	5.1	5.0	4.9	4.7	4.6	4.5	4.4	4.3	4.2	4.1	4.0	3.9	3.8	3.8	3.7	3.5	3.5	3.4	3.4	3.4	3.3
79	5.1	4.9	4.8	4.7	4.6	4.5	4.3	4.2	4.1	4.0	3.9	3.8	3.8	3.7	3.6	3.6	3.5	3.5	3.4	3.3	3.2
80	5.0	4.9	4.8	4.6	4.5	4.4	4.3	4.2	4.1	4.0	3.9	3.8	3.8	3.7	3.6	3.6	3.5	3.4	3.3	3.3	3.2
81	5.0	4.8	4.7	4.6	4.4	4.3	4.2	4.1	4.0	4.0	3.9	3.8	3.7	3.6	3.6	3.5	3.5	3.3	3.3	3.2	3.2
82	4.9	4.8	4.6	4.5	4.4	4.3	4.2	4.1	4.0	3.9	3.9	3.8	3.7	3.6	3.5	3.5	3.4	3.3	3.3	3.2	3.1
83	4.8	4.7	4.6	4.5	4.4	4.2	4.1	4.0	4.0	3.9	3.8	3.7	3.6	3.6	3.5	3.4	3.4	3.3	3.2	3.1	3.0
84	4.8	4.7	4.5	4.4	4.3	4.2	4.1	4.0	3.9	3.9	3.8	3.7	3.6	3.5	3.4	3.4	3.3	3.2	3.2	3.1	3.0
85	4.7	4.6	4.5	4.3	4.3	4.1	4.0	4.0	3.9	3.8	3.7	3.6	3.6	3.5	3.4	3.3	3.3	3.2	3.2	3.1	3.0
86	4.7	4.6	4.4	4.3	4.2	4.1	4.0	3.9	3.9	3.8	3.7	3.6	3.5	3.4	3.4	3.3	3.2	3.2	3.1	3.0	2.9
87	4.7	4.5	4.4	4.2	4.1	4.0	3.9	3.9	3.8	3.7	3.6	3.6	3.5	3.4	3.3	3.3	3.2	3.1	3.1	3.0	2.9
88	4.6	4.5	4.3	4.2	4.1	4.0	3.9	3.8	3.8	3.6	3.6	3.5	3.4	3.4	3.3	3.2	3.2	3.1	3.0	3.0	2.8
89	4.5	4.4	4.3	4.2	4.0	4.0	3.8	3.8	3.7	3.6	3.5	3.5	3.4	3.3	3.3	3.2	3.1	3.1	3.0	2.9	2.8
90	4.4	4.4	4.2	4.1	4.0	3.9	3.8	3.7	3.7	3.5	3.5	3.4	3.3	3.3	3.2	3.1	3.1	3.0	3.0	2.9	2.8
91	4.4	4.3	4.2	4.1	4.0	3.9	3.7	3.7	3.6	3.6	3.5	3.4	3.3	3.3	3.2	3.1	3.1	3.0	2.9	2.9	2.8
92	4.4	4.3	4.1	4.0	3.9	3.8	3.7	3.6	3.6	3.5	3.4	3.4	3.3	3.2	3.1	3.1	3.0	3.0	2.9	2.9	2.8
93	4.3	4.2	4.1	4.0	3.9	3.8	3.7	3.6	3.5	3.5	3.4	3.3	3.2	3.2	3.1	3.0	3.0	3.0	2.9	2.8	2.8
94	4.3	4.1	4.0	4.0	3.8	3.7	3.6	3.6	3.5	3.4	3.4	3.3	3.2	3.2	3.1	3.0	3.0	2.9	2.9	2.8	2.7
95	4.2	4.1	4.0	3.9	3.8	3.7	3.6	3.5	3.5	3.4	3.3	3.3	3.2	3.1	3.0	3.0	2.9	2.9	2.8	2.7	2.7
96	4.2	4.1	4.0	3.9	3.8	3.7	3.6	3.5	3.4	3.4	3.3	3.2	3.1	3.1	3.0	3.0	2.9	2.8	2.8	2.7	2.6
97	4.1	4.0	3.9	3.8	3.7	3.7	3.5	3.5	3.4	3.3	3.3	3.2	3.1	3.1	3.0	2.9	2.9	2.8	2.8	2.7	2.7
98	4.1	4.0	3.9	3.8	3.6	3.6	3.5	3.4	3.4	3.3	3.2	3.1	3.1	3.0	3.0	2.9	2.9	2.8	2.7	2.6	2.6
99	4.0	3.9	3.8	3.7	3.6	3.6	3.5	3.4	3.3	3.3	3.2	3.1	3.1	3.0	2.9	2.9	2.8	2.8	2.7	2.6	2.6
100	4.0	3.9	3.8	3.7	3.6	3.5	3.4	3.3	3.3	3.2	3.2	3.1	3.0	3.0	2.9	2.8	2.8	2.8	2.7	2.6	2.6
101	4.0	3.9	3.8	3.7	3.6	3.5	3.4	3.3	3.3	3.2	3.1	3.1	3.0	2.9	2.9	2.8	2.8	2.7	2.7	2.6	2.6
102	3.9	3.9	3.7	3.7	3.5	3.4	3.3	3.2	3.2	3.1	3.1	3.0	3.0	2.9	2.9	2.8	2.8	2.7	2.6	2.5	2.5
103	3.9	3.8	3.7	3.6	3.5	3.4	3.3	3.2	3.2	3.1	3.1	3.0	2.9	2.9	2.8	2.7	2.7	2.6	2.6	2.5	2.4
104	3.9	3.7	3.6	3.6	3.5	3.4	3.3	3.2	3.2	3.1	3.0	3.0	2.9	2.9	2.8	2.7	2.6	2.6	2.6	2.5	2.4
105	3.8	3.7	3.6	3.5	3.4	3.3	3.2	3.1	3.1	3.0	3.0	2.9	2.8	2.8	2.7	2.6	2.6	2.6	2.5	2.5	2.4
106	3.8	3.6	3.6	3.5	3.4	3.3	3.2	3.1	3.1	2.9	2.9	2.9	2.8	2.7	2.7	2.6	2.6	2.5	2.5	2.5	2.4
107	3.7	3.6	3.5	3.4	3.3	3.2	3.1	3.1	3.0	2.9	2.9	2.8	2.8	2.7	2.7	2.6	2.6	2.5	2.5	2.4	2.4
108	3.7	3.6	3.5	3.3	3.2	3.1	3.0	3.0	3.0	2.8	2.8	2.7	2.7	2.6	2.6	2.6	2.5	2.5	2.5	2.4	2.3

benefit from improved stride rate, check overspeed training on your test score sheet, regardless of your score. This training program will improve your stride rate.

Accessing Your Acceleration

Purpose: Your acceleration scores help interpret your 40-yard dash time as well as predict how much you should improve.

Procedure: Subtract your flying 40-yard time from your stationary 40-yard time and record the score to the right of Acceleration on your test score sheet.

What Your Acceleration Score Means: The difference between your stationary 40-yard dash and your flying 40-yard dash is the time delay required to accelerate. If there is more than a 0.7 second difference between these two scores, check ballistics, plyometrics, sprint loading, and sporting speed on your test score sheet. These training programs will improve your acceleration time. A quick method of finding out how fast you should already be sprinting a 40-yard dash is to add 0.7 seconds to your flying 40-yard dash time. For example, if your stationary 40 is 4.9 and your flying 40 is 4.0, you should be sprinting the stationary 40 in 4.7 (flying 40 of 4.0 plus 0.7 equals 4.7), not 4.9. The 0.2-second difference is probably due to faulty starting techniques. Chapter 8 gives you numerous tips to correct these problems.

ADVANCED TESTING PROGRAM

The advanced testing program is designed for athletes competing at the high school, college, and professional levels. The program requires more specialized equipment and coaches who are familiar with these procedures.

NASE Future 40

Purpose: NASE has developed a test to predict your speed potential. This test helps estimate just how much you can improve.

Procedure: Have your coach or friend test you in the 40-yard dash from a stationary start using surgical tubing to tow you as fast as possible. Connect your belt securely around the waist with the other belt attached to a partner. With your partner standing 10 feet before the finish line, back up and stretch the tubing exactly 30 yards until you reach the starting line and assume your three-point or track stance. The timer stands at the finish line, starts his watch on your first muscular movement, and stops it when you cross the finish line. After you sprint only five yards, your partner sprints as fast as possible away from you to give you additional pull throughout the test. Record your score to the right of the NASE Future 40 on your test score sheet.

What Your NASE Future 40 Time Means: Your time in this test plus 0.3 to 0.4 of a second provides an estimate of what you will be capable of after several months of training using the seven-step model for speed improvement.

Muscle Balance

Purpose: The prime movers in sprinting (knee extensors, hip extensors, and ankle plantar flexors) tend to become well-developed as a result of normal sprint training. Muscle balance testing to compare the strength of opposing muscle groups is important to prevent injury and guarantee maximum speed of muscle contraction and relaxation. Muscle imbalances can slow you down. This test can easily be completed by you and a partner or by you and your coach or trainer.

Procedure: 1RM testing (maximum amount of weight with which you can execute just one repetition) allows quick, easy comparison of the strength of your left and right limbs (upper and lower body) using the one-arm curl (biceps), one-arm military press (triceps), and the one-leg press (quadriceps). For each test, select a weight that you can lift comfortably. Add weight in subsequent trials until you find the weight that you can lift correctly just one time (1RM). Three trials with a three-minute recovery period between each trial are needed to find the true 1RM.

• *One-arm barbell curl (biceps):* Using the underhand grip in a standing position, raise the barbell from thighs to chest level and return it keeping the body erect and motionless throughout the movement. Record your 1RM.

• *One-arm military press (triceps):* Using the overhand grip in a standing position, raise the dumbbell or barbell from the shoulder to an overhead position until the elbow is locked. Record your 1RM.

Table 1.6 lists some reported values for joint agonist-antagonist ratios at slow isokinetic speeds. Your coach or trainer can test you in any of these areas where an imbalance is suspected. Your task is to find the 1RM for both movements and compare your ratio to those on the chart. Due to differences in muscle mass, you can expect some disparity (no more than 10 percent) between muscle groups such as the quadriceps and hamstrings and the plantar flexors and the dorsiflexors.

TABLE 1.6

Agonist-Antagonist Ratios for Slow Concentric Isokinetic Movements

Joint	Muscles	Desirable torque ratio at slow speed
Ankle	Plantar flexion/dorsiflexion (gastrocnemius, soleus, tibialis anterior)	3:1
Ankle	Inversion/eversion (tibialis anterial peroneals)	1:1
Knee	Extension/flexion (quadriceps/hamstrings)	3:2
Hip	Extension/flexion (spinal erectors, gluteus maximus, hamstrings/iliopsoas, rectus abdominus, tensor fascia latae)	1:1
Shoulder	Flexion/extension (anterior deltoids/trapezius, posterior deltoids)	2:3
Shoulder	Internal rotation/external rotation (subscapularis/ supraspinatus, infraspinatus, teres minor)	3:2
Elbow	Flexion/extension (biceps/triceps)	1:1
Lumbar spine	Flexion/extension (psoas, abdominals/spinal erectors)	

Note: The values expressed are a summary of numerous studies of slow-speed concentric isokinetic movements.
Reprinted, by permission, from D. Wathen, 1994, Muscle Balance. In *Essentials of Strength Training and Conditioning*, edited by T. Baechle (Champaign, IL: Human Kinetics), 425.

What Your Muscle Balance Scores Mean: In general, the further the joint agonist-antagonist muscle balance ratio is from 1:1, the more you need to be concerned. A hamstring/quadriceps ratio of 1:2 or a plantar flexion/dorsiflexion ratio of 4:1 is an indication of a speed-strength weakness that could be limiting your sprint speed. Specific weight training exercises and the proper prescription of sets, repetitions, weight, and recovery intervals can improve the ratio.

Other Tests

Strength Curve Testing. Dr. Stan Plagenhoef has developed testing procedures to measure changes in leverage and muscle mass as a limb is moved through a range of motion. Anatomical strength curves reflect the body's ability to produce muscle contractile force at given points in the range of motion. These strength curves are used to determine how far above or below the strength potential an individual falls. Data collected on Olympic sprinters such as Carl Lewis, Leroy Burrel, Chris Jones, and Lamont Smith allow valuable comparisons to athletes in other sports who are striving to improve their sprinting speed. Strength curves can also be used to compare the right and left sides of the body (dominant to non-dominant side).

On-Field Analysis (Playing Speed). For sprinting analysis, this sophisticated system uses an Olympic champion sprinter as a basis for creating a digital athletic model of performance. Performances are recorded in the computer with values assigned to points of movement. The performance of an athlete is recorded into the computer and compared to the database of the Olympic Champion Digital Model. The result is graphically displayed through differences in performance characteristics such as leg lift, arm swing, stride length, and leg extension.

Digitized analysis is also used for on-field performance to provide a complete analysis during competitive play. Coaches who are interested in the On-Field Analysis System should contact Dr. Bob Ward at 11502 Valleydale Drive, Dallas, Texas, 75230.

BUILDING YOUR PROGRAM

You now have enough information to design a speed improvement program just for you. For each test, check Yes in the Weakness column on your test score sheet if you failed to meet the standard specified. If you check Yes for a test, also check the programs listed in the far right column for that test. These are the specific training programs you need to follow to eliminate the weakness areas. These programs and the seven-step model for speed improvement are described in detail in chapters 2 through 7. Sample workouts are also shown to help you organize your training schedule. Study the following example to see exactly how the plan works.

EXAMPLE:

Ted Shanahan, age 17, is a 6'2" 185-pound inside center on the soccer team. His test scores were:

Test area	Score	Standard	
SPRINTING SPEED			
120-yard dash:	*13.3*	Everyone can improve their 40-yard dash time. Specific test scores below help to identify areas of weakness and the specific training programs needed to improve these limiting factors.	
Stationary 40:	*4.9*		
Flying 40:	*4.0*		
80- to 120-yard time:	*4.4*		
SPEED ENDURANCE (Difference between flying 40 and 80- to 120-yard time):	*0.4*	No more than 0.2 second between flying 40 and 80- to 120-yard time.	
NASE repeated 40s:	*4.9 4.9* *5.0 5.1* *5.0 5.3* *5.1 5.2* *5.3 5.2*	No more than 0.2 second difference among the ten trials.	
STRENGTH Leg press:	*400 lbs.*	Multiply your body weight by 2.5. Your leg press score should be higher.	
Leg curl (right/left):	*95/90*	Hamstring strength (leg curl) should be at least 80% of quadriceps strength (leg extension). Do each leg separately.	
Leg extension (right/left):	*180/180*		
Hamstring/quadriceps strength (leg curl divided by leg extension [right/left]):	*52/50%*		

Weakness*	Programs in the seven-step model/comments
	Good, can be improved.
	Good, can be improved.
✔ Yes ___ No	Poor; difference of 0.4 second between two 40-yard areas suggests poor speed endurance. Athlete is slowing down too much due to fatigue. Can be improved through sprint loading (step 5) and speed endurance training (step 6).
✔ Yes ___ No	A drop-off of 0.4 second (5.3 minus 4.9) also suggests the need for speed endurance training.
✔ Yes ___ No	Poor, less than 2.5 times body weight of 185 pounds. Minimum score should be 463 pounds.
✔ Yes ___ No	Poor, right hamstring strength is only 52% of right quadriceps strength. Right leg curl should be improved to 142 lbs. Left hamstring strength is only 50% of left quadriceps strength. Left leg curl should be improved to 135 lbs. (90% of quadriceps strength.) Can be improved through basic training (step 1) and functional strength/power training (step 2) and sport loading (step 5).

*If a weakness is found, check the training programs to the right that are designed to remove the weakness. These training programs are described in detail in chapter 3.

(continued)

Test area	Score	Standard	
MUSCLE BALANCE Hamstrings (right/left): Quadriceps (right/left): Arm curl (right/left): **One-arm military press** (right/left): Single leg press (right/left):	_95/90_ _180/180_ _80/78_ _130/125_ _200/198_	Find your 1RM for each arm and leg for each exercise. Right and left leg scores should not differ by more than 10%.	
STRIDE Stride length:	_80 in._	Find your range from the stride length matrix in table 1.2.	
FLEXIBILITY Sit-and-reach:	_17_	Above the 75 percentile on table 1.3.	
Practical ROM tests:	_Pass_	Successfully complete each test.	
EXPLOSIVE POWER AND QUICKNESS Standing triple jump:	_26'2"_	Males: Jr. H.S.: 20'+ ; Sr. H.S.: 25'+; college and older: 28'+. Females: Jr. H.S.:15'+; Sr. H.S.: 20'+; college and older: 23'+.	
Quick hands test:	_52_	Males: Jr. H.S.: 47; Sr. H.S.: 60; college: 80. Females: Jr. H.S.: 33; Sr. H.S.: 42; college: 57.	
Quick feet test:	_2.8_	Males: Jr. H.S.: 3.8 or faster; Sr. H.S.: 3.3 or faster; college: 2.8 or faster. Females: Jr. H.S.: 4.2 or faster; Sr. H.S.: 3.8 or faster; college: 3.4 or faster.	

Weakness	Programs in the seven-step model
✓ Yes / No Yes / ✓ No Yes / ✓ No Yes / ✓ No Yes / ✓ No	*Good. Strength scores of right and left hamstring muscles and right and left quadriceps muscles is within the 10 percent range.* *Left and right arm curl, military press, and single leg press are also within the 10 percent range.*
✓ Yes ___ No	*Poor, Ted appears to be understriding. As shown in table 1.2, a 17-year-old who is 72 inches tall should take an 87- to 95-inch stride. Can be improved through plyometrics (step 4), sporting speed training (step 6) and overspeed training (step 7).*
___ Yes ✓ No	*Excellent; above the 95th percentile.*
___ Yes ✓ No	*Ted passed each of the practical tests, which indicates that his range of motion in the key areas associated with sprinting are excellent.*
___ Yes ✓ No	*Excellent for Ted's age. Indicates high genetic potential for speed.*
___ Yes ✓ No	*Excellent score; indicates high genetic potential for quickness.*
___ Yes ✓ No	*Excellent score, potential for rapid change of direction and acceleration.*

(continued)

Test area	Score	Standard	
Right and left leg hops:	R: _2.5_ L: _2.6_ Diff: _0.1_	2.5 and below is excellent, 2.6 to 3.0 is good; if you scored above 3.0 and/or a difference of more than 0.2 second between legs, check programs at right.	
BODY COMPOSITION Biceps: Triceps: Subscapula: Suprailiac: Total:	_3 mm_ _4 mm_ _9 mm_ _9 mm_ _25 mm_	Find your percent of body fat from table 1.4. If you exceed 15% (males) or 20% (females) consult your coach or physician and follow his or her advice before beginning any weight loss attempts.	
OTHER TESTS Stride rate:	_4.5_	Use table 1.5 to find your ideal stride rate.	
Acceleration time (Stationary 40 minus flying 40):	_0.9_	No more than 0.7 second difference.	
NASE future 40:	_4.2_	This score provides an estimate of your potential for improvement. Add 0.3 second. This is approximately how fast you should eventually complete a 40-yard dash.	

Weakness	Programs in the seven-step model
___ Yes ✓ No	*Excellent score in both legs, no imbalance present between the right (dominant) and left (non-dominant) side.*
___ Yes ✓ No	*Combined skinfold readings of 25 mm for a 17-year-old male indicate that Ted possesses about 10.5 percent body fat, which is excellent for optimum sprinting speed. (See table 1.4.)*
___ Yes ✓ No	*Good, according to table 1.5, stride length of 80 inches and a flying 40-yard time of 4.0 results in an estimated 4.5 steps per second. Can be improved through overspeed training (step 7).*
✓ Yes ___ No	*Poor, suggests faulty starting form. Exceeds minimum standard of 0.7 second. Can be improved through ballistics training (step 3), plyometrics (step 4), sport loading (step 5), and sprinting form and speed endurance (step 6).*
	Ted's potential best 40-yard time is 4.5 (4.2 + 0.3 = 4.5).

Based on these test scores, the training programs needed for a soccer player such as Ted Shanahan are:

Attack areas for soccer (From table 1.7)	Training program to focus on
1. Acceleration	Overspeed training
2. Stride rate	Plyometrics
3. Stride length	Sprint loading
4. Speed endurance	Sporting speed
5. Starting ability	Speed endurance training Strength-power training

Test Weakness areas	Training programs to focus on
Acceleration	Sprint loading, sporting speed
Speed endurance	Sporting speed, speed endurance training
Leg strength/body weight ratio	Basic training, functional strength, power training
Hamstring/quadriceps ratio	Strength/power training emphasizing the hamstring muscle group, sprint loading
Stride length	Plyometrics, sporting speed, overspeed

SPORT-SPECIFIC SPEED

Regardless of your sport, there are only five ways to improve your playing speed and quickness in short distances:

1. Improve your quickness and starting ability
2. Improve your acceleration time (reach full speed faster)
3. Increase the length of your stride
4. Increase the number of steps you take per second (stride rate)
5. Improve your speed endurance

These areas are not equally important to athletes in all sports. Soccer, rugby, lacrosse, field hockey, and basketball players, and defensive backs and linebackers in football, for example, are generally moving at one-fourth to one-half speed when they go into a full-speed sprint, rather than from a stationary position like a baseball player or most football players. For these athletes, starting technique is not nearly as important as acceleration, stride rate, stride length, and speed endurance. For the track and baseball athlete, starting techniques from the blocks, the batting box, and positions in the field are quite important. Although improving your speed endurance will not make you faster, it will keep you from slowing down, due to fatigue, after repeated short sprints or at the end of a long sprint of 80 yards or more. This quality is important to most team sport athletes.

TABLE 1.7

Speed Improvement Attack Areas for Team Sports

Sport	Attack areas by priority	Comment
Soccer, field hockey, rugby, lacrosse	1. Acceleration 2. Stride rate 3. Stride length 4. Speed endurance 5. Starting ability	You sprint faster in the open field only by taking faster or longer steps. Speed endurance is important only to prevent you from slowing down after repeated short sprints.
Basketball, racquet sports	1. Acceleration 2. Stride rate 3. Speed endurance 4. Starting ability 5. Stride length	Most explosive action occurs after some slight movement has taken place (a jog, a bounce, a sideward movement). Maximum speed is never reached. Acceleration, stride rate, and speed endurance should receive the major emphasis.
Baseball	1. Starting ability 2. Acceleration 3. Stride rate 4. Stride length 5. Speed endurance	A baseball player will not approach maximum speed unless he hits a triple or inside-the-park home run. Starting ability and acceleration should receive major emphasis.
Football	1. Acceleration 2. Starting ability 3. Stride rate 4. Speed endurance 5. Stride length	Accelerating from a three- or four-point stance or standing position is critical to every position. You sprint faster in the open field by increasing stride rate and length. Speed endurance training will prevent you from slowing down at the end of a long run or on short sprints due to fatigue as the game progresses.
Track sprinting	1. Starting ability 2. Acceleration 3. Stride rate 4. Stride length 5. Speed endurance	A 100- or 200-meter dash sprinter must work in all five attack areas in nearly equal proportion, unless weakness areas have been identified.

With the importance of "push" weight and taking up maximum space well established for athletes in some positions in football and rugby, it may be not only be extremely difficult for large athletes but also counterproductive to their performance to obtain a body fat level as low as 10 percent. Yet, a significant reduction in body fat and body weight for these athletes would improve their speed in short distances.

Study table 1.7 carefully. The key speed improvement areas for each sport are listed in order of importance and help you use test scores to focus on the programs for your sport. If, for example, test scores indicate the need to improve starting technique and you are a defensive back on the football team, ignore that finding and concentrate on areas that are critical to your position.

Keep in mind that speed improvement does require a holistic approach. In other words, each part of the seven-step model discussed in chapters 3 through 9 is very important. Although you will train in each area, your test results and the key speed improvement areas for your sport reveal the areas that require special attention. Move on to chapter 2. You are now ready to begin your speed improvement program.

SEVEN STEPS TO IMPROVING PLAYING SPEED

■ ■

If you should put even a little on a little, and should do this often, soon this too would become big. —**Hesiod**

In the previous chapter, you learned the answers to the first two of these four big questions for sprinting and playing faster:

1. How quick and fast do I need to be?
2. How quick and fast am I today?
3. How do I train to get quicker and faster?
4. How do I apply my new found speed and quickness to my sport?

Now let's move on to the seven-step model and answer questions 3 and 4.

THE SEVEN-STEP MODEL

The seven-step model holds the training principles used by that privileged group of "World's Fastest Humans," many of whom have built on their God-given talents of quickness, speed, and body control by consistently applying many of the principles that make up the seven-step model.

Each of these steps brings you closer to achieving tomorrow's speed (maximum feet per second achieved in your sport) and quickness (ability to change your playing speed in all directions at the maximum feet per second) for your sport. This model uses a common sense approach that recognizes how your body works and builds a series of practical steps that systematically guides you to those new unimaginable speeds. Feel the moment of success as you break away from the competition. Each one of these steps is crucial in training for the physical demands that your new-found playing speed will be placing on your body. Climb the staircase to your athletic dreams.

TABLE 2.1

100M World-Class Sprinting

Women	Year	Time	Points*	World record
Betty Robinson	1928	12.2	588	WR
Stella Walsh	1936	11.9	640	WR
Marjorie Jackson	1952	11.5	702	WR
Wilma Rudolph	1960	11.3	744	
Wyomia Tyus	1968	11.08	785	
Evelyn Ashford	1984	10.97	815	
Florence Griffith-Joyner	1988	10.62	876	WR
Gail Devers	1992	10.82	836	
Men				
Thomas Burke	1896	12.0	620	WR
Frank Jarvis	1900	11.0	800	
Charley Paddock	1920	10.4	920	WR
Jesse Owens	1936	10.3	945	WR
Bob Hayes	1964	9.9	1038	WR
Valeri Borzov	1972	10.07	998	
Carl Lewis	1984	9.87	1045	
Ben Johnson	1988	9.79	1068	Steroid
Leroy Burrell	1995	9.85	1048	WR
Donovan Bailey	1996	9.84	1050	WR
Frank Fredericks	1996	9.86	1046	

*Computerized Running Training Programs by James Gardner and J. Gerry Purdy

> Training programs to improve speed by improving strength, power, flexibility, stride rate and length, acceleration, form, and speed endurance are important supplements to normal sprint training activities.

Principles of the Seven-Step Model

Sports Speed, Second Edition, provides you with the tools you need to sprint faster and move quicker as early in your career as possible. The tools are the basic systems of the body. As explained in the following sections, the key to speed is knowing how to exploit the power of these systems.

Building Sustained Power Output

Sufficient cardiovascular and respiratory fitness is essential for high-speed performance sports. However, training geared toward improving cardiovascular fitness for high-speed, explosively oriented sports should minimize the use of long slow distance in favor of speed play or a faster paced interval program. Once the threshold amount is achieved for these systems (see chapter 3), training can move on to sport-specific training regimes.

Training Neural Pathways for Communication and Body Control

Recent research findings support the absolute necessity of starting training very early in life. The findings support the concept of a window of opportunity—one that if disregarded will limit the achievement level of the developing child. The window of maximum learning applies to all educational disciplines, whether they be mental or physical, developed in the classroom or on the playing field. There is good reason to support the idea that a skill has to be learned early or its quality will be substantially reduced or lost completely.

Each of us has been given a wonderful instrument: the human body. The quality and quantity of skills your body performs depends on the quality and quantity of your training programs. You benefit most when you begin training early in life and progressively master gross motor patterns, then fine motor patterns, followed by specific skills for your sport. The key to effective early training in sports is to find the proper balance between training and fun and to avoid overemphasis that eventually leads to boredom and loss of interest.

Researchers have taken a new look at some long-held beliefs about accelerated learning; their findings provide athletes with a much more objective basis for making training decisions. Edward Taub of the University of Alabama at Birmingham, for example, is investigating the study of music to uncover how early training affects the nervous system. Taub's findings indicate that the magnetic images of the brain strongly support the idea that to become a violin virtuoso (or an elite performer in any sport), the artist (athlete) must start at an early age. Other findings suggest that there are more and larger complex neuron circuits in the brain circuitry of those who started training between the ages of 3 and 12 than those who began after the age of 13. According to Taub, these differences are quite dramatic. The more complex the activity, the greater the number of neural pathways in the brain and neuromuscular system. Just as adding more traffic lanes to a freeway makes traffic flow more smoothly, increasing the number of neural pathways makes the brain work more efficiently.

Even if you are a late starter, all is not lost because improvement can occur at any age. Specialization is desirable by age 13, however, if you are to increase your chances of becoming a champion athlete. Other important studies using children and senior citizens show that the more mentally and physically active receive greater positive physiological changes in the nervous system and other systems.

You must train your brain or nervous system to be quicker and swifter. Everything we do influences the nervous system positively or negatively. Brain cell studies show that neurons increase in size with use just as the visible muscles do. The key factor for you to consider in your training is to give the nervous system the opportunity to experience actions that train you to make split-second decisions. Slow-thinking programs must be replaced by faster, automatic motor programs. The Pro-Think Motorvator game and the tennis ball reaction catching workout (see chapter 3) are excellent examples of activities that can move you to faster automatic motor programs.

Combat Breathing

Combat breathing techniques bring the mind and body into a state of harmony to produce some amazing feats on the field. These techniques are based on the knowledge that all body systems work together. Athletes learn to apply the laws of pneumatics to the respiratory system for maximum protection and power output by absorbing and transmitting energy in a variety of playing situations. Because every form of human performance requires the use of energy, combat breathing is of value for all sports.

Combat breathing was developed by Dr. Rod Sackarnowski, Juko-Kai Master, to serve as a foundation course of instruction in the martial arts. Many players and coaches feel that combat breathing directly applies to virtually every sport or any form of human performance. Combat breathing is especially applicable to sports that emphasize contact such as football, basketball, soccer, and rugby, to name a few. During the Tom Landry era, the Dallas Cowboys' combat breathing sessions helped players to deliver more energy on target, receive and absorb more energy from contact, avoid injury or bruising, and avert the discomfort that is usually associated with high-energy impact forces.

The potential to prevent or minimize injury to tissues by using combat breathing is exciting. The trunk, for example, serves as the crossroads for energy transfer in all human movement. Forces can move from the lower to the upper extremities or vice versa. The back, therefore, is a common site of injury and a major source of pain, discomfort, and disability. Studies show that a healthy back with-

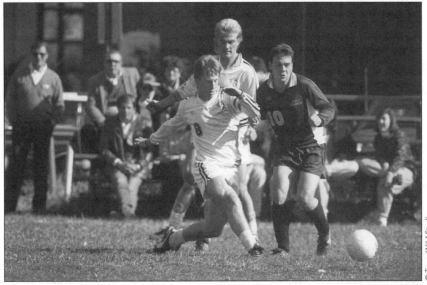

© Terry Wild Studio

stands compressive forces of 1,000 to 1,800 pounds when performing daily tasks. Maximum lifting can produce compressive forces in the 2,000 pound range.

Imagine the forces involved in the collisions of many accelerating players. Modern-day athletes who are bigger, stronger, and faster than athletes of the past can generate tremendous forces that are at or near the limits of human tolerance. Studies using Dallas Cowboys players as subjects showed that these players deliver striking forces of over 2,000 pounds when hitting blocking bags. To stay injury-free, athletes should master the science of energy transfer, a technique that is applied through combat breathing. Combat breathing techniques help to control the body's collective resources, which makes it possible to withstand the forces of a fast start, a fast stop, or the several thousand pounds of force that can be generated by players hitting one another. Releasing air pressure in the chest cavity through the mouth helps you to precisely manage the force delivered from such a hit. Chapter 3 describes a beginning program for learning combat breathing.

Improving Biomechanics

According to Adrian and Cooper, biomechanics is currently considered "the physics of human movement . . . an integrated study of the forces produced by the human body and the forces acting on the human body and the consequences of motion and tissue deformation." Biomechanics is a comprehensive science that includes every system in the body. You must take into account all systems, not just the nervous system and the skeletal system (bones, joints, and muscles), when training for sporting tasks. Biomechanics and practical coaching science work together to assist you in accomplishing your assignments during competition. Biomechanical analysis of gross and fine movements provides sound guidelines for you to follow in your skill training. Using this science greatly increases the chances that you will achieve your highest levels of performance in the most energy-efficient manner.

Maximizing the High-Speed Energy System

High-speed sprinting and short, quick burst movements are anaerobic activities that use carbohydrate (found in the blood as glucose and in the liver and muscles in its stored form as glycogen) as their primary fuel. Chapter 11 provides the principles of sound nutrition. In chapter 11, you will learn about high energy intake, energy expenditure, fluid replacement, growth and repair of body tissue, a sound method of gaining body weight and muscle bulk, and how to eat properly to maximize energy output in the glycolysis energy cycle. Anaerobic metabolism and the improvement of anaerobic endurance, called speed endurance in this text, are discussed in detail in chapter 8.

Knowing Your Resource Thresholds

Scientists have established that there are points on the work/speed curve where the body begins to shift from one source of energy utilization to another. Two commonly named thresholds are the aerobic and anaerobic thresholds. These thresholds indicate the point where there is a shift in your ability to deliver sufficient oxygen for the level of work being done. In this case, the thresholds apply specifically to your ability to utilize energy stores. Threshold, as used here, is a statistical value that relates playing performance in your sport to any off-field tests you use in your assessment program. The threshold value for each of these tests has been established at the 10th percentile.

How do you know when you are training too much? What is the threshold amount needed to perform at a given level for your sport? What is the threshold amount needed to perform at the highest level? The relationship between any given level of playing ability and strength, acceleration, power, speed, and sustained power output (endurance) is more loose than you might expect. Dr. George Kondraske, Director of the Human Performance Institute at the University of Texas, Arlington, puts it another way, "If a spoonful of sugar makes the medicine go down, do three to four teaspoons make swallowing even easier?"

The answer is no. Information acquired about NFL quarterback prospects at the University of Texas, Arlington, for example, identified the threshold or amount of a physical trait required to produce a given performance level. This study also indicated that a significant increase in an athlete's power, for example, may not improve performance at any level. The testing program described in chapter 1 will give you a good idea of the threshold amounts you need in key test areas and will identify the weak areas that you really need to focus on.

To further illustrate the threshold of training, let's examine strength, one of the essential elements in most sports. Begin by asking yourself the following questions: How strong do I have to be to sprint a 10.0-second 100-meter dash, long jump a distance of 25 feet, hit a 400-foot home run, score 30 points in basketball, swim the 100-meter freestyle under one minute, complete 80 percent of my passes in a football game, kick a soccer ball 60 yards, or drive a golf ball 250 yards? Surprisingly, the answers to these and similar questions about sport performance have not been adequately addressed by sports scientists, although this data will be forthcoming in the near future. You need the answers to these questions now because this information is extremely important in determining exactly how you should train to get faster and quicker in your sport.

Fortunately, you can use existing data to venture educated estimates to produce positive results. Until more precise answers become available, the best you can do is follow the recommendations in this book that provide close estimates of the threshold for the projected level of performance in your sport. Later chapters provide our best estimates of what these levels should be based on current information. When in doubt, the authors encourage you to spend your time performing the skills in your sport. The closer you follow the suggested path, the more rapidly you will move to higher levels of speed, quickness, strength, power, and sustained power output.

The Steps

The seven-step model categorizes various forms of exercise into seven conceptual steps. Each step places more emphasis on integrating higher levels of speed and quickness that require a faster rate of operation (force must be applied at an ever-increasing rate). This model begins with basic training in step 1. In this step, total body tissue and systems efficiency is developed to sustain the impacts of higher overspeed training in step 7 where speeds and quickness exceed normal sporting and sprinting speed by 5 to 10 percent. To improve playing speed in short distances and the speed with which you move a specific body part or change the direction of the entire body (quickness), a complete approach is required. In other words, all seven steps are important. After you have acquired a solid foundation at steps 1 and 2, you will progress into high- and super-high-speed training where you will focus on the specific act of sprinting and sprinting-type movements using specialized techniques. A critical area that can negate training gains and performance is nutrition, the very foundation of the seven-step model. Without proper sports nutrition, as discussed in chapter 11, the very best speed improvement training program will produce limited results.

Your present levels of fitness and skill determine how long you train on each of the seven steps. It will take years of hard training to reach your maximum potential. However, coaching experience has shown that a period of five to six months is required prior to your season of competition to attain sufficient resources for competition. Carefully study the general features of each step as outlined in the following text before moving on to a more detailed presentation, beginning in chapter 3, of each step.

- **Step 1: Basic training.** This step develops all qualities of human movement to a level that will provide a solid base on which to build each successive step. It includes programs to increase body control, strength, muscle endurance, and sustained effort (muscular and cardiovascular, anaerobic and aerobic).

- **Step 2: Functional strength and explosive movements against medium to heavy resistance.** Maximum power is trained by working in an intensity range of 55 to 85 percent of your maximum intensity (1RM).

- **Step 3: Ballistics.** This step focuses on high-speed sending and receiving movements.

- **Step 4: Plyometrics.** This step focuses on explosive hopping, jumping, bounding, hitting, and kicking.

- **Step 5: Sport loading.** This step focuses on precision loading at high speed. The intensity is 85 to 100 percent of maximum speed.

- **Step 6: Sprinting form and speed endurance.** This step focuses on sprinting technique and improving the length of time you are able to maintain your speed.

- **Step 7: Overspeed training.** This step involves systematic application of sporting speed that exceeds maximum speed by 5 to 10 percent through the use of various overspeed training techniques.

TRAINING WITH THE SEVEN STEPS

Research and empirical evidence have clearly shown that the elements contained in the seven-step model will improve speed and quickness and playing speed for your sport. The number of workouts per week (frequency) and the length (duration) of each workout for the various training programs used in each step are discussed in chapters 3 through 9. Just how fast results occur and how much time you devote to each step depend on the individual. An athlete who already possesses a high aerobic and anaerobic fitness level and a solid foundation in the area of functional strength and power can start to focus on steps 3 through 7. Athletes in most sports are heavily involved in strength and power training and may need only to modify their approach to conform to the type of training conducive to the improvement of speed and quickness.

Once a solid base is acquired, the programs in steps 3 through 7 become a regular part of weekly training sessions. At this point, improvement can be expected in 8 to 12 weeks. The longer you train and the more intense your training is, the greater the expected results in terms of improved speed and quickness. Although chapter 10 presents time suggestions for each training program for both the pre- and in-season period, you should remain with a specific training program until you overcome the weaknesses (and meet the standards cited in chapter 1) identified on your test score sheet. At that point, you can decide to either change to a maintenance program (to keep the gains acquired) in some areas or continue to strive for additional improvement in an attempt to produce an even greater impact on speed and quickness and playing speed.

New testing procedures now permit a more thorough analysis of the strengths and weaknesses of each athlete to help identify the most important areas for a concentrated effort. Muscle balance testing has surfaced as a critical area for some athletes who have developed one side of the body or opposing muscle groups on the same side disproportionately to the extent that speed and basic performance are adversely affected.

The biomechanics of sprinting have now been scientifically analyzed; form training in the start and during the sprinting action has been refined to the point where coaches can use high-tech computer analysis to unravel the complexity of sprinting, making it easier to identify problem areas. Couple the science of biomechanics with the trained coach's keen eye, and you have the best team to assist in removing unwanted movements that are associated with the loss of energy and forward speed required for your sport.

Exercise physiologists have uncovered important information concerning the most effective techniques to train the fast-twitch white and fast-twitch red muscle fibers critical to the improvement of sprinting speed and quickness. Studies have shown that speed strength (fast contractions through the entire range of motion) is much more important than absolute strength (maximum amount of weight that can be moved by a muscle group) in the improvement of speed in short distances. As a result, strength/power training techniques for speed improvement have been changed and now allow athletes to alter their approach in a manner that contributes to the improvement of playing speed. Techniques to improve both stride rate and stride length have also become more refined and effective. Research on plyometric training, sport loading, and overspeed training has also been encouraging. Programs in these areas have been developed that effectively improve both sprinting speed and quickness in sports performance.

Over the past 20 years, the authors of this book have also had the opportunity to determine the effectiveness of the entire seven-step model by coaching male and female athletes in practically every team sport at many age and skill levels, from beginners to the pros. Athletes who adhered to the program have turned in some surprising results. In a number of cases, high school, university, and pro athletes who had been cut from the squad have returned with their new-found speed and quickness to make the team and become key contributors.

MOVING ON TO THE NEXT STEP

Coaches and athletes are now aware that playing speed and quickness can be improved with proper training. Athletes are no longer trying to weight train their way to speed by adding as much absolute strength as possible, to wind sprint their way to speed by concentrating solely on interval sprint training, or form train their way to speed by devoting countless hours to develop the perfect biomechanics of sprinting. Research has now clearly shown that a total approach will make you faster in short distances and improve playing speed in your sport. To start reaching your potential, turn the page and begin your seven-step approach to improved speed and quickness.

CHAPTER 3

STEP 1:
BASIC TRAINING

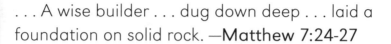

... A wise builder ... dug down deep ... laid a foundation on solid rock. —**Matthew 7:24-27**

The original basic training in the first edition of this book served as a fragmented all-systems preparation period. In this edition of *Sports Speed*, basic training is an integrated system that trains all of the elements of performance required for competition. Fundamentally, basic training is the root system that supports and sustains every play in any sport. No doubt, there will come a time when playing situations will arise that will show your weaknesses. A careful look at these situations will establish whether a direct connection exists between the weaknesses in your sport performance and some deficiency that could have been worked on.

This chapter establishes a list of core activities based on how many basic movement patterns an individual can develop. A good way to understand what basic training is all about is to take a very close look at a space shuttle launch. Initially, the shuttle is stationary on the launch pad, even after ignition. However, subtle movements are taking place as the shuttle's nervous system (computer) sends instructions to put all subsystems in motion in preparation for launch. In addition to these movements, the astronauts are preparing for the launch. Physical educators call all these actions prior to take-off, in relation to the shuttle, non-locomotor movements. The shuttle hasn't moved from the pad even though the astronauts and shuttle's systems are in motion in preparation for launch.

Likewise, any actions that you make on the field of play, without moving your body off of the playing field (launch pad), are called non-locomotor skills. Examples of non-locomotor skills include flexing, extending, rotating, bending, shifting, swaying, or faking. Just as in the shuttle, these movements are as important to your play as non-locomotor movements are for a perfect space launch. Locomotor skills, on the other hand, are basic total body actions requiring movement through space such as blocking, catching, changing directions, hitting, falling, leaping, pulling, pushing, rolling, running, sliding, starting, stopping, tackling, and throwing.

These basic movement patterns can be likened to the alphabet, which can be organized into words, phrases, sentences, and paragraphs, or to musical notes, which can be combined into scales and chords. Once you learn the basic elements of movement, you can make limitless combinations of them to form new and creative solutions to the problems faced when competing in sports. Basic training provides a solid, conceptual, and practical foundation to help accelerate you to step 7 of speed improvement.

Basic training identifies core activities including many of the movement patterns that humans perform (foot, hand, and so on). Playing basketball, boxing, dancing, playing handball, fencing, doing gymnastics, hurdling, jumping, kicking, practicing martial arts, running, throwing, walking, and wrestling require many of these basic patterns. These activities have been tagged by some physical educators as core exercises because they contain, among other things, many of the elements of a comprehensive vocabulary of human movement. Remember, these activities must be specifically applied to your specific sports needs. Try to include these activities in your physical education program at school, in your after-school extracurricular activities, and as specifically recommended in the rest of the chapters in this book.

GENERAL PREPARATION

Experts call the first part of step 1 a period of general preparation. The objective is to increase all of the body's resources to optimum levels prior to beginning your trip to faster running and playing speeds. In many programs, it is unlikely that the body's resources have been developed to threshold or optimum levels. Therefore, you should follow a threshold-based program that takes into account all the body's resources to produce an integrated program. Each of the following resources is vital in sports performance: awareness, reactions, reflexes, quickness and control of body segments in all directions, quickness in close-range movements in all directions, basic movement elements of the body, basic movement elements required for sports (movement patterns, hand-eye and foot-eye coordination), power, sustained power output, speed in all directions, maximum strength, muscular strength endurance, anaerobic conditioning, and aerobic conditioning.

Basic training also includes other organizational elements that are necessary in the operation of the total program. Use one of the variety of programs suggested for each of the basic elements. Make sure you get involved in the training process by adding your own ideas to the list of various methods that can accomplish the desired outcomes of step 1. The major outcome of basic training is to optimize the performance quality of all the essential resources required for your selected sport. You can be confident that you will accomplish this outcome if you successfully carry out the suggestions included in this chapter in combination with the assessments in chapter 1.

BASIC TRAINING SPORTS CHECK

Before venturing too far into your program planning, take a close look at your results from the assessments taken in chapter 1 and complete the sports check scorecard in this chapter. Your assessment information list includes the following:

Basic testing program

Advanced testing program

Sports check scorecard

These assessments are extremely important because you will be building your speed training on this foundation.

The basic and advanced testing programs do not collect data about resources in actual game or sport conditions. To build an effective training program, you need to measure how effectively you use all of the necessary resources during game conditions. (Because sprinting is described in detail by the measurements of the testing programs, few additional measurements are required for a comprehensive assessment of pure sprinting.)

Computer software is a good tool to use to measure the specifics of an athlete's performance. On-Field Analysis (OFAS) has developed and used a computer graphics and software package to track NFL, Senior Bowl, and East-West College All-Star Game players as they were playing the game. The data was used to develop a scientific grading system. The goal was to provide an objective method to precisely identify how the players used their resources during game conditions. Every grade is based on an objective source. The OFAS yields the most objective and precise time motion analysis data system available. Contact OFAS at 11502 Valleydale Drive, Dallas, Texas, 75230, for information. Other computer-based biomechanical systems have been designed to improve sports performance as well. Peak Performance Technologies in Englewood, Colorado, is an example of such a system.

The Coaching Association of Canada's *National Coaching Certification Program: Level 3 Coaching Theory* manual illustrates the use of a much simpler time motion analysis system to get important sport-specific training information for grading and training purposes. The association's program includes observing games with a stopwatch, paper, and pencil to chart the action on the field. The program's objective is to determine the time, motion, and intensity characteristics involved in the sport.

Using this method, coaches are able to calculate the average velocity, high- and low-intensity velocity, and schedules of repetitions. You and your coaches can use this method to evaluate your sport and your individual performance. You can make better estimates of the aerobic and anaerobic requirements of the sport by studying actual games. Sport-specific training programs and drills also can be created to duplicate the elements of the game. If you are interested in this time motion analysis method, contact the Coaching Association of Canada at 333 River Road, Ottawa, Ontario, Canada, K1L 8B9.

You can customize the sports check scorecard given in this chapter (table 3.1) for your sport by using a combination of biomechanics and time motion measurement methods. These methods assess higher level game skills to get a better understanding of how athletes are integrating their basic resources into more complex sports-related functions. The scorecards identify present performance, assess the quality of performance, and track performance.

Use the sports check scorecard as a conceptual guide. The scorecard divides the absolute performance curve into 10 labeled categories. The underlying structure of the curve is based on an absolute performance scale rather than one that has been adjusted for age. Both absolute and age-related values are important tools to assist you in program development. For more information about where you can get age-related performance scales, write the National Association for Sport and Physical Education, 1900 Association Drive, Reston, Virginia, 22091.

Sports Check Scorecard

The scorecard is a 10-level scoring scale that you can use to monitor your achievements (table 3.1). Scoring starts at the beginner performance level and proceeds progressively up to the master level where only the highly accomplished athletes can score. Do not be confused by the names given to each level. Generally, an athlete who has spent a very short time in a sport is classified as a beginner or novice.

TABLE 3.1

Sports Check Scorecard		
Level-Class	Percent level	Present score
10—Master	99+	_____
9—Elite	96-98	_____
8—Advanced	90-95	_____
7—Intermediate	79-89	_____
6—Above average	60-78	_____
5—Average	40-59	_____
4—Below average	21-39	_____
3—Apprentice	11-20	_____
2—Novice	3-10	_____
1—Beginner	0-2	_____

However, because of genetic endowment such an athlete may have a better performance score than an individual who has been involved in the sport for some time. This situation can occur because the scoring scale includes the whole spectrum of performance. Keep this fact in mind when you use the scorecard to make comparisons and program decisions. The following questions will help you determine how to use the scorecard:

What sport or skills are being assessed?

Where are you in growth and development (chronological or performance age)?

When and how often will your measurements be taken?

How will the measurements be collected and used?

Why are the measurements important?

These questions help you determine assessment process and how you compare with the best.

The 10-level sports check evaluates 11 basic elements, which are listed below and explained in this chapter:

- Sport-specific tasks
- Proper breathing mechanics
- Combat breathing

- Training the brain
- Body control
- Sport hitting power
- Starting power
- Driving power
- High-speed quickness
- Maximum playing speed
- Sustained power output-endurance base

Each of these elements is vital to your success in playing quicker and faster or sprinting higher speeds.

Sport-Specific Tasks

Sport-specific tasks should be determined and prioritized with the help of a professionally qualified person in your sport of choice. Each of the tasks that make up your sport should be grouped and evaluated according to three questions:

1. How frequently is the task done?
2. How difficult is the task to complete?
3. How critical is the task to your performance?

A scientifically based program requires an in-depth study of the sport before a training prescription can be developed. Knowing the importance of each of the tasks involved enables you to allocate appropriate training time for each of the tasks involved in the sport. Schellus Hyndeman, men's varsity soccer coach at Southern Methodist University, provided us with four sample soccer sports check scorecards. We have modified them in tables 3.2 through 3.5 in an effort to prioritize basic techniques. Use these four focus areas to help you construct a scorecard for your sport:

Technique frequency, difficulty, and importance

Technique scoring and resource recognition

Physical dimensions, thresholds, and limiting factors

Physical dimensions performance report for program assessment

Examples of a soccer goalkeeper's scorecards are shown in tables 3.2 and 3.3. Tables 3.4 and 3.5 list the physical dimensions required for soccer. Scores can be based on any familiar system that you presently use: A-B-C-D-F, 1 to 10, or 0 to 100, as shown in table 3.1. The latter is our recommendation. Whichever method you use, be consistent in its application.

TABLE 3.2

Soccer Goalkeeper Scorecard*

DEFENSIVE TECHNIQUES

	Score	Resource
1. Scooping		
Ground balls at the keeper	___	___
Ground balls to either side	___	___
2. Catching		
Catching below stomach height	___	___
Catching at stomach/chest height	___	___
Overhead catching	___	___
3. Falling/diving		
Simple falling	___	___
Footwork leading to dive	___	___
Diving for low shots	___	___
Power diving—high shots	___	___
Forward diving	___	___
4. Boxing		
Two fisted to change direction	___	___
One fisted to change direction	___	___
One fisted to keep direction	___	___
One elbow to keep direction	___	___
One elbow to change direction	___	___
Two elbows to keep direction	___	___
Two elbows to change direction	___	___
Boxing under pressure	___	___
5. Deflecting		
With one hand around post	___	___
With one hand over crossbar	___	___
One elbow to keep direction	___	___
One elbow	___	___
Two elbows	___	___
With two hands	___	___
6. Breakaways		
Sliding at opponent	___	___
Holding a long barrier	___	___
Throwing a body to block a shot	___	___
Stand up technique	___	___
7. Soccer playing skills		
Play outside of penalty area (general)	___	___
Heading	___	___
Playing to a teammate	___	___
Interception of "thru passes"	___	___
Dealing with back passes	___	___
8. Range		
Judgment of flighted balls	___	___
Ability to extend play	___	___

*Courtesy of Schellus Hyndeman, Southern Methodist University; modified by Bob Ward

TABLE 3.3

Soccer Goalkeeper Scorecard

DISTRIBUTION AND ATTACKING TECHNIQUES

	Score	Resource
1. Throwing		
Bowling	_____	_____
Sidearm sling	_____	_____
Overhead "baseball" throw	_____	_____
2. Kicking out of hand		
Volley	_____	_____
Drop kick	_____	_____
3. Goal kick and free kicks		
Short range	_____	_____
Long range	_____	_____

TACTICS

	Score	Resource
1. Positioning/angle play		
In the goal—on the goal line	_____	_____
Outside of goal area	_____	_____
2. Reading the game		
In the goal—immediate danger	_____	_____
Outside of the goal area—secondary danger	_____	_____
Outside of penalty area	_____	_____
3. Breakaways		
One versus one duels	_____	_____
4. Penalty kicks		
Tactical concerns	_____	_____
Reflex action	_____	_____

TABLE 3.4

Physical Dimensions			
	Raw score	**Threshold**	**Limiting factor**
Coordination/flow (general)			
Open/target focus			
Timing and judgment			
Kinesthetic sense			
Rhythm			
Footwork			
Handwork			
Reactions/reflexes			
Quickness			
Agility			
Kicking power			
Hitting power			
Throwing distance			
Vertical jumping			
Horizontal jumping			
Speed			
Strength			
Muscle balance			
Sustained power output			
Range of motion			
Injury recovery			
Recovery from game workout			

TABLE 3.5

Physical Dimensions Performance Report

	Time	Rate	Duration	Rest	Heart rate zone
Sleep heart rate zone (22-30%)					—
Resting heart rate zone (30-35%)					—
Aerobic zone (70-80% max)					—
Anaerobic zone (80-90% max)					—
Maximum zone (90-100% max)					—
Coordination/flow (general)					—
Open/target focus					—
Timing and judgment					—
Kinesthetic sense					—
Rhythm					—
Footwork					—
Handwork					—
Reactions/reflexes					—
Quickness					—
Agility					—
Kicking power					—
Kicking distance					—
Hitting power					—
Throwing distance					—
Vertical jumping					—
Horizontal jumping					—
Speed					—
Strength					—
Muscle balance					—
Sustained power output					—
Range of motion					—
TOTAL					—

Careful study of the information in the scorecards will give the coach and player a sound basis for constructing an evaluation and training program based on the specific skills required for the sport and the limiting factors holding the player back. Remember, your training has to match the requirements of your sport if it is to be effective. In addition, limiting factors in performance must also be corrected. Remember, this assessment should be coupled with the basic and advanced testing programs found in chapter 1.

Combat Breathing

Breathing is an essential human function that plays a major role in the production of energy at sleep, rest, or playing your sport at top speed. Not many of us have been trained to use the most efficient mechanics for meditation, relaxation, or executing the basic tasks of daily life. Most of us are walking around each day with limited breathing skills. Athletes cannot afford to lack adequate skill in any aspect of breathing while engaging in their sports. Relaxation, starting in sprinting, body contact, hitting or punching, blocking, running, sprinting, and throwing all require specific breathing skills.

Checklist for Proper Breathing Mechanics

✓ *Nose:* Breathe through the nose to warm and filter air.

✓ *Mouth:* Breathe through the nose and mouth during high oxygen demands. Regulate the release of air through the mouth during contact and high-output skills, such as body contact, hitting in baseball, punching in boxing, or throwing in all sports.

✓ *Lungs:* Use lower portions of the lungs to breathe when sleeping, meditating, relaxing, and during times of maximum oxygen transfer.

✓ *Diaphragm:* Put your hand on your stomach to check that it moves inward with each breath. Conduct your own experiment by watching a few babies breathe. Do their stomachs go in and out?

✓ *Shoulders:* Raise and roll the shoulders back to provide additional volume for combat breathing.

✓ *Rib cage:* Increase the chest volume by maximizing breathing during high oxygen demands, for protection from forces of contact, and for high force output. This added volume requires the use of all the intercostal muscles of the rib cage.

Training the Brain

In the past, training the brain to react quickly by using the latest technology has been overlooked. Amazing human feats have demonstrated that through training athletes can gain more control over their nervous systems than people ever dreamed possible.

To accelerate your speed to uncommon levels, you need to use the information that is emerging from numerous laboratories. The computer age has brought all forms of sophisticated devices to the laboratory and the field for sports scientists and coaches to use. Software and equipment have come along to monitor body functions. Heart rate monitors are now available with computer interfaces and software to collect and evaluate information for each individual heart beat and its relation to the next beat. The sports science lab is really taking the field. Today's coaches are very lucky to have such immediate and powerful objective information for training their athletes. This information is confirming what many scientists, coaches, and parents have felt for a long time: Use it or lose it; don't use it early and you'll never get "the max"; or start using it at any age and get some of it back. Some of the more important findings from these studies that will help you sprint faster and play at higher speeds are in the following list:

• Technology has given us immediate and precise information about all forms of sport. One example is the disqualification of Linford Christie in the 1996 Olympic 100-meter finals for a second false start. His gun-to-leaving-the-blocks time was below human capability. This time difference was used to confirm that he had jumped the gun. However, the time difference was so close to human capability that without today's timing devices it would have been impossible to determine. On-Field Analysis's evaluations present objective information. This specific performance information about how the players are moving on the field provides the necessary information for player evaluation, selection, and training.

Game action and sprinting takes place at such high speeds that thinking before acting interferes with your performance. Players must react to the situation and ask questions later.

• Brain research and the practical playing experiences of elite athletes reveal that there is a state of high artistic and sports performance. Many have described it as being in an effortless state called "the Zone." Research reveals that the Zone, also known as the flow state, is associated with lower heart and breathing rates coupled with brainwave frequencies of 8 to 13 Hertz. Too much or not enough stress can adversely affect your performance. You must be able to control your stress levels for maximum performance. The best known way to control stress is to get in the Zone. The information and techniques given in this chapter will help you achieve control over stress in your sport and in life. According to John Douillard in *Body, Mind, and Sport*, "[T]he coexistence of opposites—rest and alertness, composure and vigorous exercise [is] the formula for the Zone."

One of the most common faults many athletes have is trying too hard. Invariably, the harder one tries, the tighter one gets, which is just the opposite of what you want and what the Olympic motto, "Swifter, Higher, Stronger," is all about. If the athlete is in the Zone before performing, the proper muscle control or optimal coordination reaches superlative heights. Is there any question why the Zone is the most critical performance principle for the beginner or elite athlete? You cannot compete if you are fighting yourself every step of the way!

One of the most common errors in sports is that the performers monitor the response they just made rather than being open to receive a signal for the next action. We call this state "alert-mess." You can remove the mess by learning to play in a flow state.

• Athletes can control visual awareness in such a way that they can see everything in the visual field. The running back who sees all defensive players as they are positioned and then runs to daylight is using a technique called open focus, a term coined by Dr. Les Fehmi. This technique is similar to the ultimate camera that takes a clear picture, without a shutter, of anything it wants, even at the same time another picture is being taken. Can you imagine the luxury of processing all incoming information and automatically sorting out what you need at any one moment in your sport? Obviously, your performance would increase dramatically.

One way you can improve your visual awareness is by doing turns or rolls while a coach throws you a ball as you recover body control. Another way to expand your visual awareness is to juggle or use the mini-trampoline as a rebounder of two or more objects. With practice, you will be able to juggle more balls, increase the area of visual recognition, and be able to manage other sensory input with improving ability.

• We all have experienced the adaptation to high-speed travel. Driving at 70 miles per hour initially seems fast due to acceleration and the relative speeds and positions of other cars or objects in the field of vision. However, in a short period of time, this sensation is replaced by a sense that 70 miles per hour is not fast at all. This feeling is the exact playing sensation you want to have on the field. The programs for speed of movement and speed of thought provide drills and exercises that will help improve this flow state condition on and off the field. The best way to develop this "slowing" sensation is to incorporate the skills you learned in combat breathing and visual awareness. Your goal is to increase the area you are able to take in information from. Once you have learned how to expand your field of focus, your perception of motion tends to slow down.

• Training both sides of the body by developing near equal skill in both hands and feet appears to assist in improving skill levels by producing higher levels of synchrony or coordination in the nervous system. It is not uncommon to find that sensory processing or skill dominance varies on left and right sides of the body. Differences can be found in every paired organ system in the body: the brain, eyes, ears, hands, and feet. Further, research shows that hand preference affects the tissue (muscle, tendons, ligaments and capillaries, arteries and veins) composition of the upper limbs in all age groups. Significant tissue changes have been shown to occur in bone density and the fat-free soft tissues of exercised limbs. In addition to these tissue changes, you can expect to gain the functional skills required for your sport or everyday tasks.

Research by Larry Brown of Mechano-Physics and Bob Ward has shown that sprinters and cyclists produce uneven amounts of power output with their legs. This is an example of dominant and recessive motor patterns that can limit speed of movement. The suggested corrective activities and training programs can help. The sports check assessments in this chapter, along with those in chapter 1, will guide you to the proper step in the seven-step model that will help correct your deficiencies. As a simple challenge, select a few skills that you know are important in your sport and learn to do them well on both sides of the body. For instance, you could use your trail leg as the lead leg over the hurdle, jump off of the other leg in the long jump or high jump, throw a football with your weaker arm, or dribble a basketball with your less accomplished hand.

• Computers have helped create the Pro-Think Motorvator game that helps assess neuromuscular and brain function and train the neuromuscular system. Alternate hand and foot patterns, along with running patterns (for example, left arm and right leg), have been programmed into the game. These specific patterns, rhythms, and distractions are used to systematically guide players to higher levels of handwork and footwork. A powerful advantage of using the Pro-Think Motorvator game is its ability to record correct responses. There is good evidence that there are specific benefits (structural and functional changes in the nervous system) gained by playing this game that may help you sprint faster or play faster. If you are interested in receiving more information about the game, write to Pro-Think Motorvator, 11502 Valleydale Drive, Dallas, Texas, 75230.

Body Control: Learning the ABCs of Movement

The major objective that you want to accomplish with the body control program is to develop a large vocabulary of movement. The larger your vocabulary becomes, the greater the chances that you will increase your ability to move quicker and faster in a variety of directions and solve the many problems that you face on the field. The ability to use all body parts, in all of their movement patterns and in a variety of game situations, when called upon to do so, is the ultimate goal of the body control program.

We recommend a 75-minute video developed in the NFL by Bob Ward, Randy White, and Valentine Espiricueta called "Creating Big Plays" to help in this vital area. The ancient secrets of many martial arts masters have been used to create the program. The benefits of the program have been demonstrated by the outstanding play of many professional athletes. The same principles that worked for them will work for you too. Write Creating Big Plays, 11502 Valleydale Drive, Dallas, Texas, 75230, for information concerning this revolutionary method of improving body control and game performance.

Sport Hitting Power

One of the most formidable defensive players to take the field in the NFL, Randy White, needed instruction on how to improve his ability to hit with his hands properly on and off the field. Randy came to the Dallas Cowboys as a highly-recognized and decorated player. You would figure that if you ask him to hit a bag with left hand, right hand, or both together and you'd better step back! Such was not the case. The results of this simple test convinced the coaches and, more importantly, Randy that he should begin a training program to improve the power of his hits. The key point is that any skill is relative to the method used to form its value. Until an objective measurement tool is developed (like the thermometer or stopwatch) to score sport hitting power, error will be present. Furthermore, a player can get by without having to fully develop master levels of skill if the competition doesn't demand it.

Starting Power

Starting power is the ability to get moving in the appropriate direction in the most efficient way possible. A sprinter reacting to the starting gun, a linebacker reacting to a running play to fill the hole, or the Chicago Bulls fast-breaking down the court for a two-point lay up are all examples of actions that require a lot of starting power if the player or team is to be successful. If you move close to your opponent, you'd better be able to move quickly or you're in big trouble! Starting power plays a major role in the outcome of the contest.

Some of the best advice for improving this ability comes from Bruce Lee, the famous martial artist. Bruce suggested that athletes use his quickness principle of a slow, phasic, bent-knee position to move quickly into an attack, evasion, or retreat. In sports that allow movement, this position means that you keep the body in a slow movement pattern, which helps to overcome the inertia that makes it harder for you to get started from a still position. Some coaches call it dancing in your shoes. In sports where the athlete must remain still, like the start in swimming and track or the offensive linemen in football prior to the snap, the slow, phasic, bent knee position can take place in the mind: think movement.

Driving Power

Driving power applies to contact sports such as football, rugby, soccer, or basketball where initial contact is made and then the player has to follow through to clear an area by moving the opponent out of the way. Some sports considered non-contact may also involve incidental, permissible, or illicit contact. No matter how contact originates, the physical properties must be managed to minimize or avoid potential injury. Once contact is made, driving power is the ability of the player to maintain the contact and move the opponent in the appropriate direction. Repeated drills against a challenging opponent in many situations are the best way to develop driving power. This is why intersquad scrimmages are so effective and are the preferred method for high-level development.

High-Speed Quickness

High-speed quickness is your ability to adjust quickly to the movements of your opponent. Ideally, coaches would like to have athletes with outstanding speed and quickness. However, many athletes who do not have the fastest raw sprinting speed are able to make up for their lack of speed because they have a good grasp of the game. When these athletes are a reasonable distance from the action, their high-speed quickness comes into play and allows them to get the job done. Soccer and man-to-man basketball are two excellent crossover training sports to develop your high-speed quickness for any sport. Select playing situations in your sport and apply the same concept by covering your opponent as tightly as possible.

Maximum Playing Speed

Maximum playing speed is your ability to run fast in your sport. All of the tests in chapter 1 give you the necessary information to assess your maximum playing speed potential and identify and fix your weaknesses.

OFAS has analyzed over 40 NFL and college all-star football games. This highly sophisticated software package, coupled with computer graphics techniques, found that all players, no matter what position they played, had average playing speeds well below their maximum sprinting speed during the game. Table 3.6 summarizes OFAS' findings. A careful study of table 3.6 reveals that speed is not a limiting factor for playing football. Speed is very important, however; work hard on playing quickness, and it will bring you the greatest dividends.

TABLE 3.6

Speed Performance Comparisons				
Performer	Average 40 feet per sec (time in sec)	Best game feet per sec (time in sec)	40 test feet per sec	Percentage
Olympic sprinter	38 f/s (4.1)	40 f/s (3.9)	40.0 f/s	100
Wide receivers	24 f/s (5.7)	30 f/s (4.7)	31.8 f/s	75-94
Running backs	21 f/s (6.5)	29 f/s (4.8)	31.1 f/s	68-93
Defensive backs	20 f/s (6.7)	28 f/s (5.0)	30.6 f/s	65-92
Tight ends	19 f/s (7.1)	27 f/s (5.1)	31.0 f/s	61-88
Linebackers	18 f/s (7.4)	26 f/s (5.4)	29.3 f/s	61-89
Quarterbacks	14 f/s (9.2)	21 f/s (6.5)	29.0 f/s	51-72
Defensive line	13 f/s (9.7)	21 f/s (6.5)	28.3 f/s	46-71
Offensive line	12 f/s (9.9)	20 f/s (6.7)	27.7 f/s	43-72

Sustained Power Output-Endurance Base

Many contests have been won solely on an athlete's ability to persevere. Therefore, sustained power output must have a very important place in your training program. Ideally, your training program should have provisions for developing acceptable levels of fitness prior to the season of your sport. The circulatory and respiratory systems should be brought to levels that can easily handle the specific demands of your sport. Aerobic cycles and exercises have been proposed for training and evaluating your aerobic fitness. However, most sports are not purely aerobic. In fact, most sports are anaerobic. In addition, some researchers have noted a negative influence of high aerobic exercise programs on explosiveness. Therefore, we recommend that most of the running in the training program should match the speed demands of your sport.

The suggested time motion analysis methods and the sports check scorecard you develop for your sport will give you the necessary information to develop an appropriate workout program. It is important to consider other problems, such as how weight control could influence how you use aerobic exercises in your program. If you are overweight, follow the nutritional program in chapter 11. Also, you will need to spend more training time doing interval and aerobic training to help burn more calories. Start early in the off-season so there will be plenty of time to get your weight under control; don't go on any crash diet programs.

Adequate aerobic conditioning is a necessary resource for sport. How much conditioning is adequate is the question. If your sport is continuous with bursts of speed and little recovery time, higher levels of aerobic performance are in order. Your sport evaluation will determine what level you need to attain. In general, you should strive to meet the standards given in the following sections, never falling below the category of good even when you are untrained and striving for the categories of excellent or superior when you are highly trained for your sport.

Aerobic Foundation

To evaluate an athlete's aerobic foundation and test it throughout the season, the 1.5 mile test (see table 3.7) is a good, easy-to-administer test for continuous moving sports such as soccer and basketball. However, we favor faster paced tests, such as that shown in table 3.8.

TABLE 3.7

1.5 Mile Test Scores		
Men:	Under 8:45 (470 points)*	Superior
Women:	Under 9:45 (340 points)	Superior
Men:	8:45-10:15 (290 points)	Excellent
Women:	9:46-10:45 (250 points)	Excellent
Men:	10:16-12:00 (130 points)	Good
Women:	11:16-13:00 (60 points)	Good

*Points based on Computerized Training Programs, Gardner and Purdy.

TABLE 3.8

2 × 880 Yards Rest Five Minutes Repeat		
Men:	Under 2:25 (470 points)*	Superior
Women:	Under 2:42 (340 points)	Superior
Men:	2:25-2:49 (290 points)	Excellent
Women:	2:42-3:30 (250 points)	Excellent
Men:	2:49-3:15 (130 points)	Good
Women:	3:05-3:30 (60 points)	Good

*Points based on Computerized Training Programs, Gardner and Purdy.

The following test is run at a faster pace than the 1.5 mile test. It is an excellent field test for assessing aerobic fitness.

Speed Endurance: Long

The following tests are good for analyzing speed endurance for the majority of anaerobic sports or longer sprinting distances:

• 300-yard shuttle (or gassers, which are sideline to sideline on playing field). Run two 5 × 60 yard continuous shuttles. Rest one minute between sets. Keep track of the drop-off between the first and second shuttle.

• 100-meter repeat runs. Run 10 × 100 meters at 70 percent of best 100-meter time. Take 60 seconds to walk back to the starting line between each run. Keep a graph of the times. Plot best 100-meter and working 100-meter scores once a month.

- 200-meter repeat runs. Run two 4 × 200 meters at 90 percent maximum speed. Rest two minutes between sets. Keep a graph of the times; plot them once a month.

    (*Note:* The 200-meter and 100-meter runs are excellent distances for training and evaluation. The above workouts are two of the many possibilities available.)

Example:

This test or workout was designed for sports that have a work/rest cycle of play. However, it is an excellent workout for training speed endurance for most sports. Do 10 repetitions of the following.

Speed positions: 15-second run with a 60-second walk back

Medium positions: 16-second run with a 60-second walk back

Slower positions: +17-second run with a 60-second walk back

Speed Endurance: Short

The following test is good for analyzing speed endurance for short sprinting distances:

40 yard sprints. Run 10 × 40 yards at 90 percent of maximum speed with 30 seconds of rest after each sprint. Use a heart rate monitor, if possible, for a more comprehensive assessment of heart rate response during and after each 40-yard sprint and the recovery after the set of 10- to 40-yard sprints.

Basic training serves as a sneak preview of things to come and is an orientation course that prepares you for the rigors ahead. Certain goals should be established as a result of your sports check scorecard and simple tests found in chapter 1. Each goal will serve as a guide for improving your basic fitness prior to advancing to your next step. The next section will lead you through the necessary steps for developing a basic training program. It also allows you the flexibility of writing more advanced programs in the future.

ORGANIZING YOUR BASIC TRAINING

Complete the test score sheet shown in table 1.1. Develop a list of the areas you need to work on. List those areas in order of importance to your main objective. Now, complete the conditioning program schedule in worksheet 3.1. Place the sport-specific list on this sheet in the spaces provided. Each exercise is recorded in the day and time period

WORKSHEET 3.1

Conditioning Program Schedule							

Name:_____ Height:_____ Weight:_____

Date:___/___/___ Time:___:___.___

Time	M	T	W	R	F	Sa	Su
7:00	____	____	____	____	____	____	____
8:00	____	____	____	____	____	____	____
9:00	____	____	____	____	____	____	____
10:00	____	____	____	____	____	____	____
11:00	____	____	____	____	____	____	____
12:00	____	____	____	____	____	____	____
1:00	____	____	____	____	____	____	____
2:00	____	____	____	____	____	____	____
3:00	____	____	____	____	____	____	____
4:00	____	____	____	____	____	____	____
5:00	____	____	____	____	____	____	____
6:00	____	____	____	____	____	____	____
7:00	____	____	____	____	____	____	____

of your choice. This record becomes the workout schedule of exercises that will remove any of your measured weaknesses. It is important that you commit yourself to the program by writing your name in the space provided. To assure that all the necessary elements will be adequately perfected, they should be placed in a daily schedule.

How do you put a basic training program together? The first thing you must understand is that every good workout should have a primary purpose. The workout is similar to any work of art, be it a book, a dance, or a play. There is a beginning, a main purpose, and an ending. The beginning prepares the way for the main purpose, and the ending gets you back as close as possible to a normal level of body function. This theme is evident in every step of the seven-step model. You can determine the purpose of the workout by first making a list of all the critical tasks that need to be accomplished.

Then arrange this list in order of each item's importance. Finally, allocate the time you have available for practice to each item based on its importance.

General Warm-Up

An adequate structured warm-up period (10-30 minutes) that first exercises the large muscle groups (jogging, striding) and brings about perspiration and a rise in core temperature of one to two degrees should be followed by static (stretching to the maximum range of motion and holding that extreme position for 10 to 30 seconds), dynamic (stretching movements specific to the action of sprinting), or PNF stretching (Proprioceptive Neuromuscular Facilitation, which alternates contraction and relaxation of both agonist and antagonist muscles). Warm-up sessions increase your body temperature, circulation, and muscle elasticity and prepare you psychologically for the workout routine ahead. Choose your routine from the following list:

- Jog 440 to 880 yards in five minutes. Begin by jogging at an easy pace and then progressively run at a faster pace as you approach the final 220 yards. You can add a variety of footwork patterns and basic skills as you run to improve and maintain these skills.
- Build ups/walk backs on playing field. Even though your sport is confined to different playing areas, it is still worth your while to spend time in the early part of your training doing this workout. Break the circuit of 120 yards of running and 120 yards of walking into four phases:

  40 yards of gradual acceleration

  40 yards of maintained speed

  40 yards of gradual coast-down

  120 yards of recovery walk back

  Do 8 to 10 easy repetitions. Emphasize good running form while gradually increasing the speed of the run.
- Rope jumping for three to six minutes. The time can be broken into rounds that emphasize various foot and hand rhythms.
- Speed bag or shadow boxing (adapt this exercise to your specific sport: a basketball player defending an opponent, for example) for three to six minutes. Shadow boxing is an exercise in creative imagination. You are fighting an imaginary oppo-

nent and in the process have a sport-specific, meaningful way to warm up. Find those openings and use the skills to land the most effective punch. The time can be divided into rounds that emphasize various foot and hand combinations and rhythms.

- Tennis ball reaction catching. Face a wall starting at six feet and throw and catch the tennis ball at ever increasing speeds. Gradually move forward until you are able to reach a speed and distance that yields a 60 percent performance score. Maintain that position until you can perform at the 80 percent score level, and then increase the difficulty. Complete 100 catches and record the following information:

    Distance in feet at completion of 100 catches

    Speed (slow, medium, fast)

    Number of catches out of 100

    Time to complete the 100 catches

When you think you're hot stuff, have someone else throw the balls from behind you into a flat wall or corner.

- Juggling for three to six minutes. A variety of juggling techniques should be used. Two or three bags of various textures and weights can be used along with more advanced techniques such as a mini-trampoline or running as you juggle. When you get really good, use the balls from your sport. These methods fit nicely into a warm-up routine and provide an integrated way of training the brain, neuromuscular system, and visual aspects (tracking and peripheral vision).
- Balance for 30 to 60 seconds. Stand on one foot for 30 seconds. Increase the difficulty by circling the free leg or making figure-eights with it. You can add advanced variations by changing the patterns to circles, squares, triangles, and so on.

Proper warm-up and stretching reduces the incidence of soft tissue injuries, mentally prepares an athlete, and aids performance in sprinting.

The general warm-up period has adequately prepared you for the flexibility portion of your program.

FLEXIBILITY PRINCIPLES

Flexibility (stretching) exercises are often too closely associated with warm-up. Consequently, some athletes make the common mistake of stretching cold muscles before beginning their workout, rather than first warming up the body with some large-muscle activity such as walking or jogging for five to eight minutes or until perspiration is evident. At this point, body temperature has been elevated two to four degrees and muscles can now be safely stretched. Keep in mind that you warm up to stretch, you do not stretch to warm up.

Who Should Stretch?

Some athletes need to stretch more than others. Lean body types with a good range of motion may need very little stretching, whereas the stocky, more powerfully built athlete with limited range of motion needs 5 to 10 minutes of flexibility exercises before making any radical moves such as bending over to touch his toes or explosive jumping or sprinting. Athletes of all ages and skill levels can benefit from stretching exercises. Routines can be gentle, easy, relaxing, and safe or extremely vigorous.

Why Stretch?

Research has shown that a daily stretching routine will help increase your range of motion, improve your playing and sprinting performance by conserving energy and increasing fluid motion, aid muscle relaxation, aid sprinting form, and help you cool down at the end of your workout.

> An improvement in overall flexibility may improve speed by slightly increasing stride rate and decreasing energy expenditure and resistance during the sprinting action.

Regular stretching also helps to reduce the incidence of injuries that may occur in high-speed activities and sports competitions. Continuous exercise such as jogging, running, cycling, and aerobics has the effect of tightening and shortening muscles. Tight muscles are more vulnerable to injury from the explosive movements that are common in sports. A brief warm-up period followed by stretching will not only increase your range of motion but also will provide some protection from common soft tissue injuries such as strains, sprains, and tears. Striving to maintain a full, normal range of motion in each joint with adequate strength, endurance, and power throughout the range will reduce your chances of experiencing an exercise-induced injury.

When to Stretch

Stretching exercises should be used during your regular warm-up routine before each workout to prepare the body for vigorous activity, during the cool-down phase of a workout to help muscles return to a normal relaxed state, and anytime you can work exercises into your schedule to merely improve range of motion in key joints or aid in your rehabilitation from injury.

If your flexibility test scores from the assessment phase in chapter 1 were poor, you should plan to stretch for a longer period of time before and after each workout, after sitting or standing for long periods, whenever you feel stiff, or even while you are engaged in passive activities such as watching TV or listening to music. Remember, you must first elevate your body temperature and produce some sweat by engaging in large muscle group activity before you stretch.

When recovering from soft tissue injuries, focus your attention on reducing pain and swelling, returning to normal strength, and achieving full non-restricted range of motion. Unless regular stretching begins as soon as pain and swelling have been eliminated, loss of flexibility in the injured joint is almost certain.

What Stretching Techniques to Use

A well-rounded flexibility program for speed improvement must devote attention to all the body's major joints: the neck, shoulder, back, and hip, as well as the knees and ankles. You can increase your range of motion in each of these major joints in six to eight weeks by following one of the recommended stretching techniques.

Static Stretching

If you plan to work out alone, you must use the static stretching method. After moving slowly into the stretch, apply steady pressure until the point of discomfort in a particular joint for 10-30 seconds without bouncing or jerking. Complete each exercise two to three times. Many studies show static stretching to be safer than ballistic techniques that involve bouncing at the extreme range of motion. Static stretching is not likely to result in muscle soreness and is as effective as the other techniques.

Proprioceptive Neuromuscular Facilitation (PNF)

PNF stretching is a popular two-person technique based on a contract-and-relax principle. PNF stretching requires a partner to apply steady pressure to a body area at the extreme range of motion until the person being stretched feels a slight discomfort.

When stretching your hamstring muscle group, for example, lie on your back with one leg extended to 90 degrees or a comfortable stretch. Have your partner apply steady pressure while you attempt to raise your leg overhead further. As pressure is applied, you begin to push against your partner's resistance by contracting the muscle being stretched. This isometric hamstring contraction produces no leg movement because your partner will resist whatever force you apply during the push phase. After a 10-second push, relax your hamstring muscles while your partner again applies pressure for five seconds to increase the stretch even further. Repeat two to three times. Many other stretches can be devised to meet the needs of each athlete. Some other common problem sites are lower back and shoulder girdle for all throwers.

The PNF method involves four phases: an initial easy stretch of the muscle, an isometric contraction with resistance provided by a partner, relaxation of five seconds, and a final passive stretch for five seconds. As a variation, your partner may allow your leg to move slightly downward during the push phase. PNF stretching relaxes the muscle group being stretched, which produces greater muscle length and improves flexibility. Disadvantages of this method include the presence of some discomfort, a longer workout time, and the inability to stretch without a partner.

How Much Intensity to Use

Proper stretching should take the form of a slow, relaxed, controlled, and relatively pain-free movement. Disregard the "no pain, no gain" mentality when stretching; improvement occurs without undue pain. Joint pressure should produce only mild discomfort. Too much pain and discomfort is a sign you are overloading soft tissue and are at risk of injury. After experiencing mild discomfort with each stretch, relax the muscles being stretched prior to the next repetition. You will learn to judge each exercise by the "stretch and feel method," easing off the push if pain becomes intense or gets worse as the exercise progresses.

How Long to Stretch

The length of your flexibility session will increase from beginning stages to more advanced stages because the length of hold time is increased as you become more advanced. After you warm-up properly and are perspiring, complete each exercise gradually and slowly, beginning with a 10-second hold and adding two to three seconds to your hold time each workout until you can comfortably maintain the position at your extreme range of motion for 30 seconds after two to three months of regular stretching. Stretches that are longer than 30 seconds appear to only slightly increase the benefits and may be impractical.

If your main purpose for stretching is to prepare your body for vigorous exercise and to maintain existing range of motion in the major joints, 6 to 9 total minutes of stretching is sufficient. For athletes striving to increase their range of motion, 10 to 30 minutes of careful stretching daily may be necessary. Several different stretching exercises may be performed for each joint.

How Often to Stretch

Those who are just beginning a flexibility training program should use their routine three to four times weekly. After several months, two to three workouts weekly will maintain the flexibility you have acquired. As pointed out previously, stretching should also be a part of your daily warm-up routine prior to your participation in any phase of the seven-step model.

How Flexible to Become

The gymnast, ballet dancer, and hurdler must be more flexible than sprinters and athletes in most team sports. The stretching routine described in this section is geared toward improvement in all major joints and also emphasizes key areas for high-speed sprinting action.

Orthopedic surgeons are treating more injuries associated with excessive stretching and attempts to acquire a very high level of flexibility than injuries associated with failure to stretch. This increase may be partially due to a renewed interest in stretching and the popularity of yoga and aerobics that tend to overemphasize flexibility or use questionable stretching exercises. As is the case with most training programs, striving for far too much flexibility may be undesirable.

Flexibility Exercises

Choose at least one stretching exercise for each of the major muscle groups, and apply exercises equally to both sides of your body. Although there are hundreds of different stretches in use, many are unsafe and should be avoided. This section provides a sound general stretching routine for sprinting and most team sports and identifies.

Hamstring group (back of upper leg).

1. Stand erect with both knees bent slightly. Bend over and touch the ground, holding your maximum stretch position.

2. Lie on your back, sit up and reach for your toes with both knees slightly bent, holding your maximum stretch position. Keep both knees slightly bent in both exercises to remove the pressure from your lower back.

Quadriceps group (front of upper leg). Stand on your left leg, grasp your right ankle with your right hand and pull your heel toward your buttocks, holding your maximum stretch position. Repeat using your other leg.

Hip. Lie on your back and then relax and straighten both legs. Pull the left foot toward your chest and hold. Repeat using the right foot.

> Increased flexibility in the ankles, hips, and shoulders may help prevent understriding because of inflexibility.

Groin. Assume a sitting position with the soles of your feet together. Place your hands around your feet and pull yourself forward.

Calf. Stand about two feet from a wall and lean forward with the lead leg bent and the rear leg extended. Move the hips forward and keep the heel of the straight leg on the ground until you feel a stretch in your calf.

Achilles tendon and soleus. Stand approximately two feet from a wall or fence. Bend the back knee slightly, keep both heels on the ground, and lean forward.

> Increased range of motion in the ankle (extension) may favorably improve stride length.

Hold the stretched position at your maximum range of motion for 25 to 30 seconds and perform at least three sets of each exercise. Approach this session with an attitude of relaxation. You should begin the stretching session after your heart rate and body temperature have been elevated from general warm-up exercises such as those indicated previously.

THE COOL-DOWN PERIOD

The justification for a cool-down period following any of your vigorous workouts in the seven-step model is quite simple. Blood returns to the heart through a system of veins; the blood is pushed along by heart contractions, and the veins' milking action is assisted by muscle contraction during exercise. Veins contract or squeeze and move the blood forward against gravity while valves prevent the blood from backing up. If you stop exercising suddenly, this milking action will also cease, and blood return will drop quickly and may cause blood pooling (blood remaining in the same area) in the legs, leading to deep breathing, which may in turn lower carbon dioxide levels and produce muscle cramps. At this point, blood pressure drops precipitously and causes trouble. The body compensates for the unexpected drop in pressure by secreting as much as 100 times the normal amount of a hormone called norepinephrine. This high level of norepinephrine can cause cardiac problems for some individuals during the recovery phase of vigorous exercises such as a marathon or triathlon.

The final three to eight minutes of your workout should involve a period of slowly diminishing intensity through the use of a slow jog for three quarters to one mile at a pace of three to four minutes per quarter mile, each quarter mile slower than the previous one. The ideal cool-down should take place in the same environment as the workout (except in extremely hot or cold weather), last at least five minutes, and be followed by a brief stretching period. By stretching at the end of your workout as the final phase of the cool-down period, you are helping fatigued muscles return to their normal resting length and a more relaxed state and reducing your chances of muscle soreness the following day.

SUMMARY

The importance of basic training cannot be overestimated. It is the bedrock, the foundation upon which you build all the other steps. The sports check scorecard has given you the basis for your individualized program. The testing program was designed to help you consider the demands of your sport and identify any limitations that need to be corrected.

Remember, there are no make ups on the road to maximum development, no opportunities to get what you didn't get when you were supposed to get it! A later start on this road to development decreases the number of neural pathways developed, reduces the number of acquired skills, and ensures that you will not reach your maximum potential in your sport. But don't stop now just because you started a bit late, keep on going. Don't worry if you've been a little lazy in the past, our sport speed program will help you be the best you can be wherever you are. Keeping this encouragement in mind, go on to chapter 4, "Step 2: Strength and Power Training."

CHAPTER 4

STEP 2: STRENGTH AND POWER TRAINING

The main advantage of a high-horsepower automobile engine is its acceleration: it can get the automobile up to a chosen speed more quickly than a lower-powered engine can.
—Peter Brancazio

Functional strength and power training aims to improve your ability to apply sufficient force to an opponent or object at the right time, at the required performance speed, and in the right direction. The key is to discover how much force is required at various times during the game and to learn to precisely apply that force in your sport. As functional strength and power increase, so will your "horsepower reserve" that will allow you to play the game at a lower percent of your capacity with more available power for the more demanding adjustments that are certain to arise during the game. Certainly, a big benefit of a high horsepower automobile engine is its rapid acceleration. Similarly, a high-powered human body will reach a chosen speed more quickly than a lower-powered body. Improved functional strength and power can provide you with this advantage.

Speed of movement in short distances and limb strength are related; athletes with higher leg strength to body weight ratios also tend to sprint faster.

THE PURPOSE OF THE FUNCTIONAL STRENGTH PROGRAM

Before we discuss the purpose of the functional strength program, let's take a look at the basic elements that make up a game or competition to see what kind of program is required. Although these events may vary according to the situation and sport, most competitive sports have some sort of stimulus that requires a response.

Each one of us comes with built-in performance qualities that can be influenced by a functional strength program. Each of these qualities has a range (thresholds or limits) of trainability. These qualities determine how fast we recognize and respond in athletic situations. Certainly, these results determine our level of success or failure in our chosen sports.

The primary purpose of a functional strength and power program is to develop the required force and tissue capacity for your sport. Tissue capacity includes the ability of the body tissues to defend, build, repair, heal, regenerate, remodel, and regulate themselves. All functional changes bring with them structural changes in tissues and systems. These changes involve the whole organism.

Any builder knows that the materials used in construction must be able to sustain the loads in all stress ranges. The three little pigs experienced the consequences of their material selection as each encountered the Big Bad Wolf. The human body also has its limitations. These limitations were very evident when former Washington Redskins' quarterback Joe Theismann was seriously injured in a nationally televised NFL game. During a sack, functional demands were placed on his leg that exceeded the physiological limits of bone and soft tissue. As a result, something had to give, and it was Joe's leg. Doctors, coaches, athletes, and fans should recognize that forces in sport can and do go beyond human tolerance. Many times the forces exceed your tissue's capacity to protect your body, and injuries occur. Although there can be no guarantee that a high level of functional strength and power will provide protection from such injuries, it does provide some amount of basic insurance.

Specific programs, such as strength training involving heavy weight, near-maximal muscle contractions, low repetitions, and full recovery between sets, have been shown to produce greater increases in the cross-sectional area of fast-twitch fibers than slow-twitch fibers.

With proper training, the human body will take care of the needed structural changes. Tissues will be strengthened as a natural consequence of functional strength and power training. You must also develop enough additional size, strength, and power reserve so you can perform at the very high playing speeds in your sport and still protect yourself from injury. Unquestionably, the most important injury prevention factor is to be an alert, highly-skilled player with the ability to control the forces you face on the field. Proper use of the program described in this chapter will do the rest. The immediate and long-term benefits will be evident through improved performance, faster recovery time in your sport, a reduction in injuries, and a reduced recovery time should an injury occur.

The ability to propel a stationary body into rapid movement and exert maximal force requires both strength and power (speed-strength). An athlete may be quite strong, yet lack explosive power and be incapable of sprinting a fast 40-yard or 40-meter dash. Speed and power training should involve movements that are similar to those in the sport (this is the principle of specificity).

WORK AND POWER

The relationship of work and power can be illustrated by imagining yourself completing a simple task. The task is to move 100 10-pound weights onto a one-foot high train in 10 seconds. The train will depart in 10 seconds; therefore, only the weights on the train can be credited to your account. In a similar manner, the foot of the sprinter has a window of time to apply force. Accordingly, it is important that you train to meet the many specific power output requirements in your sport.

Table 4.1 summarizes the power output of an athlete who moves 10 weights from the platform to the train in a 10-second period. The key point to remember is that in most explosive sports there is about 0.1 to 0.3 second to apply additional force at the foot. The only way to increase your speed of action is to accelerate (increase the speed of work) the speed at which the 10-pound weights are moved. This illustration tells us a great deal about what we must do to run or play at faster speeds. Many of the activities in this book have been designed to identify, correct, or improve your ability to apply more force at the foot during ground contact. In good sprinting, this time you have to make this adjustment is about 0.10 second. The timing required for generating more force at the foot is like the timing required for cracking a whip. The better the sequencing of the limbs of the body, the more effective or louder the "pop" of the whip or the faster we run and play.

TABLE 4.1

Power Output			
Total pounds available	Total pounds in 10 seconds	Total work in 10 seconds	Total power in 10 seconds
1,000 lb	10 × 10 lb = 100 lb	100 lb × 1 ft = 100 ft lb	100 ft lb/10 sec = 10 ft lb/sec
100%	10%	10%	10%

The results given in table 4.1 show that the athlete was only credited with 10 percent of the power and work possible. Only the work and power you recorded in the allotted time counted. Similarly, in sprint training, a sprinter's foot is in contact with the ground for about 0.09 to 0.11 second at a time. Any force that is not applied at the foot during this time period is of no use in sprinting faster. Think of the many complicated tasks in your sport to see how important this principle becomes. Imagine the complexities of covering your opponent during the game. What if you need to move or cut left, which requires a planting of the right foot, and it's still in the air? Add this delay time into the playing equation to see how far your opponent will be from you in the time it takes you to put your foot on the ground to apply appropriate countering force.

ACCELERATION OR MASS?

Most team sports are played with multiple starts and stops and many changes in direction. Under these circumstances, it is no surprise that the average speeds players use during competition are well below their maximum sprinting speeds. It is interesting to note that All-Pro running backs like Tony Dorsett, Emmitt Smith, and Barry Sanders generate as much force as big linemen in short ranges. This fact dramatically illustrates that the amount of force generated is influenced by either changing the player's mass (weight) or acceleration (quickness of movement).

If you have a choice, the best way to generate force is to increase your acceleration. Obviously, these All-Pro running backs are able to accelerate more rapidly than the 300-pound linemen and, therefore, match the linemen's force output to make first downs on short yardage situations. The standoff between the giant linemen and smaller, quicker running backs can produce a structural problem for the running back because of his less protective body tissues. The smaller running back does give away a lot of protective tissue that could be used to absorb the forces of constant pounding. The best of both worlds is to become a big and fast running back like Hall-of-Famers Jim Brown or Earl Campbell.

WORK FAST TO BE FAST

Because the "work fast to be fast" principle is essential in all explosive sports, we recommend you make use of high power output exercises for mental and physical focus. Weights can be selectively used to train for explosive sports. It is important to recognize that there is a fine range of speeds and loads that must be adhered to if transfer to your sport is to be maximized. Tissue strength will be gained over a wide range of high-intensity explosive lifts. One guideline is to use the threshold principle discussed in chapter 2. Remember that mental quickness is an essential element of physical quickness; you must think fast to be fast.

A number of training programs have been successful in bridging the gap between strength and power to improve speed strength and sprinting speed. Combinations of weight training, explosive power training, and various forms of traditional speed training (speed endurance, overspeed, sprint loading) significantly improve speed in short distances.

Many exercises in the weight room can be used to develop functional strength and power output. Inertial impulse exercises and Olympic lifts, with their variations, are the most important of these exercises and are discussed in detail in this chapter.

INERTIAL IMPULSE

According to Albert, Hillegass, and Spiegel (1994), "functional activities and sports activities have been shown to occur between 700 to 6,000 degrees per second for the upper and lower limbs." Therefore, performance measurements and training should fall in these same ranges. Unfortunately, very few machines can step up to the plate and swing at those speeds. An exception is EMA, Inc.'s Impulse System machine, which is capable of hitting the conditioning and rehabilitation ball out of the traditional training ballpark.

Inertial impulse machines have a non-gravity, horizontal sliding loading mechanism for working the athlete. A handle and rope connection to the horizontal sliding mechanism allows the athlete to do a variety of rehabilitation and sport-specific actions. Scientific data can be collected from the exercising athlete by connecting an accelerometer and oscilloscope to the rope handle device. Inertial impulse exercise machines are available at many rehabilitation centers. These machines provide a major breakthrough in training on field power in the weight room. Although various inertial impulse training devices, such as the speed bag, have been used in the gym for other purposes (see chapter 5 for more practical suggestions), special inertial impulse machines are different in that they can be used for numerous body actions and with various loads and speeds, depending on the desired outcome. In fact, these machines provide the perfect illustration of the interrelationship between mass (weight) and acceleration (quickness).

To feel the impact of the Impulse System in a familiar skill setting, imagine putting 500 pounds in a wheelbarrow and then recording how fast you could get it moving and how quickly you could stop it. No doubt you would find that it takes a lot of time to start and stop the wheelbarrow. Suppose you took the weight out of the wheelbarrow and did the same experiment. Would you feel the difference? If you lined up some football dummies and tried to knock down the dummies with the heavy and light wheelbarrows from one foot, two feet, and 3 feet away, what would the results be? Weight and quickness apply to performance in any sport. Even if your sport is a non-contact sport, you can use this principle to improve your sports performance and reduce the likelihood of injury.

Some of the benefits you can expect to gain from using inertial impulse training include the duplication of on-field forces, functional strength and power gains that are transferable to competition in your sport, stronger tendons and ligaments, and a reduction in training time. Dr. Jim Counsilman, noted swim coach from Indiana University, coined the term for this type of training as "programmable acceleration." He believes programmable acceleration programs will form the basis of the modern sports speed training programs in the near future. However, most programs don't have the kind of equipment to apply a precise acceleration program. Still, a small level of effectiveness can still be achieved by using barbells and dumbbells.

If you don't have access to special inertial impulse equipment, you can use any system that you can hit and that hits you back or that you can respond to as a training device, including plyometrics of all kinds, speed bags, boxing, and, yes, even your pool. The pool provides the most universally available way to apply programmable acceleration techniques. Many of the major movements of the body can be exercised in the water by moving very short distances (a matter of inches to two feet) with rapid starts and stops that mimic specific positions of the skill. You can do sets of 10 with each set lasting 20 seconds. You can practice either a limited starting position or a complete joint range of motion for the desired actions. Actions can be explosive or rehabilitative in nature. Therefore, the complete exercise spectrum of training objective speeds can be included. For instance, a discus thrower can work the discus arm action with the throwing arm. The thrower does this by quickly starting, stopping, and returning to the original starting position. Be creative by designing special exercises for your sport and applying them to your program.

OLYMPIC LIFTS

The Olympic lifts are the most commonly recommended and used exercises in sophisticated power and speed training programs. Garhammer (1985), in a study of the heaviest successful snatch and clean and jerk for five Olympic gold medalists, showed that "athletes trained in the Olympic style of weightlifting have an extremely high capacity to develop power, which is necessary for success in the sport." Since Olympic lifts require high power output, they have become popular exercises in sports conditioning programs. In addition, proper lifting teaches good fundamental body mechanics that may be adapted to many sports.

These exercises provide an excellent means of improving functional strength and power. Because Olympic lifts usually do not involve a trunk-twisting action when performed with a barbell, a one-hand dumbbell will yield greater benefits and compliment the barbell exercises.

> Free weight exercises are preferred over machines for two major reasons: the actual movement and muscle involvement for which one is training can be replicated more closely, and the three-phase response of the body to stressors (Selye's general adaptation syndrome) is enhanced.

Power exercises, such as the Olympic lifts, should be included in your program for a number of reasons: they train the mind and body to develop peak force, they aid in increasing the amount of time peak force is applied, they develop force in a short period of time, and they emphasize good body position and movements that cross over into other sports.

Clean (Barbell/Dumbbell)

The major purpose of the clean (figure 4.1, a, b, and c) is to develop the large muscles of the body in an explosive action that requires the use of many joints and muscle groups in a coordinated movement. The use of dumbbells requires a twisting of the body and tends to enhance training benefits. The following suggestions will help you perform the clean correctly:

1. Assume a comfortable stance with your feet spread about hip to shoulder-width apart.
2. Grasp the bar with an overhand grip at slightly wider than shoulder width. You can use an overhand, hooked strap.
3. Bend your legs at the start of the lift and use the legs to lift the weight first.
4. Maintain a straight back and hold it tightly in that position as you bring the bar up, keeping it close to the body.
5. Place your shoulders over the bar (8 to 12 centimeters).
6. Keep the bar close to your body.
7. Rebend the legs after clearing the knees. Keep your arms straight, keeping in mind that this is a leg and back exercise.
8. Jump vertically into the lift with your legs, pulling the bar as high as possible. Your arms will blend in after the leg and back action.

9. Drive your elbows up.

10. Drop the body quickly and catch the bar on your shoulders while bringing the elbows quickly under the bar.

Figure 4.1a

Figure 4.1b

© Joe Cambioso

Figure 4.1c

Near maximum weight will require that you go into a deep knee bend to catch the bar; therefore, strong legs and back are essential in good lifting. Use the "1.3 times the clean" rule for estimating your squatting strength (maximum clean in pounds times 1.3 equals squat weight). This estimate should provide an excellent guide to ensure sufficient foundational leg and back strength reserve.

Jerk (Barbell, Dumbbell, and Machine Rack)

The major purpose of the jerk (see figure 4.1, *b* and *c*) is to develop the large muscle groups of the body with an explosive action that is total body or multi-jointed in nature. The following suggestions will help you perform the jerk correctly:

1. Take the bar from the rack to work primarily on the jerking movement.

2. Assume a comfortable stance with your feet spread about hip-to shoulder-width apart.

3. Grasp the bar with your palms facing upward. The distance

between your hands should be slightly wider than shoulder-width.

4. Rest the bar primarily on your shoulders. Keep your back vertical and tight.

5. Bend your legs with a quick dipping action. Experience will help you find the proper depth for a quick explosive return. (A depth of 10% to 15% of the athlete's height is recommended.)

6. Jump explosively into the bar, attempting to drive the bar as high as possible. The bar should move vertically overhead. The action of your shoulders and arms will blend into the explosive action of the leg jumping action.

7. Drop directly beneath the bar, catching it straight over the shoulders. The legs can be kept shoulder-width or split, as shown in the jerk sequence.

8. Experiment to determine which foot to place forward. Both feet should be turned in.

9. Straighten your arms vertically, holding them and the rest of the body rigidly.

10. Return to the erect position by moving the front foot back first with a slight jab step (this shortens the distance), and then step forward with your back foot.

Snatch (Barbell and Dumbbell)

The major purpose of the snatch (figure 4.2, *a* and *b*) is to develop the explosiveness of the muscle groups of the body in a coordinated multi-jointed action. The following suggestions will help you perform the snatch correctly:

1. Assume a comfortable stance with your feet spread about shoulder-width apart.

2. Widen the clean grip so that at full extension the height of the bar will be lower and therefore require less vertical work. Experience will help to determine the optimal grip to use.

3. Bend your legs before lifting the bar and use them to get the weight off the ground. Keep your back straight and hold it tightly.

4. Place your shoulders over the bar. Keep the bar close to your body.

5. Rebend your legs after clearing the knees.

6. Keep your arms straight to allow the legs and back to lift the bar as high as possible.

7. Jump vertically into the lift with the legs, pulling the bar with the arms as high as possible. The arms will fit in the action after the legs and back have done their part.
8. Drive your elbows upward.
9. Drop the body quickly and catch the bar directly over your head and shoulders.

Figure 4.2a

Figure 4.2b

Keep in mind that leg and back strength is essential in all aspects of lifting, but it is extremely important in the recovery phase when lifting maximum weights.

SAMPLE POWER OUTPUT PROGRAM

The Speedweek principles, covered in greater detail in chapter 10, use high-intensity work Monday through Wednesday when the body isn't as fatigued. Therefore, a power exercise program using the Olympic lifts should be used on Monday and Wednesday after completing your overspeed and sport speed programs.

The one-repetition maximum (1RM) should be used as the basis for loading. To determine a 1RM, you find the maximum weight that can be lifted for each exercise just one time. Table 4.2 shows six levels of workout intensity based on the percent of the 1RM and the quality developed.

TABLE 4.2

Rating Intensities of the 1-Repetition Maximum (1RM) for Exercise Prescription		
1RM (percent)	Rating	Quality developed*
90+	Very heavy	Strength
80-90	Heavy	Strength/strength endurance
70-80	Medium	Power/strength endurance
60-70	Medium light	Power/muscle endurance
50-60	Light	Power/muscle endurance
40-50	Easy	Threshold of training effect

*The speed of movement will determine the amount of power developed at any intensity level.
Data from P.E. Ward and R.D. Ward, 1991, *Encyclopedia of Weight Training* (Laguna Hills, CA: QPT Publications).

The sample program shown in table 4.3 indicates how Olympic lifts should be incorporated into your program to increase maximum strength. You can see from the numbers in the table that there are wide ranges in intensities, with loads increasing to at or near your 1RM. Rest between sets is maximized to minimize the effects of fatigue as a limiting factor. It is recommended that you shift the emphasis of the lifts on Monday and Wednesday. For instance, the clean can be at higher intensities and volumes on Monday, and the jerk can be at higher intensities and volumes on Wednesday. The power component in this step will be of great use as you continue to step 3: ballistics, where time for work output decreases at a tremendous rate while loads on the body increase.

TABLE 4.3

Sample Program Using the Olympic Lifts	
Monday	**Wednesday**
Warm-up	Warm-up
Cleans:	**Jerks:**
Sets: 3-6	Sets: 3-6
Repetitions: 3-5	Repetitions: 3-5
%RM: 66-100%	%RM: 66-100%
Rest: 1.5-5 min between sets	Rest: 1.5-5 min between sets
Jerks:	**Cleans:**
Sets: 3-6	Sets: 3-6
Repetitions: 3-5	Repetitions: 3-5
%RM: 66-100%	%RM: 66-100%
Rest: 1.5-5 min between sets	Rest: 1.5-5 min between sets

FUNCTIONAL STRENGTH PROGRAM FOR THE SERIOUS ATHLETE

The components of the complete workout schedule remain the same during the preseason period; however, their intensity and duration increase during the second half of this period. Phase A of the preseason should start most of the exercise at approximately 50 percent of your maximum level as a general guide. The rate of increase should be variable, such as 8 to 10 percent per week if previous maximum levels are to be regained by the time you begin Phase B.

Phase B is composed of many sets and repetitions at a high percent of your 1RM for each lift. An increased intensity in muscle endurance is also a definite objective sought during this period. The increase in intensity of the workout will require a comparable increase in the number of sets (at least five sets in most areas); as a consequence, the length of the ideal workout will increase from two to three hours.

A standard program is outlined below to help you get started:

1. **Warm-up, flexibility, body control: running or jumping techniques**
   a. Jogging one-half mile and/or rope jumping (5 minutes)
   b. Speed bags (boxing bags of various sizes, 15 minutes)
   c. Running and jumping for flexibility (10 minutes)

2. **Power position exercises (40 minutes)**
   a. Snatch: power
   b. Snatch: split-squat
   c. Clean and push jerk
   d. Pull

3. **Legs and back (23 minutes)**
   a. Dead lift
   b. Squats front
   c. Squats back
      Sets: 3-5; repetitions: 3-5

4. **Shoulders and arms (18 minutes)**
   a. Incline
   b. Bench
   c. Curls
      Sets: 3-5; repetitions: 3-5

5. **Abdominal and neck (9 minutes)**
   a. Four-way neck: 1 set, 8-12 repetitions
   b. Rotary neck : 1 set, 6 repetitions each way
   c. Abdominals: 3 sets, 25 repetitions

A minimum of two strength sessions weekly, preferably every other day, are needed to improve speed strength; one workout weekly during the season will nearly maintain off-season gains. During the first two weeks of a newly started program, more recuperation time is needed. Using maximum and near maximum weight also lengthens recovery time. Short (45 minutes or less), highly intense workouts allow athletes to train more often.

Table 4.4 shows a sample functional strength and power program for the beginner. Three sets of the leg press exercise would be performed: the first with 60 percent of your maximum for 10 repetitions, the second set at 65 percent of your maximum for 8 repetitions, and the third and final set at 70 percent of your maximum for 6 repetitions. The same procedure should be followed for each exercise.

TABLE 4.4

Sample Functional Strength and Power Program for Beginners								
Exercise	RM	Mon.	Tues.	Wed.	Thurs.	Fri.	Sat.	Sun.
Warm-up: Flexibility				Before every workout				
Leg/back:								
Leg press	___	L		M		H		
Knee extensions	___	L		M		H		
Knee flexion	___	L		M		H		
Toe raises	___	L		M		H		
Shoulders/arms:								
Lat pull-down	___	M		H		L		
Bench press	___	M		H		L		
Press (seated)	___	H		M		L		
Press (standing)	___	H		M		L		
Curls (dumbbells)	___	M		H		L		
Trunk/abdomen:								
Sit-up (bent knee)	___	3 × 15		3 × 15		3 × 15		
Neck:								
Partner four-way neck	___	3 × 8-12		3 × 8-12		3 × 8-12		

PERCENT REPETITION MAXIMUM - SETS - REPETITIONS

Light (L)	Medium (M)	Heavy (H)
60 percent 1 × 10	60 percent 1 × 10	60 percent 1 × 10
65 percent 1 × 8	70 percent 1 × 8	75 percent 1 × 8
70 percent 1 × 6	80 percent 1 × 6	70 percent 1 × 6

A sample program for the athlete at the intermediate stage of strength development is shown in table 4.5. A workout would involve three sets of 5 to 8 repetitions of each exercise with the first set at 60 percent of your maximum, the second set at 65 percent of your maximum, and the third and final set at 70 percent of your maximum.

TABLE 4.5

Sample Functional Strength and Power Program for Intermediates

Exercise	RM	Mon.	Tues.	Wed.	Thurs.	Fri.	Sat.	Sun.
Warm-up: Flexibility			Before every workout					
Power: Clean	___	H		M		L		
Legs and back:								
Squat	___	L		M		H		
Dead lift	___	M		H		L		
Knee extensions	___	M		H		L		
Shoulders:								
Bench press	___	H		M		L		
Press (seated, behind neck)	___	M		H		L		
Rowing (bent over)	___	L		M		H		
Trunk/abdomen:								
Sit-ups (medicine ball)	___	2 × 12		2 × 12		2 × 12		
Sit-ups (crunch)	___	3 × 25		3 × 25		3 × 25		
Trunk (hyperextension)	___	2 × 12		2 × 12		2 × 12		
Neck:								
Partner four-way neck	___	3 × 8-12		3 × 8-12		3 × 8-12		

PERCENT REPETITION MAXIMUM - SETS - REPETITIONS

Light (L)	Medium (M)	Heavy (H)
60 percent 1 × 5-8	50 percent 1 × 5-8	60 percent 1 × 5-8
65 percent 1 × 5-8	70 percent 1 × 5-8	75 percent 1 × 5
70 percent 1 × 5-8	80 percent 1 × 5	85 percent 1 × 5

The advanced program shown in table 4.6 is programmed for high intensity. Four sets are performed. The first set is done at 60 percent of your maximum for five repetitions, the second set at 75 percent of your maximum for three repetitions, the third set at 85 percent of your maximum for three repetitions, and the fourth and final set at 90 percent of your maximum for two repetitions.

Explosive power (acceleration of mass [weight] on-field speeds) is a critical quality to demonstrate as an athlete. Apply the following information reported by Counsilman to your explosive workouts. Counsilman stated that the Russian and East German coaches felt so strongly about working fast to be fast that they monitored the training sessions and had their athletes stop if their speeds decreased below the desired speed of movement. To apply this concept to your program, stop if your perceived speed of action decreases.

TABLE 4.6

Sample Functional Strength and Power Program for Advanced Athletes

Exercise	RM	Mon.	Tues.	Wed.	Thurs.	Fri.	Sat.	Sun.
Warm-up: Flexibility				Before every workout				
Power:								
Clean, power	___	M		H				
Snatch, power	___		M		H			
Jerk, rack	___	H		M		L		
Legs/back:								
Pull, clean	___	M		L		H		
Dead lift	___	H		M				
Squat	___	L		M		H		
Squat, front	___					M		
Shoulders/chest/arms:								
Bench press	___	H		M				
Incline press	___		M		H			
Rowing	___	H		M		L		
Flys, supine	___			L		M		
Trunk/abdomen:								
Trunk hyperextension	___			3 × 10 (60%)		3 × 10 (70%)		
Sit-ups (bent knee)	___	3 × 25		3 × 25 (60%)		3 × 25 (70%)		
Neck:								
Partner four-way neck	___	3 × 8-12		3 × 8-12		3 × 8-12		

PERCENT REPETITION MAXIMUM - SETS - REPETITIONS

Light (L)	Medium (M)	Heavy (H)
60 percent 1 × 5	60 percent 1 × 5	60 percent 1 × 5
65 percent 1 × 5	70 percent 1 × 5	75 percent 1 × 3
70 percent 1 × 5	80 percent 1 × 5	85 percent 1 × 3
		90 percent 1 × 2

The advanced athletes can train this quality by doing the following:

1. Clean, jerk, or snatch one time at 70 percent on one of the Speedweek sessions (Monday or Wednesday).

2. Work with weights at fast speeds with 70 percent 1RM for 12 repetitions.

3. Work with weights at fast speeds with 50 to 60 percent 1RM for 16 to 20 repetitions.

Table 4.7 lists performance standards in percent body weight for various feats of functional strength and power.

TABLE 4.7

Functional Strength Performance Standards

Level	Snatch	Clean	Clean-jerk	Power curl	Pull
Very poor	0.50	0.90	0.90	0.70	1.10
Poor	0.70	1.10	1.10	0.90	1.30
Average	0.90	1.30	1.30	1.10	1.50
Good	1.10	1.50	1.50	1.30	1.70
Excellent	1.30	1.70	1.70	1.50	1.90

(Numbers indicate percent of body weight; weight times the percent equals the weight lifted.)

LEGS AND BACK

Level	135° 1/4 back squat	90° 1/2 back squat	Full 3/4 back squat	Front squat	Dead lift	Good morning
Knee bend	135°	90°	Full	45°		
Very poor	1.70	1.50	1.30	1.20	1.30	0.30
Poor	2.00	1.80	1.60	1.40	1.60	0.40
Average	2.30	2.10	1.90	1.60	1.90	0.50
Good	2.60	2.70	2.50	2.00	2.50	0.70
Excellent	2.90	2.70	2.50	2.00	2.50	0.70

ARMS AND SHOULDERS

Level	Military	Incline	Bench	Dip 20 seconds	Push up 20 seconds
Very poor	0.40	0.50	0.80	4 repetitions	11 repetitions
Poor	0.60	0.80	1.10	12 repetitions	19 repetitions
Average	0.80	1.10	1.40	20 repetitions	27 repetitions
Good	1.00	1.40	1.70	28 repetitions	35 repetitions
Excellent	1.20	1.70	2.00	36 repetitions	43 repetitions

*Female athletes should use this same table. For a more accurate interpretation of your performance, use the category one level above your score. For example, a snatch using 0.90 would be a rating of Good for the female athlete rather than Average.

Leg and Back Exercises

Deadlift

For the deadlift with alternate grip (see photo), assume a comfortable stance with your feet about shoulder-width apart. Bend your knees to grasp the bar and lift it from the floor keeping your back straight. Hold bar at your thighs before bending your knees to place bar back on the floor.

Dead lift with alternate grip.

Toe Raises

Toe raises strengthen your calf muscles for powerful leg thrusts. Toe raises can be done on a machine, using a padded barbell, or with a partner sitting on your back. Repeat the exercise with your feet in the following three positions to develop all aspects of the calf: heels out, heels straight, and heels in.

Toe raises.

Front Squat

The front squat develops strength in the lower extremities and trunk. Take the bar from a weight rack using a weight belt to support your back. Position the bar on your shoulders so it rests evenly on the deltoids. Have one person on each side of the bar to spot you. Spread your feet comfortably and slightly toed-out. (Placing the toes in various positions will work different parts of the thigh.) Keep your neck and back straight and elbows lifted high throughout the lift. Inhale to support your trunk at the start and bend your knees as far as you can until your upper thighs are parallel to the ground. Exhale as you return to standing. You can also use a thick board or weight under your heels. The added height will work the front part of your thighs more. For the back squat, position the bar on your shoulders behind your head and execute the same movements as the front squat.

© Joe Cambioso

Shoulder and Arm Exercises

Incline Press

The incline press is an excellent chest, shoulder, and arm developer that closely simulates the working angles of the muscles in many sports. With the bench in an incline position, place your hands on the bar at or slightly wider than shoulder width. Hands spread wide work the shoulders and chest whereas hands positioned closer together on the bar work the triceps more. With a spotter on both sides of the bar, inhale as you bend your elbows and bring the bar to your chest. Exhale as you straighten your arms to the starting position.

© Joe Cambioso

Bench Press

The bench press strengthens the shoulders and arms for optimal shoulder girdle protection. With the bench flat, position your hands on the bar at or slightly wider than shoulder width. With one spotter on each side of the bar, inhale and lower the bar to your chest. Exhale as you straighten your arms to return to the starting position.

© Joe Cambioso

Dumbbell Arm Curls

Dumbbell curls develop arm strength to help maintain proper left to right muscle balance. The photo demonstrates an alternate dumbbell curl. Start by holding the dumbbells at your side with the palms of your hands facing your body. As you curl each arm forward, one at a time, rotate your palm upward. The curling arm moves downward as the opposite arm moves upward. Emphasize an even rhythm in the curling action and take one breath for each cycle of left and right arm curl. Also try this exercise by starting with your palms facing backwards to work the biceps more as you rotate the palm during the curl.

Lat Row

The lat row strengthens the chest, back, shoulders, and arms. Execute the lat row using many different hand positions to isolate different muscles. Inhale as you pull the cable to your low, mid, or high chest making sure your trunk is vertical. Exhale as you return your arms to the starting position, following the same path as your pull. Completely extend your arms and the end of each repetitions to stretch the lats.

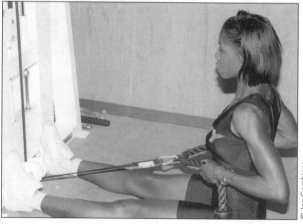

Lat Pull Down

The lat pull down strengthens the chest, back, shoulders, and arms. As in the lat row, try a variety of grips and hand widths. The wide grip, behind-the-neck action, as shown, is just one method. Vary the hands' width and position on the bar (palms away, toward, or alternated.) Inhale while pulling the bar down to the chest or to the shoulders and exhale as you bring the bar upward. Be sure to completely extend your arms at the top of each repetition to stretch the lats.

© Joe Cambioso

Flys (supine)

© Joe Cambioso

Flys are perfect for maintaining proper muscle balance of the chest, shoulders, and arms. The actions of this lift should cover the wide variety of shoulder movements. Lie on your back on a flat, incline, or decline bench. Hold the dumbbells over your body, arms extended with a slight bend at the elbow as shown in the top photo. Inhale as you lower the dumbbells to each side keeping the arms slightly bent until you reach your maximum range of motion. Exhale as you return to the starting position.

© Joe Cambioso

Abdominal and Neck Exercises

Abdominal Crunches

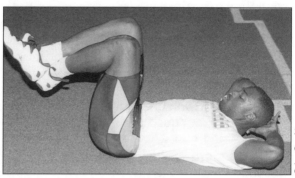

While the abdominal muscles have a limited range of motion, they play a major role in proper breathing and supporting all actions of the trunk. Start on your back with your hands behind your head and your knees up. Curl your body, flexing the abdominal muscles and forcing out air as you curl. This action will just clear the shoulders from the floor. Hold and exhale as you return to the floor. Use twisting actions in the curl to work all aspects of the trunk.

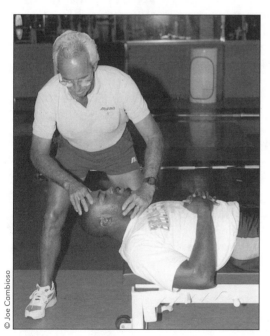

Neck Strengthening

Many athletes fail to develop their necks adequately. This two-person exercise insures that your neck will be ready for action. All actions—front, back and side—should be strengthened. With the exerciser on a bench or in a wrestler's floor position, the partner places his hands in a position on the exerciser that allows the person giving resistance a good pushing surface without undo discomfort to the exerciser. The partner applies even pressure with his hands while the exerciser pushes against this resistance.

STRENGTHENING THE HAMSTRING MUSCLE GROUP

Evaluating the hamstring/quadriceps strength ratio is more complicated than simply doing gross balance testing. Peak torque is not identical at opposing angles. Consequently, Grimby (1993) suggests that measurements be taken at the same joint angles and not at peak torque. Therefore, make sure you interpret any results from our testing as a gross indicator. Should problems arise, seek a more sophisticated testing assessment from your doctor.

The hamstring/quadriceps strength ratio test completed in chapter 1 provided you with a gross indication of the need for further testing on more sophisticated equipment that considers different joint angles. Most athletes, however, need additional training to increase the strength and power of the hamstring muscle group. Many experts feel that the hamstrings are the sprinter's weakest link. The leg curl and leg extension tests described in chapter 1 estimate the comparative strength of the quadriceps (front of upper leg) and hamstring muscle (back of upper leg) groups. Only a few elite athletes such as some champion sprinters, power lifters like world champion Dr. "Squat" Fred Hatfield, and some defensive backs in football (backward sprinting develops the hamstring group) are equally strong in both muscle groups. In over 25 years of sponsoring speed clinics and camps, we've seen only one athlete who had equal strength in both muscle groups; the large majority of athletes failed to meet our minimum standard (hamstring strength should equal 75 to 80 percent of quadriceps strength).

The power exercises (Olympic lifts) described previously are excellent hamstring exercises, as is the leg curl exercise. You also can lie on your back with your foot extended to a point several feet up on the wall. Pull down with a straight leg and hold that contraction for a period of 8 to 10 seconds. Repeat the exercise three to five times. This "paw down" motion is similar to Ralph Mann's and Tom Tellez's form drills and closely simulates that phase of the sprinting action.

Hypergravity (weighted suits, vest, or pants) training can be added to the sprint drills shown in chapter 8 for extra loading of the lower extremities. Care should be taken in selecting the training loads that allow you to maintain good sprinting action.

Roller skates or in-line skates offer a unique method of training the muscle groups responsible for the driving force for high levels of sprinting at the hip, knee, and ankle (gluteus, hamstring, quadriceps, calf muscles). Five areas of conditioning are recommended using skates:

• Range of motion in all possible directions of hip and leg movement. The legs should be moved in all directions. Begin by holding on to a chair while you complete 8 to 12 repetitions in all directions. Build up to three sets and emphasize flexibility.

• High-speed assisted drills using the sprint master or surgical tubing to focus on the sprinting action. The pull-through sprint drill shown in chapter 8 is one that can be done at high speed. Make sure that the speed is not excessive.

• Overspeed skate training. Hold onto a support and move the legs as fast as possible in a back and forth motion. Complete three to five sets of 8 to 12 repetitions with maximum rest (full recovery) between each set. When you have adjusted to the high-speed work, complete each set without holding on.

• Speed endurance exercises. Move back and forth at high speed for 10 to 30 seconds, working up to 30 to 60 seconds. You should gradually build up to 8 to 12 repetitions in sets of four, resting one and a half to three minutes between each set.

• Muscle endurance exercises for sprinting. Move the legs back and forth with a slight bend at the knee. The use of ankle weights or surgical tubing will provide the necessary loading. Complete three sets of 8 to 12 repetitions with as rapid a movement as possible with the load.

Special equipment such as Nautilus and Universal Gym also allow you to strengthen the hamstring muscle group while performing specific movements of sprinting (see figures on p.114).

Strengthening the hamstrings.

SHOULDER AND ARM EXERCISES FOR THROWERS

The biomechanics laboratory at Centinela Hospital Medical Center in Inglewood, California, under the direction of Dr. Frank Jobe, MD, Medical Director, has published a shoulder-strengthening program designed for baseball players. However, anyone interested in strengthening the shoulders and arms can follow the program. Write to the Centinela Hospital Medical Center for an illustrated copy of this program. Essentially, the exercises the Center prescribes cover every movement that the shoulders and arms can make. Multi-jointed pushing and pulling exercises recommended in our program will exercise the shoulders and arms as a unit, and the Jobe exercises will isolate the finer shoulder girdle and arm actions. A combination of both of these programs will produce the results you need for a superbly conditioned set of shoulders and arms.

The following arm and shoulder girdle actions are specifically isolated in the Jobe Dumbbell Program: external and internal rotation; shoulder flexion, extension, and adduction; scapular adduction and abduction; horizontal flexion; arm flexion and extension; forearm supination and pronation; wrist flexion and extension; and ulnar deviation.

STRENGTHENING THE KNEE

According to many experts in athletic training and rehabilitation, it is necessary to have strong legs from the ankle to the hip. However, there are 13 muscles that provide the tension to support the knee. All of them must be properly strengthened to give the knee maximum support throughout the total range of motion. All of the following actions of the knee should be included in your training program: flexion, extension, medial rotation, and stabilization.

The next chapter on ballistics training (step 3) builds upon the functional strength and power developed in step 2. Although all movements require the use of energy, chapter 5 describes the methods to develop the qualities you need to manage the explosive energy output (sending), energy input (receiving), and body toughening factors. Consequently, training for high energy movement is required. Overcoming the inertia of changing the directions of body movement and impact on the tissues of the body needs to have a special place in your conditioning program.

STEP 3:
BALLISTICS

■ ■

If one stands on the rails of a railroad track in an attempt to resist a train, he will become one with the rails. —**Martial arts saying**

Many of us sports fans have been to sporting events where the excitement, electricity, and action on the field were unbelievable. You could just feel the high levels of energy. No matter what the levels may have been in those exciting games, high-powered actions play a major role in the outcome of all sporting events. In addition, playing or sprinting at high speeds can provide much of the necessary short-term energy system development for most sports. There are three basic purposes of movement: to maintain equilibrium, to move an object, and to stop an object. The majority of sports include the following tasks:

- Multidirectional movements
- Short starts and stops with bursts of speed
- Rapid changes in direction
- Explosive power delivery of an impact through contact with the ground or an opponent
- Instantaneous power reception at contact
- Explosive power delivery to an object

Many times, these tasks occur at the same time and, in fact, should not be isolated from the total action at all.

The ability of tissues of the body to deliver, transmit, and absorb (cushion or spread the force out over time and distance) energy is fundamental to human performance and survival in athletic environments. Dr. Counsilman used a very good example in his "Advanced Theories of High-Level Performance" course at Indiana University to explain the best way to manage energy. He explained it to the class by using the sport of diving. Have you ever done a belly-flop when diving? How about a perfect dive? The difference in feelings of the two dives tells you a lot about how the energy of the dive is being managed. Obviously, in the belly-flop your body tissues have to manage all the energy of the dive in milliseconds and in a very limited distance because of the water's incompressibility. The perfect dive, on the other hand, spreads the same energy out over a much longer time and distance. How can you apply this information to your sport?

All tissues are not able to manage energy at the same level. The ability ratings for energy absorption of the most important tissues may surprise you. Their comparative ability to manage energy is shown in the following energy-absorbing capabilities scale.

(-)Low————Energy Absorbing Capabilities————High(+)

Bone   Ligament   Tendon   Muscle

MAINTAINING EQUILIBRIUM: FLOW

Prior to elaborating on the major areas of energy management, let's examine the importance of joining, resisting, and yielding into a unified whole. This state was covered in chapter 2. It is commonly referred to as the flow state or the Zone.

Technically, there are three categories of energy management:

Sending energy away from the body. This category includes all types of hitting, kicking, and throwing various implements, from footballs to medicine balls to assorted weights.

Receiving energy from outside sources. Forces that come into the body in the form of a ball or opposing players are listed in this category. Any form of catching develops the necessary sensitivity needed for receiving outside forces.

The Zone or the flow state. Whatever this state is finally discovered to be, most athletes who claim they have been there report that it is an effortless state. Time and motion slows, and performance approaches the spiritual. All of these factors permit athletes to perform at levels closer to their maximum potential. It is important to recognize that there are degrees and levels of this condition. Furthermore, each level or amount of time in the Zone will bring a different degree of performance enhancement. The higher the level, the higher the quality of energy management.

NOTING PERFORMANCE AND SKILLS

Modern technology and practical methods, like those given in chapter 3, have enabled you to reduce your play to a single performance curve by plotting every step you take during performance and identifying the actions taking place. To plot this curve, review a videotape of your performance and make a sequential list of the skills you use during each play of the game (see chapter 3). This list becomes your performance notation on how you executed each play during the game or each step of the race or jump. No matter which method you use, all the elements of your play can be recorded during a single play or movement in any sport. These patterns enable you to make a step-by-step evaluation of how you managed energy during the performance. You can study your responses to the starts, stops, contacts, and pressures of other players attempting to block, screen, or use you in some way to gain a playing advantage.

BALLISTICS TRAINING

Many programs fail to toughen the body in a systematic way during the off-season. Granted, the functional strength and power program has a toughening effect; however, additional methods are required to move the body up to higher levels of toughness. Boxers have used medicine balls for training for many years. During the Landry era, the Dallas Cowboys used medicine balls in various ways to toughen their bodies. More importantly, the balls were used to sensitize the neuromuscular system to respond instantly to contact. Many present-day systems fail to recognize the importance of giving and redirecting these outside forces to the athlete's advantage. Over the years, we have worked with many outstanding players from many different high school, college, and professional teams. The majority of the players we have worked with show very little skill in the sophisticated unity of resisting and yielding. Remember, this skill is not inherited; it must be taught. If you are searching for the edge against your competition, find a way to include this skill in training.

Medicine Ball Toughening Catches

Purpose: All sports have some physical contact even if contact with opponents isn't a part of the game. There may be unintentional contact with opponents and falls that you have to manage. These drills provide a safe way to learn how to toughen the body. The purpose of this drill is to develop the receiving skills of the body.

Equipment: You will need medicine balls or sandbags weighing from 2 to 25 pounds and a mini-trampoline. You can make a good sandbag from an inner tube of a car tire. Tie it off on one end and fill it with sand, and then tie it off again after you have reached the desired weight.

Procedure: Individually, with a partner, or in a group, perform 25 to 50 repetitions of each exercise:

• *Individual:* Throw the ball in the air or at a mini-trampoline and catch it with your body; make sure the ball contacts various body parts to get the maximum training effect. Do not catch the ball in a way that places undue stress on joints.

• *Partner or group:* Any number of players can participate. The players form a circle and stand three to four feet apart. Pass the ball any direction. If you feel there aren't enough opportunities for catching and throwing, add more balls. Include unexpected elements by throwing the ball at various speeds, at different parts of the catcher's body, and when catching the ball, absorb the shock with body movements and various body parts.

Medicine Ball Throws and Toughening Catches

Purpose: This drill develops power in all directions of movement.

Equipment: You will need medicine balls, sandbags, or weights weighing from 2 to 25 pounds.

Procedure: Individually, with a partner, or in a group, perform the following movements 8 to 10 times in each direction: seated throws; forward throw underhand and overhand; backward throw overhead; and side throw (left side and front, right side and front; left side and back, right side and back). You achieve the benefits of the toughening drills by catching the balls.

Overweight Implement Programs for All Throwing Actions

Purpose: These exercises are appropriate for pitchers, quarterbacks, javelin throwers, or any athletes that need to improve their throwing action. Although the arm is the most visible segment in the throw, the superb timing of the total body action produces the great feats in throwing. Slow-motion cameras capture the complexity and energy involved in the throw and demonstrate the importance of training the throwing action of the legs, hips, trunk, shoulders, and arms. Additional insurance is provided from functional strength and power training in step 2 of the seven-step model in the form of greater strength in supporting tissues of the joints, tendons, and ligaments.

Equipment: You can use whatever weighted implement is appropriate for your sport: football, basketball, baseball, javelin, discus, or small medicine ball. Add weighted equipment to this list.

Procedure: The sequence of throwing should proceed from heavy to light. Start your program using the heavy ball for foundation and progress to the lighter balls for throwing. The heavy ball will strengthen all the muscles and joints used in throwing and thereby establish a sound, structural and functional foundation. The normal and lighter weight instruments will provide the high-speed throwing action needed to improve your throwing skill. Throwing into a net will allow you to complete a high-intensity workout with more throws and less wasted time.

ESCAPING AND AVOIDING TIGHT SPOTS

Dan Inosanto, consummate martial artist, outlines some proven methods that will help you escape, avoid, or improve the application of ballistics and energy management to your sport. He says, "There are tight spots in every sport. Some of these are physical, and others are mental." Inosanto recommends the following techniques for all athletes because there will be situations in their sports that demand the use of these techniques, even if the sport isn't classified as a contact sport:

- Level changes (dropping from a high to a low stance)
- Angle changes (moving from the direct line of the attack player)
- Sensitivity training (bringing awareness to the level of first touch)
- Increasing energy of contact gradually, building to maximum effort
- Being aware of your natural movements and applying them to your advantage

- Being constantly in slow-phasic motion to make it easier to move and change direction
- Lateral contact (When the attack comes from the side, make level changes and simultaneously move to the line of least resistance.)
- Frontal attack (Move forward to the line of least resistance.)
- Moving in the direction from which the opponent (force) is coming to put maximum distance between you and your opponent (force) with a minimum amount of time and effort
- Mastering techniques such as ducking, slipping, rolling, and footwork (step and slide with a push, sidestep, and short steps to maintain balance and quick change in angle)
- Moving from a crouched position upward and forward
- Deceiving an opponent by giving an indication of forward motion to make the opponent commit his forward motion, and then dropping back a half step and changing the angle to your advantage in forward motion
- Linemen advantage: one hand hits the opponent's shoulder while the other pulls the opponent's opposite shoulder or arm
- Both hands hit the same shoulder of opponent to change the angle
- Both hands hit the opposite shoulder of opponent with a removal, then, one hand hits and pulls

This chapter has presented those principles and skills that answer the question, "How does ballistics training improve your playing speed?" It would be nice if all you had to do is line up and sprint as fast as you could to the finish tape, but this isn't always the case. Mary Decker Slaney was jostled off the track in the 1984 Olympics and was put out of the race. Maybe if she had had ballistics training she would have been able to recover and get back in the race.

Each new step you have taken so far has helped you to move closer to the higher reaches of playing speed. The last four steps of the seven-step model are where training and sports performance meet. Use them to lead you to exciting new levels of sports speed.

CHAPTER 6

STEP 4: PLYOMETRICS

██

. . . take power from the ground through your legs, waist, and back. —Bruce Lee

The word plyometric is derived from the Greek word *pleythyein* meaning "to increase" or from the Greek roots *plio* and *metric* meaning "more" and "measure." Plyometrics refers to exercises that enable a muscle to reach maximal strength in as short a time as possible. Plyometric exercises are important in sports requiring high levels of speed strength (ability to exert maximum force during high-speed activity) to complete movements such as sprinting, jumping, and throwing.

The term was first used in the United States in 1975 by Fred Wilt, former Olympic runner and women's track coach at Purdue University. Coach Wilt got the term from European track and field coaches who had already used plyometrics for more than a decade in the training of sprinters and athletes in jump events. Yuri Verhoshansky, coach in the Soviet Union, is credited as being one of the early pioneers and leading researchers of plyometric training. Although plyometrics was slow to be accepted in the United States, numerous articles, books, and videos produced in the 1980s and early 1990s have led to its widespread use in track and field, soccer, football, basketball, volleyball, baseball, and other team and individual sports.

HOW PLYOMETRIC TRAINING WORKS

Although plyometrics take a number of different forms, activity revolves around jumping, hopping, and bounding movements for the lower body and swinging, quick action push-off, catching and throwing weighted objects (medicine balls, shot put, sandbags), arm swings, and pulley throws for the upper body. The five medicine ball throws presented in this chapter are similar to some of the ballistic exercises described in chapter 5; however, the emphasis is placed on loading the abdominal and arm muscles prior to the movement or toss rather than on catching the ball. Exercises that simulate specific movements in a particular sport or activity are chosen.

Plyometrics are an excellent method for developing both strength and power in the muscles involved in sprinting. An athlete may have superior strength, yet be unable to produce the needed power to sprint a fast 40-yard dash. The completion of some movements in sports, such as sprinting, involve less time than it takes for the muscle to develop a maximal contraction. Evidence suggests that for such actions, an athlete will use only 60 to 80 percent of his or her absolute strength (maximum force a muscle group can produce). The key to plyometric training is to display strength as quickly and as forcefully as possible. Plyometric training has also been found to be an ideal training program to develop explosiveness and improve quickness.

Plyometric exercises use the force of gravity (by having the athlete step off a box, for example) to store energy in the muscles, and then immediately release the energy in the opposite direction.

Plyometric training is used to improve what Russian scientists of the past called *speed strength*, which is the application of maximum force during a high-speed activity such as sprinting. The unusual progress and success of Russian sprinter Valeri Borzov, 100-meter gold medal winner (10.14) in the 1972 Olympic Games, is partially attributed to the use of plyometric exercises during the six-year period prior to the games. Borzov progressed from a 100-meter time of 13.0 seconds at age 14 to 10.0 at age 20. Although you may not show such dramatic improvement, the hops, jumps, bounds, leaps, skips, ricochets, swings, and twists that make up plyometrics are an important part of your speed improvement program.

Plyometrics focus on the two key aspects of speed strength: starting strength, which is the ability to instantaneously recruit as many muscle fibers as possible, and explosive strength, which is the ability to keep the initial explosion of a muscle contraction going over a distance against some resistance. Starting strength is the key to sprinting a fast 40 to 100 meters, throwing or kicking a ball, and similar movements requiring little more than body resistance to be overcome. Examples of explosive strength are football blocking, throwing the shot put or hammer, Olympic weight lifting, power lifting, and other movements requiring considerable resistance. As Hatfield and Yessis point out in *Plyometric Training: Achieving Explo-*

sive Power in Sports (1986), "The lighter the implement you have to move and the shorter the distance, the more your starting strength becomes important; the heavier the resistance and the longer the distance, the more important your explosive strength becomes."

The main objective of plyometric training is to improve an athlete's ability to generate maximum force in the shortest time. This objective is accomplished by first loading or coiling muscles to accumulate energy before unloading this energy in the opposite direction. The force of gravity (as used in the action of stepping off a box) is used to store energy in the muscles that is immediately released in an opposite reaction (bounding or jumping up or forward upon landing). In other words, plyometric exercises involve powerful muscular contraction in response to the rapid, dynamic loading (stretching) of the involved muscles.

Most athletes already apply the basic concept of plyometrics (loading and unloading) when they cock their wrist or ankle before throwing a baseball or football, hitting a baseball, shooting a basketball, kicking a soccer ball or football, swinging a golf club, or executing the forehand or backhand stroke in tennis. The rapid stretching (loading) of these muscles activates the muscle stretch reflex, which sends a powerful stimulus to the muscles causing them to contract faster and with more power. In the actions listed above, the athletes are rapidly stretching a muscle group and then transferring the energy by immediately contracting that same group. A rapid deceleration of a mass is followed by a rapid acceleration of the mass in another direction. The loading or stretching action is sometimes called the yielding phase, and the reflex contraction of the muscles is called the overcoming phase. The object is to obtain a maximum eccentric contraction (muscle develops tension while lengthening) to load the muscle, and switch this contraction to concentric (muscle develops tension while shortening), which produces the desired explosive movement.

Rapid loading of the muscles (yielding phase) must occur just prior to the contraction phase of these same muscles. When you jump from an elevated platform to the ground, for example, your legs bend under the g-force (kinetic energy), and an immediate reactive jump occurs. How much your legs bend depends upon the g-force and the stored energy that will be used to release the powerful contraction to jump. The yielding phase produces stored energy, which is released during the overcoming phase by a powerful contraction.

Does this program sound complicated? It is really quite simple. To plan and use plyometrics properly for speed improvement and other quickness skills critical to your sport, just follow these guidelines:

1. Exercises should correspond to the form, muscle work, and range of motion in your sport or activity.

2. Exercises should correspond to the correct direction of movement. Because the leg moves toward the rear in one phase of sprinting, for example, some plyometric movements should also be directed toward the rear.

3. The rate of the stretch is strongly tied to the effectiveness of plyometric training; the higher the stretch rate, the greater the muscle tension and the more powerful the concentric contraction in the opposite direction.

4. Exercises for sprinting speed improvement should explode at the beginning of the movement and allow inertia to move the limb through the remaining range of motion. In one phase of sprinting, for example, maximum effort is exerted at the point you begin to pull the thigh through and diminishes as the leg passes underneath the body.

5. Although weights can be used to increase resistance, too much weight (vest, ankle spats) may increase strength without much effect on power. Too much weight increases your chance of injury and also makes it impossible to jump or sprint explosively, which defeats the purpose of the plyometric workout. Your body already provides considerable resistance. Adding a lot of weight is unnecessary. Light weight or your body weight is recommended to develop quick force. Alternating light (1 to 2 percent of body weight, no more than 2 to 3 pounds) and heavier weight (5 to 6 percent of body weight, no more than 10 to 12 pounds) in the same plyometric exercise is also an excellent technique to experience the feeling of higher speed action.

6. Whenever possible, a plyometric exercise should be performed at a speed faster than you are capable of producing without some assistance. The object is to use plyometric exercises that result in down time (the time your feet are on the ground, the amortization phase of plyometrics) that is less than the down time in sprinting. The faster a muscle is forced to lengthen, the greater the tension it exerts. Also, the closer the stretch of the muscle is to the contraction, the more violent the contraction. When you are jumping from boxes or bleachers, avoid hesitating after ground contact; the object is to be on

the ground as little time as possible by shortening the span between contact and take-off. The use of box jumps to increase the loading phase and surgical tubing to decrease the resistance to be overcome in speed hops are examples of techniques that allow a more forceful load or a faster contraction speed than you normally perform. You are, in effect, teaching the nervous system to experience the higher speed generated so it can duplicate it later in competition without any assistance from boxes or tubing.

7. Make a strong effort to handle the forces of landing with as little flexion of the joints as possible. When jumping on a flat surface or off boxes, too much flexion of the legs upon landing increases the time you spend on the ground, absorbs most of the force, and allows very little pre-loading or tensing. As soon as the balls of the feet touch the floor, the knees are rapidly flexed to your comfortable jumping position (never beyond right angles). This proper knee flexion position also prevents excessive ankle flexion, such as allowing the heels to touch the surface.

8. Master proper form for each exercise. A key aspect of proper technique is assuming a knee/thumbs-up position (knees bent just above a right angle, elbows to sides with hands in front of the body and thumbs facing upward) to help maintain your balance and center the workload around your hips and legs. For upper body exercise, stress proper follow-through. Emphasize the quality (proper form and speed) of each jump rather than the quantity of jumps.

9. A highly explosive movement in sports does not occur automatically. You do not sprint at maximum speed, serve at 100+ miles per hour in tennis, kick a ball 60+ yards, or jump 25+ feet without being "psyched" prior to the movement. It takes a concentrated mental effort to perform these actions.

Safety Precautions

Although surveys reveal that plyometric training is not likely to result in injury, unsound, unsupervised programs could potentially result in shin splints and knee, ankle, and lower back problems. These injuries are often a direct result of too many workouts per week, too many jumps per workout, incorrect form, jumping on hard surfaces, and using plyometrics at too early an age or without the necessary strength base. To reduce your chances of injury, follow these guidelines:

1. Preadolescent boys and girls should avoid plyometrics, unless other factors indicate more advanced maturity, because of greater susceptibility to injury prior to puberty.

2. Plyometrics should also be postponed for athletes who do not have a sufficient strength base. Avoid lower body plyometrics until you can leg press 2.5 times your body weight; avoid upper body exercise until you can perform five consecutive clap push-ups. Athletes weighing more than 260 pounds should also be capable of bench pressing their body weight; athletes weighing less than 160 pounds should be capable of bench pressing 1.5 times their body weight. Athletes falling between 160 and 260 should be able to meet the gradations of these guidelines (160-184: 1.4, 185-209: 1.3, 210-234: 1.2, 235-259: 1.1).

3. Athletes who do not respond well to the instructions of coaches are also at greater risk of injury and under- or overtraining.

4. Precede a plyometric workout with a general warm-up period consisting of walk-jog-stride-sprint cycles for one-half to three-quarters of a mile, followed by careful stretching exercises.

5. Use footwear with good ankle and arch support, lateral stability, and a wide, nonslip sole, such as a basketball or aerobic shoe. Running shoes with narrow soles and poor upper support can lead to ankle problems and are not recommended. Heel cups may be needed for those who are prone to heel bruises.

6. Plyometrics should be performed only on surfaces with good shock-absorbing properties, such as soft grassy areas, well-padded artificial turf, and wrestling mats. Never do plyometrics on asphalt or gymnasium floors.

7. Boxes should be sturdy and have a non-slip top.

8. Depth jumping from objects that are too high increases the risk of injury, particularly to larger athletes, and prevents the rapid switch from eccentric to concentric activity. The average recommended heights for depth jumps are 0.75 to 0.8 meter; athletes over 220 pounds should use heights of 0.5 to 0.75 meter.

FREQUENCY, VOLUME, INTENSITY, RECOVERY, AND PROGRESSION

Frequency. Do plyometric workouts no more than two times weekly during the off-season period in most sports and once weekly during the in-season period. Plyometric training is extremely strenuous; about 36 to 48 hours of rest is needed to fully recover. Therefore, plyometrics should be the very last session in your practice day. High-speed activity or physical contact work (such as scrimmage in soccer and football) following a plyometrics workout may be performed at less than competition speed; it could disrupt timing and increase the probability of fatigue-related injuries.

Due to the fatigue factor, avoid lower-body weight training on days when lower-body plyometrics are used. Doing both on one day negates the full effect of each of these programs. However, you can use upper-body plyometrics and lower-body weight training, or vice versa, on the same training day. A sample workout might include a general warm-up, such as jogging, stretching (flexibility exercises), overspeed training, anaerobic training, plyometrics, and a cool-down period, in that order.

> Plyometric training and heavy strength training should not be performed on the same day unless lower-body strength training is combined with upper-body plyometric work or vice versa. Neither program should be used on two consecutive days; 36 to 48 hours of recovery time is recommended.

Volume. To date, there is no magic number of jumps (foot or feet contacts with the surface) that produce the best results. Coaches at various levels differ in terms of the number of repetitions, sets, and total jumps in a single workout. Taking too few jumps is better than taking too many, however. Ideally, the number of jumps should not exceed 80 to 100 per session for beginners and athletes in early workouts, 100 to 120 per session for intermediate-level athletes, and 120 to 140 per session for advanced athletes who have completed four to six weeks of plyometric training.

Intensity. The amount of stress placed upon the muscles, the connective tissue, and the joints is referred to as *intensity*. Skipping movements provide minimum stress and are considered low-intensity exercises; box jumping, two-foot take-off and landing exercises, high-speed movements, and using additional weight, all increase the intensity of the workout. Your program should progress from low- to high-intensity exercises (see table 6.1).

Recovery. Remember that you are trying to improve your speed strength, not speed endurance. Thus, adequate rest (recovery) between

TABLE 6.1

	Sample Off-Season Plyometric Program			
Week	Drills	Set/repetitions	Rest period between sets	Sessions per week
1-2	Choose four low-intensity drills	2 × 10	2 min	2
3-4	Choose two low-intensity and two medium-intensity drills	2 × 10	2-3 min	2
5-6	Choose four medium-intensity drills	2-3 × 10	2-3 min	2
7-8	Choose two medium-intensity and two high-intensity drills	Medium: 2-3 × 10 High: 2 × 10	2-3 min Box jumps: 10-15 s between repetitions	2
9-10	Choose four high-intensity drills	Non-box jumps: 2-3 × 10 Box jumps: 2 × 10	3 min	2

Reprinted, by permission, from W.B. Allerheiligen, 1994, Speed Development and Plyometric Training. In *Essentials of Strength Training and Conditioning*, edited by T. Baechle (Champaign, IL: Human Kinetics), 323.

repetitions, sets, and workouts is required. For example, recovery for box jumping may take 5 to 10 seconds between repetitions and two to three minutes between sets. In repeated jumps where limited ground contact is stressed, there is no recovery period between repetitions; the athlete immediately "unloads" into the next repetition. Recovery between workouts is two to four days, depending on the sport and time of year. Two days is generally sufficient during the preseason; a period of three to four days is appropriate during the competitive season. The key to a successful program is to do each explosive movement with perfect form.

Progression. Exercises should progress from the low-intensity, in-place exercises for beginners to medium-intensity, and then high-intensity levels for advanced athletes. Table 6.1 outlines a 10-week program that moves from low- to medium- to high-intensity exercises over a period of six weeks. You can develop your own program with numerous variations by using this table and selecting your choices from the low-, medium-, and high-intensity exercises on pages 131-156. In six to eight weeks, when high-intensity plyometric drills become the foundation of your program, the volume of exercises should decrease. A sample plyometric program for speed improvement using these guidelines is shown in table 6.2.

TABLE 6.2

Plyometric Program for Speed Improvement

Type	Exercises	Sets/ repetitions	Rest	Progression
Low intensity (two weeks)	Squat jump	3 × 6-10	2 min	Add 1 repetition each workout
	Double-leg ankle bounce	3 × 6-10		
	Lateral cone jump	2 × 6-10		
	Drop and catch push-up	4 × 6-10		
Low to medium intensity (two weeks)	Lateral cone jump	3 × 8-10	2 min	Add 1 repetition to each workout until reaching 10
	Split squat jump	2 × 8-10		
	Double-leg tuck	2 × 8-10		
	Standing triple jump	2 × 8-10		
	Medicine ball (overhead backward and underhand forward throw)	2 × 8-10		
	Clap push-up	2 × 8-10		
Medium intensity (two weeks)	Standing long jump	3 × 8-10	2 min	Add 1 repetition each workout until reaching 10
	Alternate-leg bound	3 × 8-10		
	Double-leg hop	3 × 8-10		
	Pike jump	2 × 8-10		
	Depth jumps	2 × 8-10		
	Medicine ball throw (with Russian twist)	3 × 8-10		
	Dumbbell arm swings	2 × 8-10		Reduce weight each workout; max of 20 lb
Medium to high intensity (two weeks)	Double-leg tuck	3 × 10-12	2 min	Add 1 repetition each workout until reaching 10
	Single-leg zigzag hop	3 × 10-12		
	Double-leg vertical power jump	3 × 10-12		
	Running bound	3 × 10-12		
	Box jumps	2 × 8-10		
	Dumbbell arm swings	3 × 12		
	Medicine ball sit-up	3 × 10-15		
High intensity*	Single-leg vertical power jump	2 × 12-8	60-90 sec	Stress form and maximum explosion on each repetition. Decrease repetitions from 12-8 in two weeks
	Single-leg speed hop	2 × 12-8		
	Double-leg speed hop	2 × 12-8		
	Multiple box jumps	2 × 12-8		
	Side jump and sprint	5 × 3		
	Decline hops	2 × 12-8		
	Spring arm action	3 × 12-8		Start with 5 lb and reduce to 1 lb stressing rapid action
	Medicine ball sit-up	3 × 15-20		

*High-intensity plyometrics now becomes the foundation of your program. Total volume (number of jumps) has been reduced, and the emphasis is placed on quality.

PLYOMETRIC EXERCISES AND DRILLS

Many types of plyometric exercises are used in various sports. For playing speed improvement, we are primarily interested in a few basic jumps that involve limited ground contact time. A number of common plyometric drills result in a down time two to three times longer than in the sprinting action. Although some of these drills are important because the down time is similar to that during the start and acceleration phase of the 40-yard dash, most of your high-intensity routine should involve high-speed jumps with short down time.

In the following exercises L indicates low-intensity, M indicates medium-intensity, and H indicates high-intensity exercises.

In-Place Jumps

L

Squat Jump

Standing in an upright position with your hands behind your head, drop downward to a one-half squat position and immediately explode upward as high as possible. Repeat the sequence upon landing, stressing maximum height.

© Joe Cambioso

Double-Leg Ankle Bounce

With arms extended at your sides, jump upward and forward using your ankles.

Immediately upon landing, execute the next jump, continuing until you have completed the desired number of repetitions.

Split Squat Jump

Assume a position with one leg extended forward and the other behind the center of your body (lunge position).

Perform a vertical jump off the front leg landing with the same leg forward. Repeat with the other leg forward.

Lateral Cone Jump

Standing to one side of a cone, jump laterally to the other side. Immediately upon landing, jump back to the starting position to complete one repetition.

© Mary T. Hall

© Mary T. Hall

Upper Body

Single-Clap Push-Up

Assume a normal push-up position and lower your chest to the floor. Push your body upward with an explosive action that allows you to clap your hands and catch yourself in the upright position. Repeat the movement immediately for the desired number of repetitions.

Drop and Catch Push-Up

Kneel on both knees with your upper body erect, as though you are standing on your knees. Place both hands in front of your chest, palms down, and drop your upper body to the floor, catching your weight with both elbows bent in the bottom phase of the push-up position. Immediately push off with both hands to extend your arms and return to the upright push-up position.

In-Place Jumps

M

Pike Jump

Assume an upright stance with both arms to your sides, feet shoulder-width apart. Execute a vertical jump, bring both extended legs in front of your body, and reach out with both hands to touch your toes in a pike position. Upon landing, immediately repeat the sequence.

© Joe Cambioso

Double-Leg Tuck Jump

Assume an upright stance with both arms to your sides, feet shoulder-width apart.

Execute a vertical jump, grasping both knees while in the air. Release the knees before landing and immediately execute the next jump.

Standing Jumps

Standing Triple Jump

Assume the standing broad jump position: arms to your side, and feet shoulder-width apart. Using a two-foot take-off, jump forward as far as possible, landing on the right foot; then immediately jump to land on the left foot. Finally, jump once again and land on both feet. The standing triple jump is identical to the triple jump in track (hop, step, and jump), except for the use of a two-foot take-off. The object is to generate maximum speed and secure as great a distance as possible on each of the three phases.

Standing Long Jump

Complete only the initial jump described in the standing triple jump using maximum arm swing. Strive for both vertical and horizontal distance.

Single-Leg Hop

Assume a standing broad jump starting position with one leg slightly ahead of the other. Rock forward to your front foot and jump as far and high as possible driving your lead knee up and out. Land in the starting position on the same foot and continue jumping to complete the desired number of repetitions.

Short-Response Hops and Bounds

Double-Leg Bound

From a standing broad jump position (half squat stance, arms at sides, shoulders forward, back straight, and head up), thrust your arms forward as the knees and body straighten and the arms reach for the sky.

© Joe Cambioso

© Joe Cambioso

Double- and Single-Leg Zigzag Hop

Place 10 cones 20 inches apart in a zigzag pattern. Jump with legs together in a forward diagonal direction over the first cone keeping the shoulders facing straight ahead.

Immediately upon landing, change direction with your next jump to move diagonally over the second cone. Continue until you have jumped over all 10 cones. Execute the single-leg zigzag hop in the same diagonal direction but using one leg at a time.

Alternate-Leg Bound

Place one foot slightly ahead of the other.

Push off with your back leg, drive the lead knee up to the chest and try to gain as much height and distance as possible.

Continue by immediately driving with the other leg upon landing.

Running Bound

Run forward jumping as high and far as possible with each step. Emphasize height and high knee lift and land with the center of gravity under you.

Lateral Bound

Assume a semi-squat stance about one step from the side of an angled box or grassy hill. Push off with the outside foot to propel yourself into the box. As soon as you land, drive off again in the opposite direction, stressing lateral distance.

Ricochets

Incline Ricochet

Stand facing the bottom of the bleacher steps with your feet together and arms to the sides. Rapidly jump upward to each step as fast as possible by attempting to be "light on your feet."

Decline Ricochet

From the top of a two- to four-degree grassy hill, take a series of short, rapid hopping movements down the hill. Concentrate on being "light on your feet."

Upper Body

Push-Up With Weights

Assume a push-up position with your arms fully extended, both hands on top of the weights. Quickly remove your hands, drop to the floor, and catch yourself with your elbows slightly flexed before allowing gravity to flex the arms further until your chest nearly touches the floor. Rapidly extend your arms so your hands leave the floor high enough to again assume the position with hands on top of the weights.

© Joe Cambioso

© Joe Cambioso

Medicine Ball Sit-Up

Assume a sitting position on the floor with the knees flexed to a 90-degree angle. Have a partner toss the ball directly to your chest area. Catch the ball with arms flexed and allow the force to push your upper body back and to the floor. When your lower back touches the ground, do a sit-up and chest-pass the ball back to your partner.

© Ted Sonnier

© Ted Sonnier

Medicine Ball Overhead Backward Throw

With the medicine ball in both hands and your elbows extended, bend lightly forward and then backward as you propel the ball over your head to a partner.

Medicine Ball Underhand Forward Throw

Face your partner with the medicine ball in both hands in front of your body. Bend over slightly before propelling the ball forward to your partner.

Medicine Ball Throw With Russian Twist

While sitting, hold the medicine ball over your head in both hands. Move the ball backward slightly before throwing an overhead pass forward to your partner as you twist your body to the right. Repeat the throw, but twist your body to the left this time.

© Joe Cambioso

Double-Clap Push-Up

Perform a normal push-up with enough explosive action to allow you to clap two times while the hands are in the air before again catching yourself with slightly flexed elbows.

Dumbbell Arm Swings

With 5- to 25-pound dumbbells in each hand, assume a stance with your feet apart, hands at your sides, shoulders and upper body tilted only slightly forward, and your head straight. Drive one arm upward to a point just above your shoulder as the other arm drives backward behind your body. Before each arm reaches maximum stretch, check the momentum and initiate motions in the opposite direction.

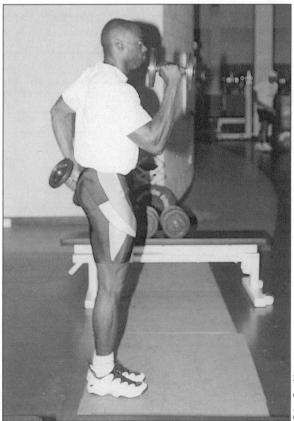

© Joe Cambioso

In-Place Jumps

Double-Leg Vertical Power Jump

Assume a standing position with your feet shoulder-width apart and your arms to your side in preparation for a vertical jump. With a powerful upward thrust of both arms, jump as high as possible. Upon landing, immediately jump again with as little ground contact time as possible.

Single-Leg Vertical Power Jump

Complete the preceding action with a one-foot take-off. Repeat the action using the opposite foot.

Single-Leg Tuck Jump

Assume an upright stance with both arms to your sides and feet shoulder-width apart. Execute a vertical jump with a one-foot take-off, grasping both knees while in the air. Release the knees before landing on the same foot and immediately execute the next jump. Repeat the jump using the opposite leg.

Side Jump and Sprint

Stand to one side of a bench or cone with your feet together pointing straight ahead. Jump back and forth over the bench for 4 to 10 repetitions.

After landing on the last jump, sprint forward for 25 yards. Two athletes begin this exercise at the same time. The first to complete the specified number of jumps and reach the finish line is the winner. Benches or cones can be set up for 100 yards. Players perform 4 to 10 jumps and sprint to the next cone before repeating the jumps and sprinting again.

Short-Response Hops

Double-Leg Speed Hop

From an upright position with your back straight, shoulders forward, and head up, jump as high as possible, bringing your feet under your buttocks in a cycling motion at the height of the jump. Jump again immediately upon contacting the ground.

© Joe Cambioso

© Joe Cambioso

Single-Leg Speed Hop

Assume the position described in the preceding exercise with one leg in a stationary flexed position. Concentrate on the height of your jump as you did in the double-leg speed hop.

Decline Hop

Assume a quarter-squat position at the top of a grassy hill with a three- to four-degree slope. Continue hopping down the hill for speed as described for the double-leg hop. Repeat the exercise using the single-leg decline hop.

Depth Jump

From an elevated box or grassy surface, drop from that height to the ground (do not jump), landing with both feet together and knees bent in an attempt to "freeze" the body and absorb the shock. Slowly return to the box and repeat the exercise for the desired number of repetitions.

Single-Leg Stride Jump

Assume a position to the side and at one end of a bench with your inside foot on top of the bench and your arms at your sides.

Drive your arms upward as the inside leg on the bench pushes off to jump as high into the air as possible. Continue jumping until you reach the other end of the bench.

Box Jumps

Step off a box that is within the recommended box heights for your weight and age and immediately jump upward and outward upon hitting the ground.

Multiple Box Jumps

Set up five boxes of differing heights three to five feet apart. Stand on the first box with toes slightly extended over the edge. Step off the first box and, upon landing on the ground, jump upward and outward to land on the second higher box. Repeat the action for the remaining boxes, alternating low and high boxes.

Upper Body

Sprint-Arm Action With Weights

Place 1- to 10-pound dumbbells in each hand. Assume a position with the upper body leaning only slightly forward, both arms bent at right angles in the correct sprinting position (left arm raised in front, elbow close to the body with the hand about shoulder height; right arm lowered, elbow close to the body with the hand no further back than the right hip). Swing the arms from the shoulder joint and execute 10 to 15 explosive movements of the arms with the correct form described in chapter 8. On the upswing, the hand rises to a point just in front of the chin and just inside the shoulder. As the arm swings down, the elbow straightens slightly and the hand comes close to the thigh.

You are now ready to continue to work on your holistic training program by adding the fifth step of the seven-step model: "Sport Loading."

CHAPTER 7

STEP 5:
SPORT LOADING

The straw that broke the camel's back.

What is sport loading? You might take the position that any kind of training is a form of sport loading. If you increase acceleration, the amount of force the body has to manage increases, thereby providing increased loading on the body. Jumping higher and farther in competition or practice produces a higher functional loading with specific positive benefits. However, we define sport loading as the systematic adding of weight to your body in any form (uniform, vest, pants, or suit) or to the implements you use in your sport (bats, balls, and so on). This method is not new. It has been used by many athletes through the years, by accident in many cases and by design in others. Interestingly, coaches of sports that involve carrying additional weight in the form of protective gear haven't placed a great emphasis on adding uniform weight to the body during training or testing and evaluating their players. The majority of the loading has been applied by using partners or field equipment such as sleds.

> **Sport loading is a technique designed to improve explosive concentric movements such as sprinting speed. A relatively light resistance that does not drastically alter sprinting form produces the best results.**

Imagine the kind of sport loading program David and Goliath might have used. Can you design a program for them? David had to rely on attributes such as quickness and precision of mind, body, and spirit. His weapon selection, a sling, was commonly used by shepherds to protect their flocks from predators. The sling perfectly matched his qualifications and the situation. Goliath, on the other hand, selected a long and heavy sword and shield. These weapons were perfectly suited to his physical attributes.

157

However, you must follow other principles to achieve victory on the battlefield or in a game. The situation and terrain have to be considered along with your own capabilities. Reliance on favorite weapons, plays, players, or favorite moves may be of little value in the ever-changing circumstances of what is taking place on the field. The results of this contest showed that David's quickness, speed, and accuracy were the deciding factors in the victory over Goliath's size and crushing, close-range strength. David won because he chose a fighting style that fit his qualifications and the demands of the situation. You must learn to do the same thing in your sport. Resolve, as David did, to be flexible, open, and unrestrained by the traditional thinking and common methods of the day. Try to find other creative solutions to getting the job done better.

Many teams in the NFL have their own version of the David and Goliath story. Most of them favor players who are Goliaths. Take the offensive line, for instance, where excessive size and strength are overvalued. The trend toward increasing size is evident in the shift from 250-pound players to 260-pound players to players over 300 pounds over the years (table 7.1). Many times the passing and running strategy is based on the idea that bigger is better, and allowances are not made for smaller players. Consequently, all defensive strategists have to do is find the proper size and performance mix that counters the size and performance qualities of the offensive line. Then the trends will change or swing the pendulum back to the more agile and explosive offensive linemen to keep up with the defensive performance. Lawrence Taylor and other similar defensive linemen create havoc in the offensive backfields in the NFL. Obviously, some NFL staffs see the performance benefits of good body mechanics, quickness, explosion, and playing speed over size.

The NBA also has its version of the David and Goliath story. In a land of seven-foot giants, few successful comparatively short players, such as Mugsy Bogues and Spud Webb, live. These short players are even short to the rest of us. These contrasting players add some excitement and enthusiasm to the game. Coaches and franchises are to be commended on their vision and openness to innovative ways of getting the job done.

Your program needs to match the range of demands you will face on the athletic field. The concepts of sport loading in this chapter will help you devise a personal program that is perfectly adapted to your needs and the playing situation in your sport. Each element of a practice session contributes different amounts to performance. Greater stress should be placed on the last three steps of the seven-step model

TABLE 7.1

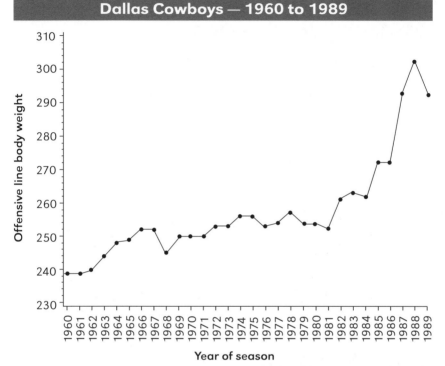

**Offensive Line Body Weight
Dallas Cowboys — 1960 to 1989**

Offensive line body weight

Year of season

(steps 5, 6, and 7) because more sport-specific skills are done in these steps. Nearly 100 percent of the work done during these last three steps has a very good chance of improving your sport performance. The first four steps work on building the best car for the race (your body), but these last three steps work on you, the driver (the nervous system that directs all the action).

> Sport loading along with strength training, speed-endurance training, plyometrics, and overspeed training produce the greatest changes in the exercised fast-twitch muscle fibers.

Although you may not have access to all the technical equipment found at many colleges or professional facilities, you can still have an outstanding sports loading program. Alternative methods of sport loading training involving little or no equipment are necessary variations in your program. A number of sport loading techniques yield effective results. Athletes of all ages can use the methods that follow to attain benefits from sport loading.

WEIGHTED BODY SUITS

Stan Plagenhoef conceptualized a weighted strap system to fit around the various segments of the body. Each strap is placed at specific biomechanical segment points. This system is the best way to load an athlete. The method distributes the load over each of the segments of one's body.

Ce'bo, a company from England, manufactures and markets a body suit design (Ce'bo Bodykit) that is available to the general public. In the literature promoting the Ce'bo Bodykit, the company states that the suit is "a weighted exercise garment that increases the gravitational pull on the body of the wearer while exercising." The suit includes four sections: upper body, arms, upper leg, and lower leg. This suit allows you to distribute the load of the weight over your body to attain more precise loading.

To our knowledge, this suit is not constructed to match one's biomechanical characteristics. However, keep a close watch on the advances in this technology because they will bring a more effective training device to you for your sport loading program.

WEIGHTED VESTS

New materials and design changes used in constructing weight vests are improving. More durable, light, tight-fitting vests with the capability to easily change weights are giving the user a greater range of usability. A weighted vest should become the foundation piece of equipment for your sports loading program. This vest can be safely utilized by male and female athletes of all ages and be adapted to practically any sport.

Research by Bosco (1985) indicated that the proper use of sport loading will improve power output and aid performance in sprinting. An average improvement of 10 centimeters in vertical jumping ability was also measured after three weeks of training. A repeat study of Bosco's design for female subjects at Brigham Young University (BYU) showed similar positive effects on vertical jumping ability with an average gain of five centimeters for the athletes. The study used a weekly increase in the vest loads of 8 percent of body weight the first week, 10 percent the second week, and 12 percent the third week. Female athletes wore the vests during the day and for practice sessions. BYU researchers also suggested that the vest could influence other aspects of power output.

Select vests that can be incrementally loaded, like The Vest by E-finity. In addition, it is desirable to be able to increase the weight on the vest in increments of half-pounds, one pound, or two pounds (figure 7.1). Table 7.2 summarizes the major purposes and weight ranges of the three vests in the E-finity system. Vest I with heavy weights is used primarily to improve basic strength. Vest II provides an opportunity to develop your speed endurance (see chapter 8), and Vest III uses lighter weights to allow you to perform at higher rates of speed to improve quickness and power.

A sample sport loading program using Vest I is shown in table 7.3. The program progresses from heavy weights (20 pounds) to lighter weights (2 pounds) over a 10-week period; you slowly progress to high-speed training with a weight that permits rapid, explosive turn-over in sprinting.

© Joe Cambioso

Figure 7.1 Select a vest that can be incrementally loaded.

You can easily use the vest during various parts of the practice session in your sport. In general, avoid using a vest during highly technical aspects of your sport that require considerable precision. The majority of precision practice should be done in a training zone that uses the

TABLE 7.2

Sports Speed Vest and Body Suit Programs			
Vest	**Name**	**General purpose**	**Weight range***
Vest I	Basic Training Vest	Power endurance	1 to 20 lb. maximum
Vest II	Speed Endurance Vest	Power endurance	1 to 16 lb
Vest III	Speed Vest	Quickness, speed, power	1 to 8 lb

*For the body suit use comparable weights.

TABLE 7.3

Sport Loading Program for Hypergravity Vest* and Body Suit** Training

Week	Repetitions	Vest	Distance	Rest (minutes)	Progression
1	3-5	I 20#	120 yd	Walk back	40 yards build to 75% speed gradually
				HR > 120	40 yards 75% speed
					40 yards ease-off
2	4-6	I 18#	120 yd	Walk back	40 yards build to 75% speed gradually
				HR > 120	40 yards 75% speed
					40 yards ease-off
3	6-8	I 20#	120 yd	Full recovery	Power starts at 85%
	3-5	I 16#	120 yd	Walk back	40 yards build to 80% speed gradually
				HR > 120	40 yards 80% speed
					40 yards ease-off
					Complete two sets
4	6-8	I 18#	120 yd	Full recovery	Power starts at 90%
	3-5	I 14#	120 yd	Walk back	40 yards build to 85% speed gradually
				HR > 120	40 yards 85% speed
					40 yards ease-off
					Complete two sets
5	6-8	I 16#	120 yd	Full recovery	Power starts at 95%
	3-5	I 12#	120 yd	Walk back	40 yards build to 88% speed gradually
				HR > 120	40 yards 88% speed
					40 yards ease-off
					Complete three sets
6	6-8	I 14#	120 yd	Full recovery	Power starts at 95%
	3-5	I 10#	120 yd	Walk back	40 yards build to 90% speed gradually
				HR > 120	40 yards 90% speed
					40 yards ease-off
					Complete three sets

(continued)

TABLE 7.3   *(continued)*

Week	Repetitions	Vest*	Distance	Rest (minutes)	Progression
7	6-8	I 12#	120 yd	Full recovery	Power starts at 95%
	3-5	I 8#	120 yd	Walk back	40 yards build to 90% speed gradually
				HR > 120	40 yards 90% speed
					40 yards ease-off
					Complete three sets
8	6-8	I 10#	120 yd	Full recovery	Power starts at 95%
	3-5	I 6#	120 yd	Walk back	40 yards build to 95% speed gradually
				HR > 120	40 yards 95% speed
					40 yards ease-off
					Complete three sets
9	6-8	I 8#	120 yd	Full recovery	Power starts at 95%
	3-5	I 6#	120 yd	Walk back	40 yards build to 95% speed gradually
				HR > 120	40 yards 95% speed
					40 yards ease-off
10	6-8	I 6#	120 yd	Full recovery	Power starts at 95%
	3-5	I 6#	120 yd	Walk back	40 yards build to 98% speed gradually
				HR > 120	40 yards 98% speed
					40 yards ease-off
					Complete three sets

*Vests I and II can be used for all loads; however, Vest III can be used for loads of eight pounds or less.
**For the body suit use comparable weights.

TABLE 7.4

Sport-Specific Training Using the Weighted Vest and Body Suit*

Practice period	Suggest load and duration
Warm-up and drills	Vest I-II-III 1# to 20# for 10-15 min.
Scrimmage sessions	Speed Vest I# to 4# until the end of scrimmage
Drills	Speed Vest 1# to 8# throughout practice
Conditioning sessions at the end of practice	Vest I-II-III 1# to 20# for 15-30 min.

*For the body suit use comparable weights.

same high-speed work levels that are expected during competition because this kind of session is best for improving skills. The loads you select should depend on the objectives set up for the practice period. If the vest is used intelligently, skill development and conditioning will occur simultaneously. Coaches can handicap elite players during training sessions to stimulate competition and force the more talented players to work harder. Table 7.4 lists some practice elements and gives some suggested vest loads and durations for each of them. Table 7.5 gives six training zones and their suggested loads and durations for organizing your training program. Be aware that Vest II and III can be used for all of Vest I weights. The big advantage for using Vests I and II is that they are designed to fit better and allow greater freedom of movement.

TABLE 7.5

Sport-Specific Training Zones Using the Weighted Vest and Body Suit*

Practice period	Distance (in meters)	Suggested load and duration
Starting zone	0-20	Vest I-II-III 1# to 20# for 15-30 min
Acceleration zone	0-30	Vest I-II-III 1# to 20# for 15-30 min
Flying zone	20-40	Speed Vest 1# to 4# for 15-30 min
90 percent zone	100-300	Speed Vest 1# to 4# for 15-30 min
Speed endurance zone	30-200	Speed Vest 1# to 8# for 15-30 min
Aerobic zone	400	Speed Vest 1# to 8# for 30-60 min

*For the body suit use comparable weights.

HARNESSES

The two-person harness is an affordable and effective tool for working on running techniques and sprinting. Two athletes of similar body weight and power use the same harness (figure 7.2). One athlete provides the resistance, and the other provides the power.

Harness use fits best in the basic training step 1 of the seven-step program. Remember, the emphasis at this level, step 5, is to perform at or near game playing speed. Speed levels should be close to 90 percent of your maximum speed.

Figure 7.2 The two-person harness allows one athlete to provide the power while another athlete provides the resistance.

PARACHUTES

Parachutes of various sizes provide some degree of resistance; however, the additional benefits that can be gained from other methods outweighs the cost and inconvenience associated with the use of parachutes. Younger athletes tend to enjoy parachutes as a sport loading technique (figure 7.3). If you choose this method, follow the guidelines shown in table 7.6.

Figure 7.3 Parachutes are a fun sport loading method for younger athletes.

TABLE 7.6

Sprint Loading Program Using Hill Sprinting, Stadium Stairs, Harness, Sand Runs, or a Weighted Sled

Week	Reps	Pulling distance*	Rest (minutes)**	Progression
1	3-5	15 yd	Walk back HR > 120	Use power starts at 75% speed in hill, sand runs, and stadium sprinting or with no weight on the sled. Complete two sets.
2	3-5	20 yd	Walk back HR > 120	Repeat above at maximum speed.
3	6-8	25 yd	Full recovery	Repeat power starts above at maximum speed.
	3-5	30 yd	Walk back HR > 120	Use power starts at 75% speed in hill, sand runs, and stadium sprinting or with no weight on the sled. Complete two sets.
4	7-9		Full recovery	Power starts at 90%.
	3-5	40 yd	Walk back HR > 120	Repeat above power starts and power sprints. Add weight to the sled that allows you to sprint with good form. Complete two sets.
5	7-9	50 yd	Full recovery	Repeat above workout. Add more weight. Complete three sets.
6-9	7-9	60 yd	Full recovery	Repeat above workout. Add more weight each week. Complete three sets. Include one final run to exhaustion by continuing your sprint for as long as possible. Record the distance and try to improve it each week.

*Actual distance you are pulling the sled or sprinting uphill or up stadium steps.
**Rest—no walk back for a weighted sled.

UPHILL SPRINTING

Most parts of the country provide suitable terrain for sprinting uphill. Although a wide range of grades can be used, it is recommended that the degree of incline allow you to run with good starting and sprinting form. When Bob Ward designed the Incline/Decline course for the Dallas Cowboys in the 1980s, he included the best features for uphill training. The angles and distances were selected from extensive research, consultation with many experts from around the world, and practical coaching experience. These angles and the distances are shown in table 7.7. If you can find similar angles and distances, apply them as shown in the uphill use column. In general, steep angles (8.0 degrees) can be used for the starts and acceleration loading, and angles of 1.0 degree, 2.5 degrees, or 3.0 degrees can be used for starts and speed endurance workouts. A 10- to 30-yard incline of 8 to 10 degrees should be covered in 2.5 to 3.5 seconds, followed by a near full-speed sprint of 20 to 80 yards at the same incline. These values have proven to be very effective for sprint loading programs at the Dallas Cowboys' training facility. Attempt to come as close as possible to these guidelines, although precise values are not absolutely necessary.

TABLE 7.7

Dallas Cowboys Incline/Decline Course				
Total distance in yards	Distance in yards	Distance in meters	Featured angles	Uphill use
0.00	0.00	0.00	Start	
27.25	27.25	25.00	Flat	Recovery
33.81	6.56	6.00	8 degree angle	Starts
34.90	1.09	1.00	Flat	Recovery
67.70	32.80	30.00	3.5 degree angle	Acceleration
89.57	21.87	20.00	Flat	Recovery
122.37	32.80	30.00	3.0 degree angle	Acceleration
131.12	8.75	8.00	Flat	Recovery
196.72	65.60	60.00	2.5 degree angle	Speed endurance
278.72	82.00	75.00	1.0 degree angle	Speed endurance
328.72	50.00	45.87	Sand run	Body control Speed endurance

STADIUM STAIRS

Stadium stairs or other stairs can be used in the same manner as hill sprinting. Try to locate stairs that have the same approximate angles of incline (figure 7.4). Make sure the steps provide a safe environment for training.

© Joe Cambioso

Figure 7.4 If using stadium stairs to simulate hill sprinting, make sure the steps are safe.

SAND RUNS

Herschel Walker said that his father had him running over plowed fields in Georgia when he was a youngster. While running in a sand session with the Cowboys, Walker looked as if he were running on the top of the sand while most of the other players labored or dug deep holes in the sand. The early training must have given him that kind of control.

Sand running is an excellent way to stress the total body, especially the lower extremities. The foot, knee, and hip muscle joint systems are required to adjust to the unstable sandy running surface. This adjustment develops and toughens your body's ability to handle unexpected stability changes. There aren't many activities that you can include in your program that can work all joint actions like sand running can. It's almost like a form of wrestling for the lower extremities.

WEIGHTED SLEDS

Both expensive and inexpensive sleds are available. Metal and plastic models are also available that allow quick and easy weight changes. For very little cost, you can use a spare tire with a rope and weighted belt. Regardless of the device you choose, make sure you use a load that allows proper form and high-speed sprinting. Too much weight will cause you to lose form and will prevent explosive movements. Time yourself over various starting and sprinting distances of 5 to 40 yards using both a stationary and a flying start.

WHEN TO USE SPORT LOADING

The ideal point to include sport loading training in your program is at the latter part of Wednesday's workout or later in Speedweek. There are two training objectives you need to consider in your program plan:

1. *Power Start and Explosive Close-Range Movement (Acceleration Phase I)*. Phase I helps you overcome inertia to get started in any of your sport-tasks. It is extremely important in sports that deal in close ranges. Phase II acceleration marks the end of the majority of your ability to run faster. This leveling in speed has been noted by many other researchers during maximum and near-maximum speed runs.

Unique studies conducted on the Dallas Cowboys by Bob Ward and Larry Brown have shown that maximum acceleration takes place very close to the start (one to three feet) and rapidly diminishes to zero or to very low amounts somewhere around 50 to 60 yards. The rate of drop-off is a very good indicator of your running skill and conditioning level. The timeline of an athlete's run shows that the length of an athlete's ability to accelerate and apply power continues for about six to eight seconds from the start in the case of all-out sprinting. Further, it has been demonstrated that world-class sprinters can accelerate slightly even in the last few yards to the finish. This slight increase could mean the difference between winning and losing a close race.

In most sports, usable force (essentially acceleration) is attained within approximately 10 to 15 yards (0.6 to 1.5 seconds). Therefore, you should train multidirectional peak power by playing games such as handball, basketball, badminton, and racquetball, as mentioned in chapter 3. Doing 10 to15 starts that cover 0 to 20 yards will help train the straight ahead aspects.

2. *Power Sprint*. This phase trains you to develop power at high speeds. The speed curves of sprinters show that deliverable power drops off as they move faster. The best way to train high-speed power is to do sprint loading work from a flying start, using the vest or incline sprints at maximum or near maximum levels. Six to ten

repetitions for 10 to 80 yards should be used with weights or resistance that does not reduce performance speed by more than one to five percent. Adding weight to a vest, for example, of no more than one to five percent of body weight should put you in this range.

A sample sprint loading program for hill sprinting, stadium stair sprinting, and weighted sleds is shown in table 7.6. A sample sport loading program for hypergravity vest training is shown in table 7.3.

All the work you have done from step 1 through step 5 has prepared you to sprint faster and play faster in your chosen sport. Step 6, covered in the next chapter, will show you the methods used by world-class performers in all sports to accomplish their outstanding feats. These methods will help you do the following:

- Improve your playing speed
- Improve playing speed endurance
- Develop world-class sprinting form and speed

CHAPTER 8

STEP 6: SPRINTING FORM AND SPEED ENDURANCE

Those who are enamoured of practice without science are like a pilot who goes into a ship without rudder or compass and never has any certainty where he is going. —**Leonardo da Vinci**

No two athletes run precisely the same way; however, sprinting mechanics should remain the same for all athletes. This chapter explains the mechanics of sprinting, including stride length, stride frequency, and arm action. In addition, the proper technique in the 40-yard dash is explored.

> An analysis of correct sprinting form has allowed research-ers to identify key factors contributing to efficient movement. It has also revealed a diversity of styles and techniques among champion athletes. This diversity suggests the need for athletes to improve their basic style without trying to mimic the exact techniques of others.

Running is instinctive, but the misinterpretation of the fundamental phases of running sometimes interferes with the natural and correct form. As an athlete, you must be aware of what is natural and what is unnatural. If you are unaware of this difference, your efforts can make you run slower. Often athletes feel that they have to "bear down" and "stay low and pull" in order to run fast. The scientific analysis of running suggests just the opposite. Reaching maximum speed depends greatly upon how relaxed you can keep your body in a naturally upright position. The human machine is much better at pushing than pulling, partly because the formation of the leg is unsuited as a pulling force. Therefore, the suggestion to "stay low and pull" prevents maximum speed. If you want to run faster, remember that sprinting is primarily a pushing action against the ground.

© Joe Cambioso

SPRINTING SPEED:
STRIDE LENGTH × STRIDE FREQUENCY

Sprinting speed is the product of stride length and stride frequency. Maximum speed exists only when these components are in correct proportion. Stride length is best improved by increasing your force against the ground. The resulting reaction from the ground drives the body's center of mass farther forward, lengthening the stride naturally (figure 8.1). When your foot makes contact with the ground, it must be directly under your body's center of gravity (figure 8.2). For example, if your foot lands too far out in front of your body and ahead of your center of gravity when you are sprinting (a condition known as overstriding), it will cause a braking effect resulting in a loss of speed.

Stride frequency is the time required to complete a stride and is limited by the length of the stride. Thus, although stride length is determined when force is applied by pushing against the ground, stride frequency is merely the time required to complete that stride. Again, maximum speed is achieved when stride length and stride frequency are in correct proportion. Forcing a greater stride frequency will only produce a shorter stride length and result in a loss in speed. The emphasis should be on improving stride length naturally, without overstriding, and not on forcing a greater stride frequency.

Figure 8.1

Figure 8.2

Sprinting involves a series of jumps from one foot to the other; stride is lengthened by increasing the power of the push-off and jumping farther without touching the lead foot down ahead of the center of gravity. Stride length is increased by exerting more force during high-speed movement. This force requires additional strength, power, and flexibility.

THE STRIDE CYCLE

During any running stride, the leg cycles through three different phases: the drive phase, when the foot is in contact with the ground; the recovery phase, when the leg swings from the hip while the foot clears the ground; and the support phase, when the runner's weight is on the entire foot.

During the drive phase, the power comes from a pushing action off the ball of the foot (figure 8.1). Recall that stride length, and therefore sprinting speed, is the result of a pushing action. The goal of the drive phase is to create the maximum push off the ground. The ball of the foot is the only part of the foot capable of creating an efficient and powerful push. Some misinformed sport professionals believe that the drive phase's pushing action comes from the toes. However, pushing from the toes reduces both power and stability and slows the runner. The drive phase contributes to overall speed only when the runner pushes off the ground using the ball of the foot.

The drive of the supporting leg during the sprinting action takes approximately 0.09 to 0.11 second though maximum strength in contracted muscles can occur after only 0.7 to 0.9 second. Obviously, maximum strength is not reached during the sprinting action. Fast training that improves speed strength, therefore, has the best chance of decreasing supporting leg time and thus improving sprinting speed. After an adequate strength foundation has been acquired, direct your attention toward the improvement of speed strength.

During the recovery phase, the knee joint closes and the foot cycles through as it comes close to the body (figure 8.2). As the knee joint opens and the leg begins to straighten, the foot comes closer to the ground in preparation for the support phase. An important point to remember about the recovery phase is that the runner does not reach for the ground or force a stamping action. The leg should remain relaxed and allow the foot to naturally strike the ground.

During the support phase, the foot makes initial contact with the ground on the outside edge of the ball of the foot. The weight of the body is then supported at a point that varies according to the speed of the athlete (figure 8.3). The faster the speed, the higher the contact point on the ball of the foot. Striking the ground first with this part of the foot serves to maximize speed but takes great energy. At slower speeds (jogging, for example), the contact point moves toward the rear of the foot between the arch and heel. During longer and slower runs, energy is saved by using a flat foot plant. At all running speeds, the support phase begins with a slight load on the support foot that then rides onto the full sole. Even during sprinting, the heel makes a brief but definite contact with the ground. This analysis of the support phase shows how it is impossible to reach your maximum speed by running on your toes.

ARM ACTION

Arm action in sprinting is critical when developing the most efficient stride length. The arms work in opposition to the legs, with the right arm and left leg coming forward as the left arm and right leg go backward and vice versa. The shoulders should be as relaxed as possible, with the swing coming from the shoulder joint. The shoul-

© Ted Sonnier

Figure 8.3

ders should stay square (perpendicular) to the direction of the run. The swing should be strong but relaxed. The hands should be also be relaxed. On the upswing, the hand should rise naturally to a point just in front of the chin and just inside the shoulder (figure 8.1). During the upswing, the arm angle is about 90 degrees or less, coordinating with the quick recovery of the forward swing of the leg (figure 8.2).

During the downswing, a natural straightening at the elbow corresponds with the longer leverage of the driving leg on the opposite side of the body to allow horizontal drive. As the arm swings down, the elbow will extend slightly (figure 8.1). At the bottom of the swing, the hand should be next to the thigh. However, toward the end of its backward movement, the arm bends and speeds up again to match the final, fast stage of the leg drive. The elbows should stay close to the body. Attempts to keep the elbows away from the body will prevent relaxation of the shoulders and limit efficient running mechanics. The arm action in sprinting is never forced or tense.

The mechanics of sprinting dictate that athletes who want to run faster must concentrate on pushing off the ground, landing with the proper foot placement, using the correct arm action, and staying relaxed.

SHARPENING YOUR 40-YARD DASH

Many different sports professionals use the 40-yard dash to evaluate an athlete's speed. However, most athletes do not understand how to start or race the 40-yard dash. Team-sport athletes rarely take the time to work on an effective start and the proper way to run the 40-yard dash.

> Correct sprinting form is important for team-sport athletes and can result in significant improvement in acceleration, maximum speed, and overall times in short distances.

The following information was prepared for team-sport athletes. In addition to providing advice on proper sprinting mechanics, the sections below examine faulty techniques commonly suggested to increase speed in the 40-yard dash.

The Start

Because the 40-yard dash is a very short distance, the start is critical to a peak performance. The first phase to examine in the start is the stance. Choose either the three-point or four-point stance (figures 8.4, *a* and *b*, and 8.5, *a* and *b*). For the three-point stance, have your stronger leg, usually the leg you jump with, in front. For most athletes, if you are right-handed, your left leg will be your stronger leg. We illustrate a start from a left-handed athlete (figure 8.4*a*). From a kneeling position, place the right (stronger) foot forward so that the edges of your toes are approximately 16 to 20 inches behind the starting line. With the knee of your back leg on the ground, position it even with the ball of your front foot. Extending your left arm out just behind the line, raise your body up to a position where the angle of the front leg is about 90 degrees, and the angle of the rear leg close to 135 degrees. The left hand should be extended up on the fingertips with the fingers far apart. Spreading your fingers will give you more stability. The right arm should rest on the thigh of the

Figure 8.4*a*

Figure 8.4*b*

right leg or in a position behind the body as if in a running position. Assume a relaxed position with most of your body weight on the legs and a small amount of your weight on the extended front arm.

The power at the start comes from your legs, not your arm, so don't lean too far forward so that too much weight is on your arm. If most of the weight is on your arm, there will not be enough pressure on the legs to drive and push out properly. In addition, if there is too much pressure or weight on the arm, you will have to stumble out and catch yourself before you can regain balance. You must drive and push out with your legs when starting; don't try to throw your arms out and forward. Your arms are just working to create proper stride length and frequency; they do not replace the power of the legs.

Drive off your front leg in a straight line from the foot through the top of your head (figure 8.4b). A good start will combine a balanced and stable position followed by the correct driving and pushing with the legs. In addition, emphasis should be on pushing backward and downward to set the body in motion.

The four-point stance is the same as the three-point stance except both arms are extended to the ground. From a kneeling position, place your stronger leg forward with your toes approximately 16 to 20 inches behind the starting line (figure 8.5a). With the knee of your back leg on the ground, position it even with the ball of the front foot. Extend and spread out both of your arms behind the starting line about shoulder-width apart (figure 8.5a). Keeping your fingers spread apart and the arms straight, rise up to a set position where the front leg is at a 90-degree angle. The back leg should be at a 135-degree angle (figure 8.5b).

© Ted Sonnier

Figure 8.5a

Figure 8.5*b*

Keep most of the weight on your legs so that you are comfortable and balanced. The driving action will come from the legs. Keep your arms straight in the set position and not bent at the elbows. Balance and the driving and pushing action are the two key factors when starting the 40-yard dash. Like the three-point stance, drive off the front leg in a line through the top of your head. In addition, emphasize pushing backward and downward to set the body in motion.

The Race

When racing the 40-yard dash, it is important to accelerate from start to finish. Although this sounds simple or even obvious, athletes who fail to understand acceleration are cheating themselves of their best times. The scientific analysis of sprinting has proven that you cannot run at your very top speed for much more than one second. In the 40-yard dash, most athletes believe they have to run at maximum speed over the entire distance. In addition, they also believe that if they focus on increasing their stride frequency, they will run a fast time. The more efficient approach to running the 40-yard dash is to accelerate over the entire distance and through the finish in order to reach the top speed toward the end of the race. Your fastest times will be recorded when you feel yourself accelerating *through* the finish line.

Drive out of the starting position and gradually come up into full running position. Don't stay low or bent at the waist during the race as this will only keep you from running with the correct body position. In addition, you must *stay relaxed*. Speed over any distance requires the athlete to be disciplined enough to relax through the entire race.

Troubleshooting Sprinting Mechanics

Arm Action. If you run with tense arms, practice loose, swinging movements from a standing position. Remember to swing from the shoulder and keep the arms relaxed at all times. Although the arms work in opposition to the legs, they must be coordinated with the action of the legs for maximum sprinting efficiency.

Body Lean. Many athletes and some sport professionals suggest too much body lean. Your body should have a slight lean in the direction that you are running. It is important to note that the lean comes from the ground and not from the waist. The lean is only a result of displacing the center of gravity in the direction you are running. Leaning by bending at the waist interferes with the correct mechanics of sprinting.

Foot Contact. *Don't run up on your toes.* The toes have no power or stability. If you run on your toes, you will not be able to run fast. Stay on the balls of your feet and push against the ground. Don't reach for and pull toward the ground; this strategy will develop injuries and result in poor sprinting mechanics and slow times. Allow the heel to make contact with the ground when running at any distance.

Overstriding. Overstriding is the worst and most misunderstood element of sprinting. Don't reach and overstride to increase stride length. Push against the ground and let the foot land underneath your center of gravity. Any placement of the foot in front of the center of gravity will cause the body to slow down.

Understriding. Try not to be too quick. Too much turnover will cause you to run fast in one place, and you will not cover any ground. Quality sprint speed is a combination of both stride frequency and stride length. One does not replace the other.

Tension. Don't try to power your way through a race or sprint effort. You will not run fast if you are tight. To run fast, you must stay relaxed.

Reaching your maximum speed requires training. Many sport professionals believe that running is a natural act that needs no special focus. Such a belief has prevented many athletes from improving their performance. As you consider your training, concentrate on the principles of sprinting mechanics, and your speed will improve.

KEY SPRINTING FORM DRILLS

Ralph Mann—former Olympic silver medalist in the 400-meter hurdles and current speed improvement specialist—evaluated over 1,000 drills for down time, proper technique, and duplication of skills. The following bounding, sprinting, and workout drills have been successfully used by Mann and Coach Tom Tellez to improve speed in short distances.

> Form sprinting drills help establish correct neuromuscular movement patterns. Establishing as near error-free movement as possible may improve stride rate and stride length and eliminate wasted energy that does not contribute to forward movement.

Bounding Drills

These drills are designed to develop the explosive leg power required in starting. They are stressful enough to be a workout, or they can be part of a workout. They are *not* designed to be warm-up or cool-down drills.

© Joe Cambioso

Straight Bounding

Beginning from a slow jog, try to bound as high into the air as possible using a running form that emphasizes a high knee lift. Land on the opposite leg and continue bounding down the field. The intensity of this drill is controlled by altering the height and the number of repetitions. For beginners and heavier players the height of the bound should be limited and the number of bounds kept at no more than four with each leg. As your experience and training progress, you can increase the height and the number of repetitions.

Inside Bounding

This drill is similar to outside bounding except that the foot is placed laterally inside the normal landing position, and the body is projected laterally as well as up and forward. This drill should be used after you have had experience with straight bounding.

© Joe Cambioso

© Joe Cambioso

Outside Bounding

This drill is similar to straight bounding except that the foot is placed laterally outside the normal landing position, and the body is projected laterally as well as up and forward. The drill should be used after you have had experience with straight bounding.

Sprinting Drills

The following drills are designed to develop the mechanics, strength, and power needed to produce maximum performance in sprinting. They are designed for use while you warm up before a workout. The length and difficulty of each drill can be altered to any desired distance and intensity.

Butt Kickers

From a jog, the lower leg is allowed to swing back and to bounce off the buttocks. The upper leg should not move much. Place emphasis on allowing (not forcing) the heel to come up to the butt.

Wall Slide

From a jog, the action is the same as for butt kickers except that the heel of the recovery leg must not travel behind the body. Imagine a wall of glass running down the back, and do not allow the heel to break the glass. This action will produce knee lift without forcing the action. As in butt kickers, when this drill is done properly, the heel with bounce off the butt.

© Joe Cambioso

Start and Sprint

From a stationary position, start quickly, and feel the power being applied behind your body. Ten yards out, quickly shift from running in back of the body to sprinting in front of the body. This drill should emphasize the difference between starting technique (behind the body) and sprinting technique (in front of the body).

Quick Feet Drill

From a jog, increase your stride rate such that you take as many steps as possible in a 10-yard interval. Jog for 10 yards and repeat. Emphasize quick turnover with the legs moving in front of, not behind or under, the body.

Workout Drills

These drills were designed as a workout or as part of a workout. Typically three sets of each drill are performed. Start each of these drills on your toes and make an effort to remain in this position during the drill.

Cycling

Leaning against a wall, bar, or any support, one leg is cycled through in a sprinting manner. Emphasize keeping the leg from extending behind the body, allowing the foot to kick the butt during recovery, and pawing the ground to complete the action. Ten cycles with each leg make up one set.

Butt Kickers

This drill is the same as butt kickers in the sprinting drills except that the emphasis is more on quickness. Ten kicks with each leg make up one set.

Down and Offs

From a high knee position, the emphasis is to decrease your foot/ground contact by hitting the ground with the ball of the foot and getting off as quickly as possible. In turn, the effort on the ground should bounce your leg up into the high knee position. Ten down and offs make up one set.

© Joe Cambioso

Pull-Throughs

Extending the leg in front of the body (like a hurdler), the leg is then brought down and through ground contact in a power motion. Ten pull-throughs with each leg make up one set.

Stick Drill

Twenty sticks (18 to 24 inches in length) are placed 18 inches apart on a grass surface. Athletes sprint through the sticks as fast as possible, touching one foot down between each. Emphasize high knee lift and quick ground contact. Coaches can time athletes by starting a stopwatch when the foot contacts the ground between the first and the second stick and by stopping the watch when a foot contacts the ground after passing the final stick. One completion of the drill makes up one set.

African Dance

While running forward, raise each leg to the side of your body as in hurdling, and tap each heel with your hand. A 10-yard run equals one set. Start this drill easily and gradually build up the intensity.

© Joe Cambioso

Drum Major

While running forward, rotate your leg inward to the midline of your body and tap your heel at the midline. A 10-yard run equals one set.

© Joe Cambioso

SPEED ENDURANCE TRAINING

Speed endurance training will not help you take a faster or longer step. It will, however, prevent you from slowing down late in the game, at the end of a long sprint, or after sprinting several times with little rest in between. You have seen many examples of poor speed endurance in different sports. A halfback is tackled from behind by a slower player. A sprinter is passed in the final 10 meters of a race. A baseball player runs out of steam and is tagged out at home. A basketball player is beaten to the ball by a slower player. All these are examples of poor speed endurance, which causes a player either to slow down or to fail to accelerate as fast as normal due to fatigue. In most sports, a player is expected to make repeated bursts of speed. Ideally, the fourth or fifth sprint is run as fast as the first. This is often not the case due to poor speed endurance. By becoming well-conditioned for speed endurance, you will have several advantages in your sport: (a) repeated short sprints all at the same speed can be made with minimum rest, (b) maximum speed is reached more quickly, and (c) maximum speed is held for a longer distance before slowing occurs.

High levels of speed endurance provide you with a fresh start on each short sprint. Speed endurance training is a vital phase for athletes in team sports such as football, basketball, and baseball. It is the phase that can give you the edge.

Speed endurance is easy to improve. You only need to sprint short distances two to three times per week and keep a record of how many repetitions you sprinted, how far you sprinted, and how much recovery time you took between each repetition. The rest is easy. On each workout, you simply increase the sprint distance and decrease the recovery time between each repetition. In a period of six to eight weeks, your speed endurance scores will be better.

The following guidelines will help you understand how to devise the best program for your sport:

• Sprinting (up to 200 meters) is 90 to 95 percent anaerobic, and training should reflect this percentage. Aerobic training (lap running and jogging) should occupy only a small portion of your training regimen. Improved aerobic conditioning has little or no effect on speed in short distances. Too much distance running in the pre-season has been shown to decrease speed in short distances.

• Use maximum sprints for short durations (10 to 60 seconds).

• Rest periods of a few minutes should follow each maximum effort.

• All-out sprints—covering approximately the same or greater distances than those normally sprinted in your sport (football, 20 to 60 yards; basketball, 10 to 30 yards; and baseball, 30 to 120 yards, etc.)—should be used.

• A one-minute maximum effort sprint followed by four to five minutes of rest before repeating the effort improves speed endurance. Repetitive 400-meter runs in 60 to 75 seconds followed by a four- to five-minute rest period are also an effective technique.

Pickup Sprints

Pickup sprints are an easy, effective training program to improve speed endurance for football, baseball, soccer, basketball, and other sports. Pickup sprints involve a gradual increase from a jog to a striding pace, and then to a maximum effort sprint. Use a 1:1 ratio of the distance and recovery walk that follows each repetition. For example you may jog 25 meters, stride 25, sprint 25, and end that repetition with a 25-meter walk. The walk or slow jog should allow some recovery prior to the next repetition. This jog-stride-sprint recovery cycle tends to develop speed endurance and reduce your chances of muscle injury in cold weather. The cycle is an example of early-season training, and the exact number of repetitions depends on your conditioning level. As you improve, the distance is lengthened, with late-season pickup sprints reaching segments of 120-meters.

New Zealand athletes use a routine similar to pickup sprints that involves a series of four 50-meter sprints and near-maximum speed (6 to 7 seconds) per 400-meter lap, jogging for 10 to 12 seconds after each sprint and completing the 400-meter run in 64 to 76 seconds. Athletes have performed as many as 50 sprints with little reduction in speed on any repetition.

The majority of speed endurance work for athletes in football, basketball, soccer, and baseball should involve segments of 25- to 50-meter sprints because the object is to train the fast-twitch fiber and improve both conditioning and speed. Sprinting longer distances (50, 75, 100, or 125 meters) can be used occasionally as the final one to three repetitions of a workout.

You can retest yourself in the 120-yard dash and compare your flying 40 time to your 80- or 120-yard time to check your speed endurance. Another check test involves completing six consecutive 40-yard dashes at 30-second intervals and then comparing the drop-off. Ideally, none of the timed 40s should be more than 0.2 second off your best effort. Assume the three- or four-point stance at the starting line and have a coach or friend time you in the 40-yard dash. Now walk forward 10 yards slowly and begin your second timed 40 when 30 seconds have elapsed. Repeat this procedure once up and once down the area until you have completed six timed 40-yard dashes with a 30-second rest between each.

You are now ready to move on to the seventh and final step in the seven-step model for speed improvement: overspeed training.

CHAPTER 9

STEP 7: OVERSPEED TRAINING

Resetting the speed clock.

Overspeed training is the seventh and final step of your speed improvement program. You now possess the foundation to engage in the most demanding phase of sport speed training. This phase is also the most fun. With overspeed training, you may run a 40-yard dash faster than Olympic sprinters such as Mike Morris, Leroy Burell, Michael Johnson, Gail Devers, or Gwen Torrence, or NFL speedsters such as Deion Sanders or Darell Green. The feeling of raw power and speed is very exciting. If you use overspeed training correctly, you will be amazed at the results.

NEUROMUSCULAR TRAINING

The purpose of overspeed training is to increase both your stride rate and stride length by forcing you to perform at a much higher level than you are capable of without assistance. Overspeed or "sprint-assisted" training produces this effect on the neuromuscular system. During overspeed training, you are getting your nervous and muscular systems accustomed to higher contraction rates. A neurosurgeon, speaking at the National Convention of the National Association of Speed and Explosion, put it in layman's terms, "After several weeks of overspeed training, the nervous system allows you to continue these higher rates without any help. As a result, you can now take those faster steps and longer steps without any assistance." Although this statement is only theory, research clearly shows that the number of steps you take per second and the length of your stride will improve following four to eight weeks of overspeed training.

Stride rate can be increased with proper overspeed techniques such as towing and downhill sprinting.

GUIDELINES FOR OVERSPEED TRAINING

To receive maximum results, you must use overspeed training correctly. Adhere to the following guidelines for each of the four overspeed methods discussed in this chapter:

• Warm up thoroughly before any type of overspeed training. Begin every workout with a general warm-up routine to increase core temperature. Use the large muscle groups first with a slow jog for 400 to 800 meters, followed by a faster jog and three-quarters speed striding for an additional 400 meters or more. When you are perspiring freely, stop and complete the stretching routine presented in chapter 3 for 8 to 10 minutes. You are now ready for the walk-jog-stride-sprint cycle (walk 15 steps, slow jog 15 steps, stride 15 steps at three-quarters speed, and sprint 15 steps); continue this cycle for 400 meters or until you feel prepared to execute your all-out overspeed sprints.

• Take overspeed training seriously, and pay attention to the specific suggestions for each method to avoid muscle or equipment-related injuries that may occur due to horseplay or carelessness.

• Use towing only on a soft, grassy area. Inspect the surface for broken glass and other objects.

• Expect to experience muscle soreness one to two days after your first overspeed session. Overspeed training is demanding and will recruit motor units and muscle fibers that you are not accustomed to using. Even if you have been involved in some form of sprint training for several weeks, you can still expect to experience considerable soreness. This soreness is an excellent sign that overspeed training is going beyond your normal training routine.

• Always use overspeed training in the beginning of your work-out, immediately after completing your general warm-up and stretching session. You can only take ultra-fast, long strides when you are free from fatigue. Avoid any type of overspeed training after you are fatigued from drills, calisthenics, scrimmages, speed endurance training, weight training, or plyometrics.

• Remember, you are trying to take faster and longer steps than ever before, not improve your conditioning level for short sprints (see the speed endurance discussion in step 6). Take advantage of the entire rest period specified between each repetition and make certain you are fully recovered before completing the next overspeed sprint.

• Emphasize quality form in all repetitions. If you are sprinting out of control, the pull must be reduced on subsequent repetitions to allow you to complete the run with perfect form. The most effective training of the neuromuscular system for speed improvement occurs when your overspeed training program forces you to run no more than five percent above your unaided speed.

• Be patient and progress slowly. On your first workout, sprint only three times at three-quarters speed; sprint four times two days later, and sprint five times on your third workout of the first week.

TYPES OF OVERSPEED TRAINING

There are four basic methods of overspeed training: downhill sprinting; high-speed cycling; towing with surgical tubing, pulley devices, and the Sprint Master; and high-speed treadmill sprint training. Not every method is equally effective. Some are also less costly and more practical than others. Read this section carefully and decide how you want to proceed. Table 9.1 describes the advantages and limitations of each overspeed techniques.

Overspeed training has been shown to efficiently and naturally increase both stride rate and length. Athletes have also improved their 40-yard-dash times by as much as 0.6 second during an 8 to 12 week period. Track athletes in the 100-meter dash have improved their times by more than 0.8 second. Keep in mind that such improvement won't happen overnight. Training the neuromuscular system takes time, so you need to stay with the program a minimum of eight weeks. Eventually, you will move to an ongoing maintenance program involving one to two workouts per week to avoid losing your acquired gains.

Downhill Sprinting

Downhill sprinting is one of the safest, most practical forms of overspeed training and requires no special equipment. Refer back to table 7.7 for guidelines in selecting slope angles and distances for overspeed sprinting workouts. The trick is to find a slope that fits your objectives. A general guideline is to locate a 50-meter area with a slope of no more than one to three and one half degrees. Consult your coach for suggestions. Decline areas greater than three and a half degrees increase your chances of falling, produce overstriding, cause you to land on the heels of the feet, and force ground contact beyond your center of gravity, which produces a braking effect. As a result, a forceful push-off on such a slope is nearly impossible. The braking effect and a deviation from one's natural sprinting form is

TABLE 9.1

Comparison of Five Overspeed Training Programs

Method	Cost	Advantages	Disadvantages	Effectiveness
Downhill sprinting	$0	Practical, only slight chance of injury due to falls or muscle pulls. You can easily reduce pace and stop if you lose balance.	Does not provide as much assistance; less increase in stride rate and stride length than some other methods.	Good, will increase both stride rate and length and sprinting speed.
High-speed stationary cycling	$200-600	Can be performed in your home or gym. Eliminates wind resistance and gravity to permit higher pedaling rates than an outdoor bicycle.	Rather unproved; increased rate of leg movement per second on the cycle should help increase stride rates in sprinting.	Fair, focuses on leg turnover; more research needed. Should be used with another method.
Towing (tubing/ pacer)	$25-85	Inexpensive, allows you to train alone safely; provides excellent controllable pull.	Falls may occur; No bailout since tubing or pacer is fastened to your waist. Tubing occasionally breaks or comes lose.	Excellent, increases stride rate and length and speed in short distances.
Sprint Master	$2,000 or more	Operator controls the pull and can back off if form is broken or athlete stumbles; athlete can bail out by merely releasing the grip.	Very expensive; not practical for group sessions because of time requirement; requires two people for only one to train.	Excellent, same as above.
High-speed treadmill sprinting	$4,000-10,000	Can be performed inside; elicits very high stride rates. You can grab guard rails or allow safety belt to protect you if you lose balance.	Very expensive; requires use of a spotting belt, an assistant, and time to learn to step on and off at very high speeds ("greyhound effect").	Excellent, produces high stride rates and a long stride; increases speed in short distances.

even noticeable in some athletes when using slopes of more than four degrees. The ideal area will allow you to sprint 20 meters on a perfectly flat surface (to accelerate to near-maximum speed), sprint down a 15-meter downhill slope of one to three and one half degrees (to force higher than normal stride lengths, stride rates, and speed), and then end by sprinting 15 meters on a flat area to allow you to attempt to maintain the higher speed rates without the assistance of gravity.

> Combined downhill-uphill sprinting has been shown to force runners to take more steps per second than flat-surface sprinting.

Carefully examine the grounds in your school, university, park, and neighborhood, looking in the surrounding areas of soccer and football fields and other grassy areas, or ask your coach to consider building an area specifically for downhill sprint training. Once you find a suitable place to train, follow the program shown in table 9.2; pay attention to the rest or recovery period between each repetition.

High-Speed Stationary Cycling

During high-speed cycling, wind resistance, gravity, and body weight are eliminated to allow you to complete more revolutions (similar to steps in sprinting) per second than you are capable of doing on a road bicycle or during the sprinting action. This overspeed technique should be used with one other method, such as towing or downhill sprinting, to guarantee your success in increasing stride rate and length. Preliminary evidence indicates that high-speed cycling programs may increase your stride rate in sprinting. A sample program is described in table 9.2.

TABLE 9.2

Downhill Sprinting and Cycling Program				
Week	Repetitions	Acceleration distance	Overspeed distance*	Progression (repetitions)	Rest (min)
1	2-3	10-15 yards (1.5-2 seconds)	20-25 yards (1-1.5 seconds)	Add one to two per workout	2
2	4-6	15-20 yards (2-2.5 seconds)	20-25 Yards (1.5-2.0 seconds)	Add one each workout	2.5
3	7-9	20-25 yards (2.5-3 seconds)	20-25 yards (1.5-2.5 seconds)	Add one each workout	3
4	9-10	20-25 yards (2.5-3 seconds)	20-25 yards (1.5-2.5 seconds)	Add one each workout	3.5
5	9-10	20-25 yards (2.5-3 seconds)	20-25 yards (1.5-2.5 seconds)	Add one each workout	3.5

*Overspeed distance is the actual distance (or time) you are sprinting downhill or pedaling at high speeds.

Towing

Towing or pulling athletes to sprint faster is not a new approach. Prior to the use of surgical tubing and two-person pulley arrangements, currently outdated methods such as motor scooters, motorcycles, and even automobiles were used. In 1956, towing was used to train Olympic medal winner Al Lawrence, who held on to a rigid bar attached to a car four times per week for distances of 100 to 600 yards. In the 1960s, towing was successfully used in Australia to reduce the 100-meter time of one subject who held on to the side of a tram car. Young sprinters increased their stride length considerably (an average of six inches) and improved their 100-yard dash time from an average of 10.5 to 9.9 seconds. In 1976, a four-station tow bar attached to an automobile was used to improve 40-yard dash times with a flying start. Towing has also been a regular part of our annual speed camps since 1970, and overspeed training has been an important part of our training programs to improve 40-yard dash times for team sports.

Towing produces higher stride rates and increases stride length more effectively than downhill sprinting and high-speed cycling. It also will improve your 40-yard dash time more than most other overspeed training techniques. You can choose from three unique modern methods: towing with surgical tubing, towing with the Ultra Speed Pacer, or towing with the Sprint Master, if available.

Towing With Surgical Tubing

Surgical tubing can force you to take faster and longer steps and complete a 40-yard dash at world-record speed simply by providing you with a slight pull throughout the high-speed portion of your sprint. A 20- to 25-foot piece of elastic tubing is attached to your waist by a belt. The opposite end can be attached to another athlete or to a stationary object such as a tree or a goalpost to allow you to work out alone (see figure 9.1). Back up to stretch the tubing 15 yards (about 20 yards total from your partner) and run at three-quarters speed with the pull until you learn to adjust by keeping your balance and using proper sprinting form. After four or five practice runs, you should be ready for the full ride.

Back up until you are approximately 30 to 35 yards from your partner before sprinting at high speed with the pull. Most good surgical tubing will safely stretch to six times its unstretched length (20 feet × 6 = 120 feet or 40 yards). Avoid stretching the tubing beyond this recommended limit. You also can make stationary runs from a three-point or track start. Athletes in our speed clinics and camps have completed 40-yard dashes in less than 3.9 seconds when being pulled with surgical tubing.

Training Suggestions.
Surgical tubing allows you to train anytime with or without a partner. You can use a number of different drills:

© Mary T. Hall

Figure 9.1 Towing with surgical tubing will make you faster.

• Attach one end of the tubing to a goalpost and the other to your waist with the tubing tied in front. Stretch the tubing by walking backward about 20 yards. Jog forward toward the goalpost with the pull. Repeat this drill again four times, two with a three-quarter speed run and two with a full-speed sprint. Within the next three sprints, back up an extra five to eight yards each time to increase the pull and the speed of your sprint.

• Repeat the last part of the preceding drill, emphasizing a high knee lift.

• Complete four or five all-out sprints using the exact rest interval recommended in table 9.3. Allow the tubing to pull you at approximately a half of a second faster than your best 40-yard dash time. It takes only a slight pull to produce this effect. Place two marks 40 yards apart and have someone time you as you are being towed.

• For athletes who are required to do so in their sport (defensive backs in football; baseball, field hockey, lacrosse, rugby, soccer, and tennis players), repeat the preceding drills by sprinting backward and/or in a sideward position. Turn your belt around to the center of your back or to the hip.

• Choose a faster athlete and race him or her while you are being towed. You will be amazed at how fast you are sprinting. You will also win the race.

- Do the quick feet drill by measuring one of your strides before placing 20 sticks at a distance two to three feet shorter than your normal stride. Repeat the first drill described in this section, emphasizing rapid stride frequency.

- Complete the two-person drill by attaching one end of the tubing to your waist and the other to your partner's back. Have your partner sprint 25 to 30 yards ahead against the resistance, and then stop. You now sprint toward your partner in your overspeed run. Continue for two to three more repetitions before reversing the position of the belt. You are now sprinting against resistance (sprint loading), and your partner is sprinting with assistance (overspeed training). This drill should be the last drill in your overspeed workout because it does not allow adequate time between each sprint to fully recover.

Sprint loading is a technique designed to improve explosive concentric movements such as sprinting speed. A relatively light resistance that does not drastically alter sprinting form produces the best results.

Follow the overspeed training program in table 9.3 two to three times per week (every other day) during the preseason period in your sport and one to two times per week during the in-season period.

Safety Precautions for Surgical Tubing. Surgical tubing can be dangerous. Adequate supervision is recommended at all times. Tubing can break if stretched too far, and belts can come loose if they are carelessly fastened. Follow these tips carefully to guarantee your safety:

- Inspect the tubing before your first run of each workout by allowing the tubing to slide through your hand as you back up. Any rough marks should be carefully examined. If a nick is detected, discard the tubing and replace it with other tubing.

- Inspect the knots on both belts and retie them if they are not tight or appear to be coming loose.

- Examine the knot that ties the tubing to the belt to make certain it is firmly in place and secure.

- After you attach the belt to your waist, tie a knot with the remaining portion to make certain it cannot come loose.
- Avoid standing with the tubing fully stretched for more than a few seconds. During this stretched phase, knots come loose and tubing breaks.
- Use tubing that attaches to a belt around your waist rather than a harness. With only slight differences in height between you and your partner, a broken tubing or a loose belt could snap upward and strike you in the eye. Tubing attached to the waist that does come loose when stretched is unlikely to produce any serious injury.
- Use shoes without spikes for the first several workouts until you have fully adjusted to the high speed and can complete each repetition with correct form.
- Use surgical tubing on soft grassy areas only.

Towing With the Ultra Speed Pacer

The Ultra Speed Pacer is a simple pulley device that relies on leverage. The pulley (fulcrum) is fastened to a fixed object in the gym or on the athletic field. Each side of the rope going through the pulley is attached to an athlete using a belt. As one athlete sprints at a 45-degree angle away from the pulley, the other athlete is forced to sprint toward the pulley while receiving considerable pull. After a few trials, you and your partner will easily determine how fast the angle sprinter should run to increase or decrease the pull. The device has the potential to provide a strong pull and produce very high stride rates, stride lengths, and sprinting speed. Because this device merely provides a straight pull at various speeds, you cannot use the drills described for surgical tubing with this device.

Towing With the Sprint Master

Following a summer speed camp in 1981 at Virginia Commonwealth University in Richmond, Virginia, there was frustration over the problems with the use of a motor scooter to tow athletes at high speeds. It was then that Dr. Dintiman indicated the need for a motorized device that could be attached to a wall and used indoors or outdoors that was also capable of towing athletes at high, regulated speeds. John Dolan, who assisted in the speed camp, was immediately enthusiastic. He and a highly mechanical friend, Michael Watkins, constructed more than 20 prototypes before the Sprint Master was perfected. The machine is precisely engineered to pull athletes at speeds faster than any human can sprint. It attaches to the goalposts of a football or soccer field or to the wall in a gymnasium and provides controlled, variable speed for each athlete. It is also a safe device that eliminates the cumbersome, dangerous use of a vehicle and allows the athlete to merely release his or her grip if balance is lost. For information on the purchase of a Sprint Master, write NASE, 1400 W. First St., Kill Devil Hills, NC, 27948.

> **Towing to force runners to take more steps than would otherwise be possible has improved stride rate and 40-yard dash times by more than 0.6 second.**

The Sprint Master also allows you full use of your arms while being towed at speeds of up to one second faster than your best flying 40-yard dash time. The athlete grasps the two handles and is literally reeled in by the Sprint Master.

Use the following steps to start an overspeed program with the Sprint Master:

- Use the workout schedule shown in table 9.3 two to three times per week (every other day).

- Have your coach or friend pull you at approximately half of a second faster than your best flying 40-yard dash time. The operator quickly learns how to judge pace and can group athletes of similar speed together. It is also quite simple to place two marks 40 yards apart and time athletes as they are being pulled. The set screw on the machine can then be fixed at the proper speed.

- When you are being pulled, grasp the tow-rope handles and accelerate slowly for 10 to 15 yards. The Sprint Master will then exert its proper pull as you reach full speed and will continue to pull you for the recommended 20 to 25 yards; longer distances tend to produce fatigue and cause you to lose your balance. Pump your arms as you would in normal sprinting form instead of placing your hands and arms in front of the body and letting yourself be pulled in water-ski like fashion.

- Practice the art of letting go of the rope handles if you lose your balance. On an athletic field, especially in full uniform, a high-speed fall and a roll is generally safe. Very few runners fall at any towing speed once the operator learns the technique.

Operating the Sprint Master is easily learned and is described precisely in a brochure. Speeds can be individually determined for each athlete, and the operator can make the pull safely. In the Chicago Bears training camp, one runner completed a 2.9-second flying 40-yard dash (equivalent to a 3.6 or 3.7 stationary 40-yard dash and faster than sprinter Leroy Burell) while being towed with the Sprint Master. Chicago Bears coaches who timed the runner were surprised at the results and now use a Sprint Master in their training program. Most of the towing drills described previously for surgical tubing cannot be used with the Sprint Master because it allows only straight-ahead sprinting at various speeds.

TABLE 9.3

Overspeed Training Using Surgical Tubing or the Sprint Master				
Week	Repetitions	Overspeed distance (yards)*	Rest (minutes)	Progression
1	3-5	10-15	2	Three-quarter speed runs only to acclimate
2	3-5	10-15	2	Maximum speed
3	5-7	15-20	3	Maximum speed
4	7-9	20-25	3	Maximum speed
5	7-9	20-25	3	Maximum speed
6-9	7-9	25-30	3.5	Maximum speed with weighted vest that progresses from one to five pounds over three weeks. Used for the final two repetitions of the workout only.

*Represents the total distance you are sprinting at maximum speed.

Treadmill Sprinting

In the Virginia Commonwealth University Laboratory, the A.R. Young high-speed treadmill (capable of speeds of 0 to 26+ miles per hour and a 100-meter dash under ten seconds) is used to improve stride length, stride rate, form, speed endurance, and sprinting speed. Cinematography identifies differences in stride length and rate at various speeds in both treadmill and unaided, flat-surface sprinting. Form is corrected by an expert standing on a stool facing and looking downward at the subject during high-speed sprinting. The treadmill is also an excellent piece of equipment for overspeed training.

The following guidelines were developed for use on the treadmill as an overspeed training technique:

- Athletes use a standard warm-up procedure and stretching prior to entry on the treadmill.

- A harness that also attaches to the support rails and allows free arm movement, balance, and safety is used. One spotter is also placed on each side of the treadbelt.

- A one-week acclimation period is used to allow sprinters to adjust to entry on the treadbelt at high speeds and to treadmill sprinting.

- Because the treadbelt accelerates slowly and would introduce a fatigue factor if sprinters were required to jog, stride, and sprint until higher belt speeds were reached, treadbelt speeds are preset prior to entry. After six to eight practice attempts, sprinters can easily enter at high speeds. The so-called greyhound effect allows athletes to reach maximum speed in approximately two seconds.

High-speed treadmill sprinting (up to a 9.8-second 100-meter dash) improves stride rate and speed in short distances.

The sample program shown in table 9.4 has been used in a number of experiments at Virginia Commonwealth University over the past decade.

Treadmill sprinting is not without its special problems. The sprinting action produces a slight slowing effect each time the foot strides the treadbelt; however, aiding factors predominate and allow a faster rate for most individuals even without training. The braking or slowing effect when each foot strikes the treadbelt has been found to be greater for heavier athletes (over 200 pounds) and for athletes of all sizes in the initial stages of training and tends to be eliminated as acclimation occurs and form instruction is given. At high speeds beyond one's maximum speed (in early training sessions), the braking effect almost reduces treadbelt speed to a sprinter's maximum speed. This problem is soon overcome.

TABLE 9.4

High-Speed Treadmill Sprint Program

Purpose	Speed	Repetitions
Acclimation	90% of maximum	6-20 at 2-minute intervals for 10 seconds
Entry practice	75% under maximum 90% under maximum At maximum speed	10-30 for two seconds
Improved stride rate and length	1-2 mph and 3-4 mph above maximum speed	2-6 for 3-5 seconds allowing full recovery after each

The program described in table 9.3 can also be used in treadmill sprint training. Overspeed distances are converted to seconds on the treadmill (10 yards = 1 second; a 25-yard sprint requires 2.5 seconds on the treadmill). The number of repetitions, length of the rest interval, and progression are similar for both techniques.

There are additional problems, however. It is difficult to determine true treadbelt speed with and without a sprinter on the treadmill. In one study (Dintiman 1984), a highly accurate surface speed indicator was used to determine belt speed variations with a sprinter (a 159-pound individual and a 197-pound individual) and without a sprinter. Several findings deserve attention:

- A heavier sprinter has a greater braking effect.
- The percent of braking increases as treadbelt speed increases for both light and heavy subjects.
- As training progresses in several weeks, the amount of braking is reduced in both light and heavy sprinters at the higher speed rates.
- At speeds in which the sprinter is being supported by the belt and is unable to maintain belt speed, only a normal expected braking occurs.

Most of the problems of treadmill sprint training can be overcome for athletes of all sizes by using an ample number of practice sessions at various speeds (acclimation), seeing that athletes master proper sprinting form, and avoiding a treadbelt speed too far beyond the subject's present maximum speed (the point at which proper sprinting form cannot be maintained). Ongoing research with high-speed treadmill sprinting continues to show improvements in stride rate and length, with this effect carried over to unassisted sprinting.

Advanced Overspeed Training Techniques

A number of effective overspeed variations have been tested in our camps and clinics with athletes at the middle school, high school, university, and professional levels. These advanced methods are designed only for older, mature athletes who meet the leg strength standard (2.5 times body weight) described in chapter 1 and have used the basic overspeed program described previously for at least four weeks. Three different types of advanced towing can be used in each session in addition to the basic program:

- Towing with a shortened stride for two to three repetitions at high speed while you consciously increase your stride rate greatly
- Towing with an exaggerated stride for one to two repetitions at high speeds while you consciously lengthen your stride
- Sprint-loaded towing for two to three repetitions at high speeds with weight added to the body (one to five pounds using the weighted vest described in chapter 7)

Overspeed training is one of the most important steps in the seven-step model. Everyone can benefit from this type of training, regardless of their 40-yard dash times. It is nearly impossible to reach your maximum speed potential without overspeed training. A 6- to 12-week program can produce dramatic results.

CHAPTER 10

DESIGNING YOUR PERSONAL PROGRAM

THE ATTACK PLAN FOR YOUR SPORT

You now have enough information in four main areas to design your personal program: (1) an understanding of the five key areas to emphasize for improving your speed, (2) knowledge of just how important each of these areas is to your specific sport, (3) an awareness of your weakness areas based on test results, and (4) the knowledge to utilize all aspects of the seven-step model to speed improvement to improve your weakness areas and make you quicker and faster for your sport.

The five ways you get faster are listed in table 10.1 along with the specific training programs designed to strengthen these areas. Return to chapter 1, table 1.7 to review the key areas for your sport. Write these areas in a column on the left side of a piece of paper. Now list your key weakness areas and the training programs prescribed in your test score sheet (chapter 1, table 1.1) in a second column next to the critical areas for your sport. Although you have done a similar procedure in chapter 1, it is important once again to make sure you are focusing the majority of your efforts on the right training programs. In general, you don't need to concentrate on any of the training programs specified in table 10.1 unless test results revealed a weakness area. You do, however, need to maintain what you already have. Sometimes it is beneficial to focus on speed and quickness improvement in an area such as stride rate even when a weakness in that area has not been revealed. Such areas, however, should not be the major focus of your program.

PRESEASON SPEED IMPROVEMENT

You now have everything you need to improve your speed. You have been tested and your scores have been evaluated. You have also

TABLE 10.1

Sprinting Speed Improvement Through Various Training Programs

How sprinting speed is improved	Specific training programs
Improve your reaction time, starting ability, and acceleration (reach full speed faster)	Starting form training for your sport Muscle imbalance training Functional strength power training Overspeed and acceleration training
Increase the length of your stride	Functional strength power training Muscle and imbalance training Plyometrics Sprint loading Overspeed training Form training Flexibility training
Increase the number of steps you take per second (stride rate)	Overspeed and advanced overspeed training Quick feet training Muscle imbalance training
Increase your explosive power and quickness	Quick feet and quick hand training Ballistics Overspeed acceleration training Plyometrics Functional strength and power training
Improve your form and speed endurance	Form training Speed endurance training Ballistics Sprint loading

The table assumes that athletes already possess an acceptable level of body fat, general conditioning, and strength (steps 1 and 2).

studied the speed improvement areas critical to your sport and learned the seven-step model. You are finally ready to begin your program. The final order for your preseason speed improvement program is listed in table 10.2. Follow this order carefully during the preseason period. Functional strength and power training (weights) and plyometrics are alternated every other day. Overspeed training is used only three times weekly.

The preseason period begins four months from your first scheduled practice day next season. For best results, count back 16 weeks from the start of your in-season period (first day of competition). Use

TABLE 10.2

Order of Use for Your Training Programs

Training program	Length	Order	Frequency	Explanation
General warm-up and stretching	8-12 min	1	Daily	Jog half a mile or more first to increase body temperature and follow with stretching and five sets of 25-yd walk-jog-stride-sprint.
Overspeed training	30 min	2	Two to three times a week	You should be completely fatigue-free before using any overspeed program.
Form training	15-20 min	3	Twice a week	Practice both starting and sprinting form.
Speed endurance	20 min	4	Two to three times a week	Your main objective is to develop explosive power and exhaust the anaerobic system using a combination of short- and long-distance pick-up sprints.
Ballistics	10-15 min	5	Twice a week	Use upper body ballistics before a plyometric workout; schedule this program near the end of your workout.
Functional strength and power training	30-40 min	6	Every other day	Always the last program in your workout because it produces extreme fatigue.
Plyometrics	15-20 min	6	One or two times a week	Always the last program in your workout; should not be used on days that you engage in weight training.
Cool-down	8-12 min	7	Daily	Light jogging and stretching.

the first eight weeks of this 16-week period to devote major attention to steps 1, 2, 3, and 4 of the seven-step model to lay on additional muscle mass and body weight, to improve your strength/weight ratios, and to increase explosive power. Use the second eight-week period (see the sample eight-week programs for various sports in tables 10.3 through 10.6) to concentrate on steps 5, 6, and 7.

This 16-week time frame is the longest training period you will ever have to concentrate specifically on these foundation areas that may be preventing you from sprinting faster and moving quicker (first eight weeks) and the sport loading, sprinting form/speed endurance, and overspeed training in steps 5, 6, and 7 (second eight weeks). You will not have time during the in-season period to improve these areas; your only hope then is to maintain them. Use the time wisely, and it will pay big dividends next season.

Your Preseason Program

Sample eight-week preseason programs are shown in tables 10.3 through 10.6 for football, baseball, basketball, and soccer. Athletes in other sports can devise their own program by completing the worksheet presented in appendix A. Plan to retest yourself at the end of the first eight-week period and again after completing four weeks of the second eight-week period. Use the speed profile form displayed in appendix B to chart your progress. Your coach will test you at the start of the in-season period. Take each training program seriously and practice proper nutrition during this critical improvement period. This is the key time for you to focus only on improving your speed in short distances. No other period of time allows you to totally devote your efforts to one objective. Make it pay off.

IN-SEASON SPEED IMPROVEMENT

The normal practice session during the in-season period in most sports is not long enough to bring about great improvement in most basic training areas. Coaches may also have difficulty deciding where to place the key supplementary programs that will prevent their athletes from losing much of their off-season gains. This section provides some guidelines for the proper placement of various training programs and a reasonable time frame that does not significantly detract from the practice schedule and still maintains off-season gains in speed, quickness, strength, power, flexibility, and speed endurance. Without a well-designed in-season program, it is quite common in most sports for athletes to lose a percentage of the gains acquired in the off-season period. Although additional improvement can also occur in an attempt to peak for a specific event at the latter part of the season, the primary objective of an in-season program is to prevent loss of strength, power, flexibility, speed endurance, speed, and quickness.

Order of Use During the In-Season

Fortunately, there is a logical order for coaches and athletes to follow during the in-season period. Let's review this order along with the purposes of each key training program because it is important for you to follow this sequence as closely as possible to get the full benefits of the program and to avoid injury and overtraining. Your coach should consider a similar order during the in-season period.

1. General warm-up (jogging, striding, and light sprinting) and flexibility training or stretching exercises have very little conditioning value. Their main contribution is to increase range of motion, help prevent injuries, and warm the body to prepare it for the more vigorous aspects of your program.

2. Overspeed training is specifically designed to improve your stride rate (number of steps per second) and stride length. Overspeed training should be scheduled second in the workout, immediately following your general warm-up period and stretching exercises, since it requires the complete absence of fatigue.

3. Scrimmage should follow overspeed training. Keep in mind that the body is still unfatigued, less apt to be injured, and more likely to execute skills at high speed under game conditions.

4. Drills, specific to your sport for the purpose of skill development if applicable and needed on a particular day, are fourth. At this point in the practice session, you are still relatively free from fatigue and can execute at high speed under game conditions.

5. Calisthenics are used to improve general conditioning, develop strength and muscular endurance, and improve aerobic fitness. They are conditioning-oriented and should not be at the beginning of your workout. Thirty minutes of hard calisthenics will only change a fresh athlete into a fatigued athlete. Such fatigue will interfere with skill and timing and make you more susceptible to injury.

6. Speed endurance training such as wind sprints and interval sprint training as commonly used in soccer, rugby, lacrosse, field hockey, football, baseball, and basketball is also a conditioning activity. Because such training brings about a high level of fatigue and makes it difficult to continue a workout much longer, speed-endurance training should be near the end of the workout, rather than at the beginning.

7. Ballistics can be incorporated here if practice time allows. Because this is also a conditioning activity, it should occur near the end of the workout.

TABLE 10.3

Sample Preseason Speed Improvement Program for Football Players

Phase	Week	Training programs	Length	Progression
Preparatory	3-8	Form training	25 minutes	Practice the start for your position for 8-10 minutes each workout along with the sprinting form drills described in chapter 8 (step 6). Have your coach re-evaluate your form in both the starting and the sprinting action.
		Overspeed	30 minutes	Continue with the progression described in the overspeed program in step 7. Work up to the highest number of repetitions. Begin the advanced overspeed program. Think turnover, shorten strides slightly on some repetitions.
		Football skill session	45 minutes	Integrate your newly found speed and quickness into football drills to improve your sports-specific skills.
Monday-Wednesday		Weight training	60+ minutes	Continue with the recommended methods given in steps 1 and 2 of the seven-step model. Be certain to explode through each repetition.
Wednesday at breakpoint		Sport loading		"Hillbursts" (2.5- to 7-degree stadium steps or hill) for 10 to 60 yards for four to six repetitions of 10-second bursts. Follow the recommendations given in step 5 of the seven-step model.
Tuesday-Thursday		Form training (starting and sprinting)	25 minutes	Speedform drills, acceleration, overspeed training.
		Football skill session		Integrate speed into your football drills.
		Sporting speed		(Tuesday) High-speed sprinting is the major objective; think speed and quickness as you work out; apply the methods described in step 6. (Thursday) Speed endurance is the major objective; use repeated high-speed sprints following the program described in step 6. Use some backward high-speed sprints on both a level surface and a slight incline to develop the hamstring muscle group.

(continued)

TABLE 10.3 *(continued)*

Phase	Week	Training programs	Length	Progression
		Sport loading	10-15 minutes	Follow the program described in step 5.
		Plyometrics	15-20 minutes	Continue the program described in step 4.
		Aerobics		(Thursday) 15-30 minutes of continuous work at your target heart rate.
Friday		Football skill session		Integrate speed into your football drills.
		Muscle endurance		Circuit weight training; do three sets at 50-85% RM, 8-12 repetitions, resting 15-40 seconds between exercises.
		Aerobics	15-30 minutes	15-30 minutes of continuous work at your target heart rate.
Saturday		Body control	160 minutes	Games, martial arts.
Sunday		Rest		
D-Day	0	Football practice begins		
Competition begins	1-2 prior	Super refueling program		These two weeks are necessary to allow your body to gain all the refueling benefits from your hard work to this point. Reduce the amount of work you do. Continue to include a few high-intensity workouts (speed and strength) to keep your high-quality edge. You want to begin your football season with enthusiasm; therefore, load your tanks both mentally and physically with rest and high-energy nutrition (see chapter 11).

Note: Each workout begins with a general warm-up period consisting of light jogging and striding until you are perspiring freely and body temperature has risen one or two degrees, a relaxed session of stretching exercises, and a series of walk-jog-stride-sprint cycles. Workouts end with a cool-down period. Retest yourself in your key weakness areas at the end of the preparatory period, just before D-Day.

TABLE 10.4

Sample Preseason Speed Improvement Program for Baseball Players

Phase	Week	Training programs	Length	Progression
Preparatory	3-8	Form training	25 minutes	Practice the start for your position for 8- to 10-minutes before each workout along with the form drills described in step 6. Work on the cross-over step, breaking right and left, and over-the-shoulder sprinting. Have your coach analyze your starting and sprinting form.
		Overspeed training	30 minutes	Continue with the progression described in the overspeed program in step 7. Work up to the highest number of repetitions before beginning the advanced program. Think turnover; shorten strides slightly on some repetitions.
		Baseball skill session	45 minutes	Integrate your newly found speed and quickness into baseball drills to improve your high-speed sports-specific skills.
Monday-Wednesday		Weight training	60+ minutes	Continue with the recommended methods given in steps 1 and 2 of the seven-step model. Be certain to explode through each repetition.
Wednesday at breakpoint		Sport loading	25 minutes	"Hillbursts" (2.5- to 7-degree stadium steps or hill) for 10 to 60 yards for four to six repetitions of 10-second bursts. Follow the recommendations in step 5.
Tuesday-Thursday		Form training (starting and sprinting)	25 minutes	Speedform drills described in step 6.
		Baseball skill session		Integrate speed into your baseball drills.
		Sporting speed	30 minutes	(Tuesday) High-speed sprinting is the major objective; think speed and quickness as you work out; apply the methods described in step 6. (Thursday) Speed endurance is the major objective; use repeated high-speed sprints following the program described in step 6.

(continued)

TABLE 10.4 (continued)

Phase	Week	Training programs	Length	Progression
				Use some backward high-speed sprints on both a flat surface and an incline to develop the hamstring muscle group.
		Sport loading	30 minutes	
		Plyometrics	10-15 minutes	Follow the program described in step 5 of the seven-step model.
		Aerobics	15-20 minutes	Continue the program described in step 4.
		Baseball skill session		(Thursday) 15-30 minutes of continuous work at your target heart rate. Integrate speed into your baseball drills.
		Muscle endurance	30+ minutes	Circuit weight training; do three sets at 50-85% RM, 8-12 repetitions, resting 15-30 seconds between exercises.
		Aerobics	15-30 minutes	15-30 minutes of continuous work at your target heart rate.
		Body control	160 minutes	Games, martial arts.
Sunday		Rest		
D-Day	0	Baseball practice begins		
Competition begins	1-2 prior	Super refueling program		These two weeks are necessary to allow your body to gain all the refueling benefits from your hard work to this point. Reduce the amount of work you do. Continue to include a few high-intensity workouts (speed and strength) to keep your high-quality edge. You want to begin your baseball season with enthusiasm; therefore, load your tanks both mentally and physically with rest and high-energy nutrition (see chapter 11).

Note: Each workout begins with a general warm-up period consisting of light jogging and striding until you are perspiring freely and body temperature has risen one or two degrees, a relaxed session of stretching exercises, and a series of walk-jog-stride-sprint cycles. Workouts end with a cool-down period. Retest yourself in your key weakness areas at the end of the preparatory period, just before D-Day.

TABLE 10.5

Sample Preseason Speed Improvement Program for Basketball Players

Phase	Week	Training programs	Length	Progression
Preparatory	3-8	Form training	25 minutes	Practice the speedform drills described in step 6. Work on the cross-over step, breaking right and left, and over-the-shoulder sprinting. Have your coach evaluate your form in both the starting (preparatory position for basketball) and sprinting action.
		Overspeed training	30 minutes	Continue with the progression described in the overspeed program in step 7. Work up to the highest number of repetitions before beginning the advanced program. Think turnover; shorten strides slightly on some repetitions.
		Basketball skills	45 minutes	Integrate your newly found speed and quickness into basketball skills.
Monday-Wednesday		Weight training	60+ minutes	Continue with the recommended methods described in steps 1 and 2 of the seven-step model. Be certain to explode through each repetition.
Wednesday at breakpoint		Sport loading	25 minutes	"Hillbursts" (2.5- to 7-degree stadium steps or hill) for 10 to 60 yards using four to six repetitions for 10-second bursts. Follow the program described in step 5.
Tuesday-Thursday		Form training (starting and sprinting)	25 minutes	Speedform drills.
		Basketball skills		Integrate speed into your basketball drills.
		Sporting speed	30 minutes	(Tuesday) High-speed sprinting is the major objective; think speed and quickness as you work out; apply the methods described in step 6. (Thursday) Speed endurance is the major objective; use repeated high-speed sprints following the program described in step 6. Use some backward high-speed sprints on both a level surface and an incline to develop the hamstring muscle group.

(continued)

TABLE 10.5 (continued)

Phase	Week	Training programs	Length	Progression
		Sport loading	30 minutes	Follow the program described in step 5.
		Plyometrics	10-15 minutes	Continue the program described in step 4 of the seven-step model. Emphasize the vertical leaps and bounds.
		Aerobics	15-20 minutes	(Thursday) 15-30 minutes of continuous work at your target heart rate.
		Basketball skills		Integrate speed into your basketball drills.
		Muscle endurance	30+ minutes	Circuit weight training; do three sets at 50-85% RM, 8-12 repetitions, resting 15-40 seconds between exercises.
		Aerobics	15-30 minutes	15-30 minutes of continuous work at your target heart rate.
		Body control	160 minutes	Games, martial arts.
Sunday		Rest		
D-Day	0	Basketball practice begins		
Competition begins	1-2 prior	Super refueling program		These two weeks are necessary to allow your body to gain all the refueling benefits from your hard work to this point. Reduce the amount of work you do. Continue to include a few high-intensity workouts (speed and strength) to keep your high-quality edge. You want to begin your basketball season with enthusiasm; therefore, load your tanks both mentally and physically with rest and high-energy nutrition (see chapter 11).

Note: Each workout begins with a general warm-up period consisting of light jogging and striding until you are perspiring freely and body temperature has risen one or two degrees, a relaxed session of stretching exercises, and a series of walk-jog-stride-sprint cycles. Workouts end with a cool-down period. Retest yourself in your key weakness areas at the end of the preparatory period, just before D-Day.

TABLE 10.6

Sample Preseason Speed Improvement Program for Soccer Players

Phase	Week	Training programs	Length	Progression
Preparatory	3-8	Form training	25 minutes	Practice the speedform drills described in step 6. Work on the cross-over step, breaking right and left, and over-the-shoulder sprinting. Have your coach re-evaluate your starting (preparatory position for soccer) and sprinting form.
		Overspeed training	30 minutes	Continue with the progression described in the overspeed program in step 7. Work up to the highest number of repetitions before beginning the advanced program. Think turnover; shorten strides slightly on some repetitions.
		Soccer skill session	45 minutes	Integrate your newly found speed and quickness into soccer to develop your sports-specific skill.
Monday-Wednesday		Weight training	60+ minutes	Continue with the recommended methods given in steps 1 and 2 of the seven-step model. Emphasize lower body weight training and neck, shoulder, and arm strength and power. Be certain to explode through each repetition.
Wednesday at breakpoint		Sport loading	25 minutes	"Hillbursts" (2.5- to 8-degree stadium steps or hill) for 10 to 60 yards using four to six repetitions for 10-second bursts. Follow the program described in step 5 of the seven-step model.
Tuesday-Thursday		Form training (starting and sprinting)	25 minutes	Speedform drills.
		Soccer skill session	25 minutes	Integrate speed into your soccer drills.
		Sporting speed	30 minutes	(Tuesday) High-speed sprinting is the major objective; think speed and quickness as you workout; apply the methods described in step 6 of the seven-step model.

(continued)

216

TABLE 10.6 *(continued)*

Phase	Week	Training programs	Length	Progression
				(Thursday) Speed endurance is the major objective; use repeated high-speed sprints following the program described in step 6 of the seven-step model. Use some backward high-speed sprints on both a level surface and an incline to develop the hamstring muscle group.
		Sport loading	30 minutes	Follow the program described in step 5 of the seven-step model.
		Plyometrics	10-15 minutes	Continue the program described in step 4 of the seven-step model. Emphasize the vertical leaps for heading and bounds for quick movements.
		Aerobics	15-20 minutes	(Thursday) 15-30 minutes of continuous work at your target heart rate.
		Soccer skill session		Integrate speed into your soccer drills.
		Muscle endurance	30+ minutes	Circuit weight training; do three sets at 50-85% RM, 8-12 repetitions, resting 15-40 seconds between exercises.
		Aerobics	15-30 minutes	15-30 minutes of continuous work at your target heart rate.
		Body control	160 minutes	Games, martial arts.
Sunday		Rest		
D-Day	0	Soccer practice begins		
Competition begins	1-2 prior	Super refueling program		These two weeks are necessary to allow your body to gain all the refueling benefits from your hard work to this point. Reduce the amount of work you do. Continue to include a few high-intensity workouts (speed and strength) to keep your high-quality edge. You want to begin your soccer season with enthusiasm; therefore, load your tanks both mentally and physically with rest and high-energy nutrition (see chapter 11).

Note: Each workout begins with a general warm-up period consisting of light jogging and striding until you are perspiring freely and body temperature has risen one or two degrees, a relaxed session of stretching exercises, and a series of walk-jog-stride-sprint cycles. Workouts end with a cool-down period. Retest yourself in your key weakness areas at the end of the preparatory period, just before D-Day.

8. Strength and power training (weight training, plyometrics, or sport loading) is the most fatiguing of any program. It leaves you weak and vulnerable to injury. It is therefore placed as the very last item in your workout.

9. A cool-down period is desirable and may involve a slow jog or walk and a relaxed, brief stretching period, particularly after a strength and power training session.

Although time becomes precious during the competitive season in most sports, it is not difficult to work with the maintenance loads shown in table 10.7 to prevent loss of speed.

TABLE 10.7

Maintenance Loads During the In-Season Period	
Quality	In-season maintenance loads
Flexibility	Two to three sessions weekly
Speed	Two one-half hour overspeed workouts per week (five to eight towing pulls each session)
Strength and power	One vigorous weight training workout weekly plus one plyometric session
Muscle bulk	Two weight training sessions weekly
Speed endurance	Two pick-up sprint training workouts weekly
Sport speed	Four or five practice sessions weekly in your specific sport

Maintenance Programs In the Practice Schedule

Only a slight adjustment and departure from the normal practice routine will be necessary to work the maintenance program into the regular practice schedule. To make this adjustment, coaches should consider the following:

1. Commit a part of each practice day to speed improvement.
2. Include testing at least twice per season in the major areas described in chapter 1 to locate weaknesses that are restricting fast and quick movement and preventing athletes from reaching their genetic speed potential.
3. Assign a sprint coach specifically to the task of testing. The track coach is generally an excellent choice.
4. Eliminate traditional wind sprints from the program; substitute one of the speed endurance programs described in chapter 8 that maintains adequate records and guarantees progress and improvement.

5. Use explosive power and strength training and overspeed training one to two times weekly to maintain the strength, power, quickness, and speed acquired during the preseason.
6. Use plyometric training no more than one to two times weekly (on days when maintenance weight training is not scheduled).
7. Use the speed improvement maintenance programs in the proper order.

Exactly how would this work in a scheduled practice session? Table 10.8 shows you the minimum times needed per session for each program and the order in which it should take place. As you can see, you can add speed improvement programs with only minor adjustments to the practice session.

TABLE 10.8

Practice Placement of Speed Improvement Training Programs During the In-Season Period in Team Sports

Time	Order	Program	Purpose	Comment
6-7 minutes	1	General warm-up, stretching exercises	Increased range of motion, warm-up effect, increased stride length	Mental preparation. Little conditioning value, warm up and complete flexibility routine without becoming fatigued
12-15 minutes	2	Overspeed training	Increased stride rate and length, improved acceleration	Short maintenance session while athletes are free from fatigue
75-120 minutes	3	Normal session in football, basketball, baseball, and other sports	Mastery of skills, strategy, and conditioning	Major portion of practice session
20 minutes	4	Calisthenics, speed endurance training	General conditioning	Major thrust of conditioning program
15-30 minutes	5	Weight training or plyometrics	Power, strength, acceleration	Two to three times weekly for improvement, once weekly to maintain

Speedweek

The Dallas Cowboys used a unique approach under Bob Ward, referred to as Speedweek, that they found easy for players to understand and apply and that was very effective. Speedweek divides each seven-day period into three phases, as described in the following sections.

© Terry Wild Studio

Early Non-Fatigued Phase (Monday, Tuesday, Wednesday Morning)

No leg work (strength and power training or endurance training) is permitted during this period. High-intensity work with overspeed training (tubing, downhill sprinting) dominates this three-day period while athletes are relatively fatigue-free. The proper order described previously is still followed. Upper body strength and power training takes place.

Late Fatigued Phase

This phase starts on Wednesday afternoon (breakpoint) and continues through Friday. Training now moves to strength and power training activities (sprint loading, weight training, plyometrics) and speed endurance. The final four to eight weeks of the preseason period, plyometrics involves only short jumps and hops of 30 to 50 meters at very high speed, as opposed to longer jumps at a moderate pace. Overspeed training is not used during this period. Again, the proper order described previously in this chapter is carefully followed.

Rest Period (Saturday)

A light workout is combined with team strategy sessions and one-on-one meetings with specialty coaches.

You are now ready to begin a personalized program designed specifically for you. Don't put it off. This is your chance to move to a higher level for your sport and significantly improve your speed and quickness. Take a serious approach and master every phase of the seven-step model. You will be amazed at the results.

CHAPTER 11

SPORTS SPEED NUTRITION

—by Barry Sears

Tell me what you eat and I will tell you what you are. —Anthelme Brillat-Savarin

Athletes, unlike average people, have uncommon goals and drives that keep pulling and stretching the limits of their souls, minds, and muscle functions. In doing the hard workouts necessary to reach these goals, athletes' systems must be able to operate at near maximum output over and over again. To do so, they have to stay in the Zone. Athletes often talk of the Zone as if it were some mystical, magical place. In reality, it is a hormonal zone, ultimately controlled by the diet. Therefore, for an athlete to be able to function within this zone, the biochemically run units of the body—the cells or power-houses—must be supplied with all the essential materials that are practical, healthy, and legal.

Sports nutrition is a far more complicated science than most athletes are led to believe, just as speed training is more complicated than doing drills and running wind sprints. In the past, sports nutrition has focused solely on the caloric aspects of the diet, such as the percentage of carbohydrates or fats deemed appropriate for an athlete. In reality, performance depends upon hormonal responses that are controlled by an adequate supply of water and macronutrients (proteins, carbohydrates, and fats) as well as micronutrients (vitamins, minerals, and phytochemicals).

Within the microenvironment of the cell, the biochemistry, molecular biology, immunology, and hormonal regulation will ultimately determine its maximum performance. Each of these factors is vitally important to any serious athlete. Macronutrients and micronutrients work together like a well-trained team. As maximum human performance is approached, the inadequacy of any single factor becomes the main limitation. The future of sports nutrition is likely to be focused on molecular factors within the microenvironment of the cell that can be supported and enhanced by diet. Of these molecular factors, it's the regulatory hormones' control as influenced by one's diet that can have the greatest impact. Your control of the diet in turn regulates hormonal responses that can dramatically improve your sports speed training or conversely retard your potential progress. Just as there is a training zone in which your progress reaches its maximum, there likewise is a hormonal zone within your cells in which you maximize your performance through your diet.

THE MACRONUTRIENTS

Unlike training, which is done periodically, eating occurs throughout the day. Every time you eat you start a new hormonal activation cascade that lasts for the next four to six hours. The balance of macronutrients (protein, carbohydrate, and fat) in a meal dictate the type of hormonal response that occurs four to six hours after that meal. The following sections explain how these macronutrients affect hormones.

How Carbohydrates Affect Hormones: Insulin

When you consume carbohydrates, they are broken down in the stomach and duodenum into simple sugars that can be absorbed. Because only simple sugars are absorbed by the body, terms such as *simple* and *complex carbohydrates* don't have much meaning in regard to macronutrition. What is important is the rate of entry for simple sugar into the bloodstream. As the rate of entry of these simple sugars increases, the release of the hormone called insulin increases as well. Insulin is an anabolic hormone in that it drives different nutrients to their respective storage sites. For instance, it drives sugar to the muscles and liver for storage as glycogen; it also drives amino acids to the muscles and drives fat to the adipose tissue for storage.

You need enough insulin to get nutrients to where they can be utilized for performance, but too much insulin in the bloodstream is like a loose hormonal cannon on the deck of a ship. That is, excess insulin drives down the blood sugar levels so low that the brain cannot function at peak efficiency. This hypoglycemic condition is commonly called *bonking*. Excess insulin also prevents the release of stored body fat for energy, forcing the muscles to use stored glycogen to a greater extent than should be required. Finally, excess insulin prevents the liver from restoring blood sugar levels to maintain a stable energy source for the brain. On the other hand, if insulin levels are too low, essential nutrients such as carbohydrates, amino acids, and fat will not be driven to their appropriate utilization sites. Therefore, there is an optimal insulin zone that you are trying to maintain by controlling the carbohydrate content of every meal.

How Proteins Affect Hormones: Glucagon

Just as insulin is stimulated by carbohydrates in a meal, protein primarily stimulates another hormone called glucagon that has the opposite effects of insulin. In many ways, the balance of protein and carbohydrates in a meal is like a hormonal carburetor. The ratio of carbohydrates to protein controls the relative levels of insulin to glucagon every time you eat. When this insulin to glucagon carburetor is fine-tuned, the body runs at a higher efficiency. Nutrients are being delivered (because of the correct levels of insulin) to the appropriate storage sites, and then being released (because of glucagon) due to increased demands by the muscles during training and competition. Excess glucagon (induced by eating excessive protein) stimulates a catabolic condition that ultimately reduces carbohydrate levels and eventually stimulates an abnormal metabolic state known as *ketosis*.

How Fats Affect Hormones: Eicosanoids and Essential Fatty Acids

Contrary to what is commonly believed, fats are exceptionally useful to athletes in training. First, they contain essential fatty acids, which are the building blocks for the most powerful hormones in the body, known as *eicosanoids*. Eicosanoids control oxygen transfer and the release of other hormones, such as growth hormone, that are required for optimal training, competition, and recovery. In addition, fats (especially monounsaturated fats) slow the entry of carbohydrates into the bloodstream from the intestines and thereby prevent insulin surges, which are contrary to optimal training.

THE DIETARY BALANCING ACT

Your diet is a constant balancing act of protein, carbohydrate, and fat to optimize the production of glucagon, insulin, and eicosanoids. The better you balance the diet, the better the resulting hormonal response. The better the hormonal response, the better your physical performance. Although you should try to maintain a consistent diet (and therefore a consistent hormonal environment), there are three distinct critical hormonal windows for maximizing performance:

1. The first of these windows is 30 to 45 minutes prior to exercise or competition. In this pre-exercise window, you should begin the hormonal changes that allow you to lower insulin and

therefore tap into your stored body fat more effectively. The number of calories consumed should be small (less than 100) so as not to divert any significant amount of energy toward digestion, but should provide enough protein and carbohydrate to begin changing hormonal levels prior to exercise. An example of a useful snack might be one ounce of turkey breast and half of a fruit.

2. The second hormonal window occurs immediately after exercise. Again, you want to have a small snack of approximately 100 calories to set the appropriate hormonal balance between insulin and glucagon for the maximum release of growth hormone that occurs 15 to 30 minutes after exercise.

3. The final window occurs in the two-hour time period after exercise. In this time frame, you want to eat a fairly large meal (but still maintain the appropriate hormonal balance) to replenish muscle glycogen levels more effectively.

All snacks or meals eaten within the three critical hormonal windows should have the same ratio of protein to carbohydrate to generate the optimal hormone response. The other meals eaten during the day should also have a similar protein-to-carbohydrate balance to maintain a consistent hormonal status within your body. To achieve maximum results, you have to treat eating as an integral part of your training process. The question is what is the appropriate balance? It's not based on any percentages, but is determined by the nutrient athletes neglect most: protein.

Your Protein Menu

No athlete should ever consume more protein than he or she needs, but to consume less is equivalent to protein malnutrition. Recent research has indicated that protein requirements, especially for athletes, are much higher than previously thought.

Protein requirements

1. If you are active (less than one hour of exercise per day, five times per week), you need 0.7 grams of protein per pound of weight.

2. If you are very active (one to two hours of exercise per day, five times per week), you need 0.8 grams of protein per pound of weight.

3. If you are doing heavy weight training or doing two workouts a day, five times per week, you need 0.9 grams of protein per pound of weight.

To calculate your daily protein requirement, multiply your lean body mass by the appropriate gram protein requirements for your listed activity level. For example, if you are doing the speed training outlined in this book, you will probably require about 0.8 grams of protein per pound of weight. If you weigh 160 pounds and have 12% body fat, you will require about 130 grams of protein per day.

One hundred and thirty grams of protein can be divided easily into three meals and two snacks per day. For the 160-pound athlete, this requirement could be met in three meals each consisting of 35 grams of protein and two snacks of 10 grams of protein each. Keep in mind that the human body can't metabolize more than 45 grams of protein at any one meal; if you eat more than that amount of protein at a meal, the excess gets converted into fat.

Excellent sources of low-fat protein include skinless chicken and turkey, very lean cuts of red meat, fish, egg whites, tofu, protein powder, or soybean products. Thirty-five grams of protein can be found in a five-ounce chicken breast, five ounces of sliced turkey, eight ounces of fish, ten egg whites, or two soybean hamburger patties.

Your Carbohydrates Menu

Now that you have your protein requirements, plan to consume about one-third more carbohydrates than protein at each meal. This amount equals about four grams of carbohydrates for every three grams of protein.

Remember that carbohydrates stimulate insulin, but too much insulin is detrimental to your performance. The importance of maintaining the correct amount of insulin is why the ratio of protein to carbohydrate is so critical. Not all carbohydrates are the same when it comes to insulin, however. Complex or starchy carbohydrates such as pasta, grains, cereals, and breads tend to stimulate insulin to greater degrees than fruit and vegetable sources of carbohydrates. The fiber in fruits and vegetables causes them to have a lower glycemic index. A lower glycemic index means that the carbohydrate enters the bloodstream more slowly, with a resulting decreased insulin response.

Therefore, you want the bulk of your carbohydrates to come from fruits and vegetables. Treat grains, cereals, bread, and pasta like condiments, not the main source of carbohydrates. Fruits and vegetables are also low-density carbohydrates as opposed to the high-density pastas, starches, and grains. Thus, you have to eat a lot of fruits and vegetables to adversely affect insulin levels. On the other hand, it is very easy to overconsume high-density carbohydrates and induce an adverse insulin response.

Good sources of 46 grams of low-density, low-glycemic carbohydrate might be (1) two pieces of fruit and a cup of steamed vegetables, (2) three cups of steamed vegetables and a piece of fruit, or (3) one cup of pasta and half of a piece of fruit. As you can see, you have to eat a lot of fruits and vegetables to get your carbohydrate needs.

Your Fat Menu

Fat is an exceptionally powerful hormonal modulator for the athlete, if the fat is primarily composed of monounsaturated fat. Therefore, you always want to add extra monounsaturated fat to each meal. Good sources of monounsaturated fat include olive oil, macadamia nuts, almonds, cashews, pistachios, avocados, and olives. Monounsaturated fat acts like a control rod in a nuclear reactor: It slows the rate of entry of carbohydrates (whatever their source) into the bloodstream, thereby reducing the extent of the insulin response. Fat also interacts with receptors in the stomach to send other hormonal signals to the brain to govern satiety so that you are not constantly hungry. In addition, fat supplies the building blocks for the most powerful hormone system for an athlete: eicosanoids. Table 11.1 shows the fat requirements for a 160-pound athlete.

TABLE 11.1

Diet Requirements* for a 160-Pound Athlete						
	Breakfast	Lunch	Snack	Dinner	Snack	Total
Protein:	35	35	10	35	10	125
Carbohydrates:	46	46	14	46	14	166
Fat:	16	16	3	16	3	54

*All measurements are in grams.

Your Total Menu

The content of one's diet influences the release and production of cell regulatory hormones. Table 11.1 includes fat requirements to show a balanced diet for the hypothetical 160-pound athlete. The balanced composition of this diet maximizes hormone responses that ultimately foster maximal athletic performance. Depending on your weight and physical activity level, you can construct an individualized hormonal-control menu using the outline in table 11.2.

TABLE 11.2

Individualized Hormonal-Control Menu					
	Breakfast	Lunch	Snack	Dinner	Snack	Total
30 percent protein:	_____	_____	_____	_____	_____	_____
40 percent carbohydrate:	_____	_____	_____	_____	_____	_____
30 percent fat:	_____	_____	_____	_____	_____	_____

The first thing in table 11.1 you will notice is that the optimal hormonal control diet suggested for the 160-pound athlete advocates less carbohydrate than has typically been recommended. But if you understand the importance of controlling insulin, the reduction in carbohydrates makes perfect sense. The table probably also suggests consuming more protein than you have been consuming. Yet many elite athletes tend to be protein-deficient for their level of activity. Finally, even with the extra fat, this is still a low-fat diet in terms of total grams of fat, according to U.S. government guidelines. Table 11.3 breaks down the requirements into actual meals.

Although this diet for the hypothetical 160-pound athlete is less than 2,000 calories, it would be difficult to consume all the food if the carbohydrate portion is mainly fruits and vegetables. Furthermore, any extra calories required for training would need to come from body fat. As a result, one doesn't need to consume excessive calories to maintain high physical performance. If you need more calories, add them as extra monounsaturated fats since this type of fat has *no* affect on insulin. As you can see from these meals, grains, starches, and breads are not the major component of a hormonal control diet. Remember to introduce any change in your eating habits at least one week prior to competition to give your body adequate time to adapt to these new hormonal changes.

Your Game Day Menu

The only difference on game day and the normal daily diet would be the following:

- Eat your last meal prior to the game at least three to four hours before the game.
- Eat a small hormone-balancing snack of less than 100 calories about 30 to 45 minutes before the game.
- Eat another hormone-balancing snack of 100 calories at halftime.

TABLE 11.3

Typical Meals for a 160-Pound Athlete

Breakfast

5" omelet (consisting of 1 egg and 4 egg whites, 2 oz. non-fat cheese, 2 tsp. olive oil)

1/2 cantaloupe

1 piece toast

Lunch

6 oz. of tuna fish with 2 tsp. mayonnaise

1 orange

1 apple

2 cups steamed vegetables

Afternoon snack

2 oz. sliced turkey

1 piece fruit

Dinner

5 oz. chicken breast

4 cups steamed vegetables

1 piece fruit

Late-night snack

2 oz. cottage cheese or 1 oz. sliced turkey

1/2 piece fruit

A suitable snack might be two hard-boiled egg whites and one-half piece of fruit.

KEEPING INSULIN AND GLUCAGON IN THE RIGHT ZONE

Now we have come full circle to why it is important to maintain the hormones insulin and glucagon in a tight zone. The degree of control of these two hormones (governed by the protein to carbohydrate ratio of your last meal) controls the activity of a key enzyme, delta-5-desatierose, that determines whether the body ultimately produces "good" or "bad" eicosanoids. Good eicosanoids increase oxygen transfer and bad eicosanoids decrease oxygen transfer. And oxygen transfer determines athletic performance regardless of the fuel source (carbohydrate or fat) being used by the muscles. This hormonal understanding begins to explain why no study in the sports medicine literature shows any improvement in performance following a high-carbohydrate diet compared to following a moderate-carbohydrate diet (like the one proposed), *if* each of the diets is held constant for more than seven days. Within seven days of any consistent dietary change, the body will make the necessary hormonal adjustment. Even though a high-carbohydrate diet will increase muscle glycogen levels, the corresponding increase in insulin levels triggers the increased production of bad eicosanoids, which decrease oxygen transfer. The net result is that the expected increase in performance due to increased muscle glycogen levels is never realized due to decreased oxygen transfer. For those athletes who are genetically sensitive to a high insulin response to carbohydrates, their athletic performance can be severely decreased on a high-carbohydrate diet.

The hormonal control program proposed in this chapter is neither a high-carbohydrate diet nor a low-carbohydrate diet. Because this dietary program consists of more carbohydrate than protein, it is best described as a carbohydrate-moderate program. The protein requirements are based on the athlete's need to maintain his or her existing muscle mass. Therefore, this diet should also be described as protein-adequate. Finally, fat (primarily monounsaturated fat) is added as a caloric ballast to maintain the necessary calories so that an athlete maintains himself or herself at a percent body fat in which he or she can compete and train most effectively. Because monounsaturated fat has no effect on insulin levels, its addition to the diet maintains a constant hormonal environment from meal to meal. This consistency of hormonal response allows the athlete to recover faster from one bout of exercise to another in addition to maximizing performance during training or competition.

You don't have to be mathematically precise with every meal to optimize your hormonal balance, although the better your balance of the ratio of protein to carbohydrates, the better the results. For most athletes, this balance can be achieved by following these guidelines:

- Eat more low-fat protein at meals.
- Cut back on pasta, cereals, grains, and breads.
- Eat more fruits and vegetables (remember, they are also carbohydrates).
- Don't be afraid to add monounsaturated fats to your diet.

Two other suggestions that have been shown to be of great value to entering and staying in the Zone are to make two lists:

- The low-fat protein foods you will eat
- The fruits and vegetables you will eat

These foods should be your primary choices at every meal. Just think of the analogy of a hormonal carburetor in which you are adjusting the balance of protein to carbohydrate to get the most appropriate hormonal response for the next four to six hours. How do you know if you are doing a good job? Listen to your body. If you're not hungry until five hours after a meal and have good mental focus, your last meal was hormonally correct. On the other hand, if you're hungry within two to three hours after a meal and have a low mental focus, you probably consumed too many carbohydrates relative to the amount of protein at your last meal.

Eventually, your eyes become your best tool. For any particular meal, look at the volume of the low-fat protein on your plate because it determines the amount of carbohydrate you can consume. If you're eating pasta, grains, starches, or breads, the volume of carbohydrate you eat should be the same size as the protein portion. If you're eating fruits and vegetables, you can eat twice as much protein. The secret is knowing when to stop eating carbohydrates.

PROPER HYDRATION FOR SPEED TRAINING

The most important nutrient for any athlete is water. An athlete can never drink enough of it. The fact that 75 to 85 percent of the body is water proves how vitally important water is for cellular life. Water's role in forming a gel in cells makes life possible. Dehydration is probably the greatest factor to adversely affect performance.

Practical experience and scientific studies support the following recommendations:

- Water at temperatures of 40 to 50 degrees Fahrenheit is most efficiently absorbed by the body.
- Drink at least eight 10-ounce servings of water per day.
- During exercise, drink water every 15 to 20 minutes.

Plain water provides the most effective results. Carbohydrate sports drinks have the effect of increasing insulin, and as discussed previously, excessive insulin formation is the worst hormonal enemy of any endurance or strength performance athlete.

LOSING AND GAINING WEIGHT

Athletes are just as obsessed about excess body fat as the rest of the population. The way to lose excess body fat is to lower insulin levels, which can be achieved by decreasing carbohydrate intake and increasing exercise output. The following actions will help you lower insulin levels:

- Do aerobic exercise (which, if done long enough, will lower insulin).
- Control your total amount of carbohydrate intake.
- Maintain adequate protein and monounsaturated fat intake.

Unfortunately, many athletes employ the starvation method and focus on eliminating all sources of fat, which includes protein. Such caloric thinking leads to hormonal disaster. The hormonally correct way to lose excess body fat is increased aerobic exercise coupled with tight insulin control using the diet. For the elite athlete, increased aerobic exercise is no problem. However, paying attention to diet requires some responsibility. It does you no good to do more aerobic exercise to lower insulin and then increase insulin by consuming excessive amounts of fat-free carbohydrates during the day.

Body Fat for Optimal Performance

Of course, it is possible to become too lean. For every sport, there is a zone of body fat percentage in which athletes will perform at an optimum level. If you are following the hormonal control diet described earlier in this chapter and find that your body fat percentage is dropping below a desired level, add more monounsaturated fat to your diet to increase your caloric intake and maintain your desired percent of body fat. If your body fat increases beyond a desired level, decrease the amount of added monounsaturated fat while maintaining the same protein-to-carbohydrate ratio.

Adding Muscle Mass

The other holy grail for athletes is adding new muscle mass. Athletes are lead to believe that they have to consume megadoses of extra protein to achieve that goal. In reality, the extra amount of required protein to build new muscle is surprisingly small. To build one pound of new muscle per month is a noble goal. However, realize that about 70 percent of the weight of muscle is water. This means that each pound (454 grams) of new muscle developed each month contains only 136 grams of extra protein. There are about 30 days in a month, so the extra protein beyond the amount required to maintain your existing muscle mass is something like five extra grams of protein per day. Of course, you still want to maintain the correct ratio of protein to carbohydrate, so you will need to adjust your carbohydrate portion to account for this extra protein.

The release of growth hormone from the pituitary gland coupled with testosterone transforms this extra protein into new muscle mass. Although you can't affect either hormone directly by the diet, you can use diet to set the appropriate micro-environment for the maximum release of growth hormone. The primary stimulus for the release of growth hormone is anaerobic training, such as speed training. Not surprisingly, insulin can have an adverse hormonal consequence on muscle mass development as it tends to block the release of growth hormone. Without adequate levels of growth hormone, maximum muscle building is impossible. Therefore, maximum new muscle development requires a hormonal control program to maintain insulin in a tight zone (not too high nor too low) coupled with a well-designed resistive training program. The other time growth hormone is released is during deep sleep just prior to REM sleep. For this reason, having a small hormonally balanced snack before you go to bed can also set the hormonal environment for maximum sleep-induced release of growth hormone for tissue repair following maximum effort and exhaustion.

Remember that muscle mass gain and excess body fat loss are both governed by hormonal events. Likewise, training and performance are governed by the same hormonal events. Your diet remains the primary tool to control these hormonal events. You have to eat, so you might as well eat smart. Seasoned athletes often note that intelligence and emotional maturity often determine the winner on the field of competition. Newly developing knowledge is putting an additional premium on mental preparation and intelligence for diet during training and before competition. These qualities can influence who gets the gold and who is split seconds behind with the silver.

For more sports nutrition information, contact Ward Enterprises at 11502 Valleydale Drive, Dallas, TX 75230.

DESIGNING YOUR OWN PLAYING SPEED IMPROVEMENT PROGRAM

Step 1: All possible weakness areas identified on your test score sheet (table 1.1) that relate to table 10.1 are listed below in the left column, How playing speed is improved. Check only the items where a weakness was found in your test scores.

How playing speed is improved	Specific training programs
Improve reaction time and starting ability ___ All athletes should make starting form training specific to their sport a regular part of the practice session at least twice weekly.	Starting form training for your sport Muscle balance training
Improve acceleration time ___ There was more than 0.7 seconds difference between your flying 40-yard dash and your stationary 40.	Starting form training Strength and power training Muscle balance training Overspeed acceleration training
Increase the length of your stride ___ Your stride length was less than recommended for your age and height.	Strength and power training Muscle balance training Plyometrics Sport loading Overspeed training Form training Flexibility training
Increase your stride rate* ___ Your stride rate was less than 4.5 steps per second. ___ Your percent of body fat exceeded 15 (men) or 20 (women).	Overspeed and advanced overspeed training Quick feet training Muscle balance training Consultation with parents and physician about possible loss of body fat
Increase your quickness ___ Your leg press/body weight score was less than 2.5 × your body weight. ___ Your hamstrings (leg curl) test score was less than 75 percent of your quadriceps (leg extension) score.	Quick feet training Ballistics Overspeed acceleration training Plyometrics Strength and power training

(continued)

How playing speed is improved	Specific training programs

___ Your right or left hamstring or quadriceps scores differed by more than 10 percent.

___ Your standing triple jump scores were below the standard for your age.

___ Your 20-yard single leg bound test scores were below the standard for your age.

___ Your quick feet test scores were below the standard for your age.

Improve your form and speed endurance

Form training
Speed endurance training
Ballistics
Sprint loading

___ Your flying 40-yard time was more than 0.2 seconds faster than your 80-120 yard time, or there was more than 0.2 seconds difference among the ten trials of the NASE repeated 40s test.

___ Your sit-and-reach test scores fell below the 75th percentile.

___ Sprint form errors were noted by you or your coach.

Step 2: To the right of each item you checked, circle the specific training programs listed. These are the programs you need to emphasize.

Step 3: Devise your personal program for your sport that emphasizes these programs using one of the models in tables 10.3 to 10.6.

Field hockey, lacrosse, rugby	Use the model in table 10.6.
Tennis, handball, racquetball, and squash	Use the model in table 10.5.
Softball	Use the model in table 10.4.

Step 4: Return to the section on "Your Preseason Program" in chapter 10 to refresh your memory on how to complete your program.

Step 5: Return to table 1.7 in chapter 1 to refresh your memory on the relative importance of each of the ways speed is improved for your specific sport. This information can help you determine how much emphasis you want to place on the improvement of a weakness area.

*All athletes should check this item and work on stride rate improvement regardless of their test scores.

YOUR SPEED PROFILE

Name:_____ Birth date:_____

Sport(s) and position:_____

Test weakness areas:_____

	Test date	Initial scores	1 month later	2 months later	3 months later
Sprinting speed:					
Stationary 40	_____	_____	_____	_____	_____
NASE 40	_____	_____	_____	_____	_____
Flying 40	_____	_____	_____	_____	_____
Acceleration	_____	_____	_____	_____	_____
80-120	_____	_____	_____	_____	_____
Speed endurance	_____	_____	_____	_____	_____
Stride:					
Stride rate	_____	_____	_____	_____	_____
Stride length	_____	_____	_____	_____	_____
Strength:					
Leg press/ weight ratio	_____	_____	_____	_____	_____
Leg extension (quadriceps)	_____	_____	_____	_____	_____
Leg curl (hamstring)	_____	_____	_____	_____	_____
Hamstring/ quadriceps ratio	_____	_____	_____	_____	_____

(continued)

	Test date	Initial scores	1 month later	2 months later	3 months later
Power and quickness:					
Standing triple	_____	_____	_____	_____	_____
Quick hands test	_____	_____	_____	_____	_____
Quick feet test	_____	_____	_____	_____	_____
Flexibility:					
Sit-and-reach	_____	_____	_____	_____	_____
Pass/fail tests	_____	_____	_____	_____	_____
Body composition:					
Percent body fat	_____	_____	_____	_____	_____
Muscle balance	_____	_____	_____	_____	_____
Height	_____	_____	_____	_____	_____
Weight	_____	_____	_____	_____	_____

BIBLIOGRAPHY

Albert, M. 1991. *Eccentric muscle training in sports and orthopaedics.* New York: Churchill Livingstone.

Albert, M., S.S. Hillegass, and D. Spiegel. 1994. Muscle torque changes caused by inertial impulse exercise training. *Journal of Sport and Physical Therapy* 20(5):254-261

Anderson, P., and J. Kenriksson. 1975. Training induced changes in the subgroups of human Type II skeletal muscle fibers. *Acta Physiologica Scandinavica* 99:123-125.

Baechle, T., ed. 1994. *Essentials of Strength Training and Conditioning.* Champaign, IL.: Human Kinetics.

Baechle, T., and R.W. Earle. 1989. *Weight Training: A Text Written for the College Student.* Omaha: Creighton University.

Beaulieu, J.E. 1981. Developing a stretching program. *The Physician and Sportsmedicine* 9(11):59-69.

Berger, R. 1972. Strength improvement. *Strength and Health* (August):44-45, 70-71.

Blattner, S., and L. Noble. 1979. Relative effects of isokinetic and plyometric training on vertical jumping performance. *Research Quarterly* 50(4):583-588.

Bosco, C. 1985. Adaptive response of human skeletal muscle to simulate hypergravity condition. *Acta Physiologica Scandinavica* 124(4):507-513.

Bosco, C., H. Rosko, and J. Hirvonen. 1986. The effect of extra-load conditioning on muscle performance in athletes. *Medicine and Science in Sport and Exercise* 18(4):415-419.

Bosco, C., S. Zanon, H. Rosko, A. Dal-Monte, P. Bellotti, F. Latteri, N. Candeloro, E. Locattelli, E. Azzaro, R. Pozzo. 1984. The influence of extra load on the mechanical behavior of skeletal muscle. *European Journal of Applied Physiology* 53(2):149-154.

Burkett, L. 1970. Causative factors in hamstring strains. *Medicine and Science in Sports and Exercise* 2:39-42.

Chu, D. 1983. Plyometrics: The link between strength and speed. *NSCA Journal* 5(2):20-21.

Chu, D. 1992. *Jumping Into Plyometrics.* Champaign, IL: Human Kinetics.

Clarke, D., and F. Henry. 1961. Neuromotor specificity and increased speed from strength development. *Research Quarterly* 32:315-325.

Costello, F. 1985. Training for speed using resisted and assisted methods. *NSCA Journal* 7(1):74-75.

Davis, G., D. Kirkendall, D. Leigh, M. Lui, T. Reinbold, and R. Wilson. 1981. Isokinetic characteristics of professional football players: Normative relationships between quadriceps and hamstring muscle groups and relative to body weight. *Medicine and Science in Sports and Exercise* 13:76.

Dibrezzo, R., B. Gench, M. Hinson, and J. King. 1985. Peak torque values of the knee extensor and flexor muscles of females. *Journal of Orthopedics Sports and Physical Therapy* 7:65-68.

Dintiman, G. 1964. The effects of various training programs on running speed. *Research Quarterly* 35:456-463.

Dintiman, G. 1966. The relationship between the leg strength/body weight ratio and running speed. *The Bulletin of the Connecticut Association for Health, Physical Education, and Recreation* 11:5.

Dintiman, G. 1968, 1985. A survey of the prevalence, type, and characteristics of supplementary training programs used in major sports to improve running speed. Richmond, VA: Virginia Commonwealth University.

Dintiman, G. 1970. *Sprinting Speed: Its Improvement for Major Sports Competition.* Springfield, IL: Charles C Thomas.

Dintiman, G. l974. *What Research Tells the Coach About Sprinting.* Reston, VA: AAHPER.

Dintiman, G. 1980. The effects of high-speed treadmill training upon stride length, stride rate, and sprinting speed. Unpublished work. Virginia Commonwealth University.

Dintiman, G. 1980. *How to Sprint Faster: A Do-It-Yourself Book for Athletes in All Sports.* Richmond, VA: Champion Athlete.

Dintiman, G. 1984. *How to Run Faster: Step-By-Step Instructions on How to Increase Foot Speed.* Champaign, IL: Leisure Press.

Dons, B., K. Bollerup, F. Bonde-Peteron, and S. Hancke. 1979. The effect of weightlifting exercise related to muscle fiber composition and muscle cross-sectional area in humans. *European Journal of Applied Physiology* 40:95-106.

Douillard, J. 1995. *Body, Mind, and Sport: The Mind-Body Guide to Lifelong Fitness, and Your Personal Best.* New York: Crown.

Figoni, S., C.B. Christ, and B.H. Mossey. 1988. Effects of speed, hip, knee angle, and gravity on hamstring to quadriceps torque ratios. *Journal of Orthopedics Sports and Physical Therapy* 9(8):287-291.

Fox, E.L. 1979. *Sports Physiology.* Philadelphia: Saunders.

Friedl, K.E., R.J. Moore, and L.J. Marchitelli. 1992. Steroid replacers: Let the athlete beware. *NSCA Journal* 14(1):14-19.

Fugl-Meyer, A.R., L. Gustafsson, and Y. Burstedt. 1992. Isokinetic and static plantar flexion characteristics. *European Journal of Applied Physiology* 45:221-234.

Gambetta, V. 1978. Plyometric training. *Track and Field Quarterly Review* 80(4):56-57.

Gardner, J., and J. Purdy. *Computerized Running Training Programs.* TAFNEWS Press, P.O. Box 296, Los Altos, CA, 94022.

Garhammer, J.G. 1985. Biomechanical profiles of Olympic weight lifters. *International Journal of Sport Biomechanics* 1:122-130.

Getchell, B. 1979. *Physical Fitness: A Way of Life.* New York: Wiley.

Gilliam, T.B., S.P. Sady, P.S. Freedon, and J. Valamacci. 1979. Isokinetic torque levels for high school football players. *Archives of Physical Medicine and Rehabilitation* 60:110-114.

Grace, T., E.R. Sweetser, M.A. Nelson, L.R. Ydens, and B.J. Skipper. 1984. Isokinetic muscle imbalance and knee joint injuries. *Journal of Bone and Joint Surgery* 66A:734.

Grimby, G. 1993. Clinical aspects of strength and power training. In *Strength and Power in Sport*, edited by P. Komi, 338-354. London: Blackwell Scientific.

Häkkinen, K., and P.V. Komi. 1982. Specificity of training-induced changes in strength performance considering the integrative functions of the neuromuscular system. *World Weightlifting* 3:44-46.

Hatfield, F., and M. Yessis. 1986. *Plyometric Training: Achieving Explosive Power in Sports.* Canoga Park, CA: Fitness Systems.

Henry, F. 1960. Factorial structure of speed and static strength in a lateral arm movement. *Research Quarterly* 31:440-447.

Henry, F. 1960. Increased response latency for complicated movements and a memory drum theory of neuromotor reaction. *Research Quarterly* 31:448-458.

Herman, D. 1976. The effects of depth jumping on vertical jumping and sprinting speed. Unpublished master's thesis. Ithaca, NY: Ithaca College.

Hill, A.V. 1970. *First and Last Experiments in Muscle Mechanics.* London: Cambridge University Press.

Hilsendager, D., M.H. Strow, and K.J. Acklerman. 1969. Comparison of speed, strength, and agility exercises in the development of agility. *Research Quarterly* 40:71-75.

Holt, L.E. 1976. *Scientific Stretching for Sport.* Halifax, Nova Scotia: Sport Research.

Housh, T.J., W.G. Thorland, G.O. Tharp, G.O. Johnson, and C.J. Cisar. 1984. Isokinetic leg flexion and extension strength of elite adolescent female track and field athletes. *Research Quarterly* 55:347-350.

Hunter, S., T.E. Cain, and C. Henry. 1979. Preseason isokinetic knee evaluation in professional football athletes. *Athletic Training* 14:205-206.

Jordan, J. 1969. Physiological and anthropometrical comparisons of negroes and whites. *Journal of Health, Physical Education, and Recreation* 40:93-99.

Klein, K., and F. Allman. 1970. *The Knee in Sports.* Baltimore: Williams & Watkins.

Klinzing, J. 1984. Improving sprint speed for all athletes. *NSCA Journal* 6(4):32-33.

Korchemny, R. 1985. Evaluation of sprinters. *NSCA Journal* 7(4):38-42.

Laird, D.E. 1981. Comparison of quadriceps to hamstring strength ratios of an intercollegiate soccer team. *Athletic Training* 16:666-667.

Leimohn, W. 1978. Factors related to hamstring strains. *Journal of Sports Medicine* 18:71-76.

Letter, W. 1960. Relationships among reaction times and speeds of movement in different limbs. *Research Quarterly* 31:141-155.

Luhtanen, P., and P.V. Komi. 1978. Mechanical factors influencing running speed. In *Biomechanics VI-B*, 23-29, edited by E. Asmussen and E. Jorgensen. Baltimore: University Park Press.

Malan, E. 1960. The effects of rest following warm-up upon physical performance. Proceedings of the College Physical Education Association, 63:45.

Mann, R. 1984. Speed development. *NSCA Journal* 5(6):12-20, 72-73.

Masley, J., A. Hairabedian, and D. Donaldson. 1953. Weight training in relation to strength, speed, and coordination. *Research Quarterly* 24:308-315.

Matveyev, L. 1983. *Fundamentals of Sports Training.* Moscow: Progress Publishers.

McFarland, B. 1984. Speed: Developing maximum running speed. *NSCA Journal* 6(5):24-28.

McFarland, B. 1985. Special strength: Horizontal or vertical. *NSCA Journal* 7(1):64-66.

Meriam, J. 1978. *Engineering Mechanics. Vol. 2: Dynamics.* New York: Wiley.

Moore, J., and G. Wade. 1989. Prevention of anterior cruciate ligament injuries. *NSCA Journal* 11(3):35-40.

Moore, M.A., and R.S. Hutton. 1980. Electromyographic investigation of muscle stretching techniques. *Medicine and Science in Sports and Exercise* 12(5):322-329.

Ostemig, L.R., J.A. Sawhill, B.T. Bates, and J. Hamill. 1981. Function of limb speed on torque ratios of antagonist muscles and peak torque joint position. *Medicine and Science in Sports and Exercise* 13:107.

Parker, M.G., D. Holt, E. Bauman, M. Drayna, and R.O. Ruhling. 1982. Descriptive analysis of bilateral quadriceps and hamstring muscle torque in high school football players. *Medicine and Science in Sports and Exercise* 14:152.

Pauletto, B. 1986. Let's talk training: Periodization-peaking. *NSCA Journal* 8(4):30-31.

Pauletto, B. 1986. Rest and recuperation. *NSCA Journal* 8(3):52-53.

Powers, S.K., and E.T. Howley. 1990. *Exercise Physiology.* Dubuque, IA: Brown.

Reser, J. 1961. The effects of increased range of motion on vertical jump. Master's thesis. Los Angeles: University of California.

Rogers, J. 1967. A study to determine the effect of the weight of football uniforms on speed and agility. Master's thesis. Springfield, IL: Springfield College.

Sale, D.G., J.D. MacDougall, S.E. Alway, and J.R. Sutton. 1983. Muscle cross-sectional area, fiber type distribution, and voluntary strength in humans (abstract). *Canadian Journal of Applied Sports Science* 2:21.

Schlinkman, B. 1984. Norms for high school football players derived from Cybex data reduction computer. *Journal of Orthopedics Sports and Physical Therapy* 5:410-412.

Seyle, H. 1978. *The Stress of Life,* revised edition. New York: McGraw-Hill.

Smith, D.H., H.A. Quinney, H.A. Wenger, R.D. Steadward, and J.R. Sexsmith. 1981. Isokinetic torque outputs of professional and elite amateur ice hockey players. *Journal of Orthopedics Sports and Physical Therapy* 3:42-47.

Smith, L. 1961. Individual differences in strength, reaction latency, mass, and length of limbs and their relation to maximal speed of movement. *Research Quarterly* 32:208-220.

Spassov, A. 1989. Bulgarian training methods. Paper presented at the symposium of the National Strength and Conditioning Association in Denver, CO, June.

Stone, M.H., H. O'Bryant, and J.G. Garhammer. 1981. A hypothetical model for strength training. *Journal of Sports Medicine and Physical Fitness* 21:342-351.

Stull, A.G., ed. 1980. *Training, Environment, Nutrition and Fitness.* Vol. II. of *Encyclopedia of Physical Education, Fitness, and Sports,* edited by T. Cureton. Salt Lake City, UT: Brighton.

Thomas, L. 1984. Isokinetic torque levels for adult females: effects of age and body size. *Journal of Orthopedics Sports and Physical Therapy* 6:21-24.

Verkhoshanski, Y. 1973. Depth jumping in the training of jumpers. *Track Technique* 51:1618-1619.

Ward, B., and G.B. Dintiman. 1986. *Speed and Explosion Consultant Manual.* National Association of Speed and Explosion, Box 1975, Nags Head, NC, 27959.

Ward, B., and G.B. Dintiman. 1987. *Speed and Explosion* (60:00 videocassette). National Association of Speed and Explosion, Box 1975, Nags Head, NC, 27959.

Ward, P.E., and R.D. Ward. 1991. *Encyclopedia of Weight Training.* Laguna Hills, CA: QPT.

Wathen, D. 1993. NSCA position stand: Explosive/plyometric exercises. *NSCA Journal* 15(3):16.

Weiss, L. 1991. The obtuse nature of muscular strength: The contribution of rest to its development and expression. *Journal of Applied Sports Science Research* 5(4):219-227.

Willgoose, C. 1950. Relationship of muscular strength to motor coordination in the adolescent period. *Journal of Educational Research* 44:142.

Williams, M. 1995. *Nutrition for Fitness and Sport.* 4th ed. Dubuque, IA: Brown.

Wilmore, J., and D. Costill. 1994. *Physiology of Sport and Exercise.* Champaign, IL: Human Kinetics.

INDEX

Acceleration, 32, 169
Acceleration and mass, 88-89
Advanced testing program, 32-35
Arm action in sprinting, 173, 175-176

Ballistics, 116-121
  maintaining equilibrium: flow, 117
  noting performance and skills, 118
  tight spots, escaping and avoiding, 120-121
Ballistics training, 118-120
Basic testing program
  illustrated, 35-42
  test score sheet for, 4-9
Basic training
  core activities for, 56-57
  defined, 52
  flexibility principles for, 78-83
  general preparation, 56-57
  identifying core activities, 56
  organizing, 74-78
Basic training sports check
  measuring performance specifics, 57-58
  scorecard for, 58-60
  sport-specific tasks, 60-65
Biomechanics, 49-50, 53
Body composition, 25-29
Body control, 47-48, 69
Bounding drills for sprinting form, 181-182
Brain training, 47-48, 66-69, 117

Carbohydrates, effect on hormones, 222-223
Cardiovascular and respiratory fitness, 47
Combat breathing, 48-49, 65
Cool-down period, 83

Downhill sprinting for overspeed training, 193-195
Driving power, 70

Eicosanoids, 223, 229
Energy-absorbing capabilities of body tissues, 117
Energy management, 117-118
Explosive close-range movement, training for, 169
Explosive power and quickness tests, 20-25
Explosive strength, 123, 123-124

Fat
  body fat percentage for optimal performance,
    231-232
  as percentage of body weight, 28
Fats, effect on hormones, 233
Flexibility
  exercises to increase, 82-83
  joint-specific nature of, 15
  need for, 81
  principles of, 78-83
  proprioceptive neuromuscular facilitation
    (PNF), 80
  and stretching, 78-81
Flexibility tests, 15, 17-19
Flow state, 66-67, 117
40-yard dash, 177-180
Functional strength performance standards, 103

Functional strength program
  purpose of, 86-87
  sample programs, 100-102

Glucagon, 223, 229

Hamstring/quadriceps strength, 11-14
Harnesses, 164-165
High-speed energy system, maximizing, 50
High-speed quickness, 70-71
High-speed stationary cycling, 194, 195
Hormones
  diet influencing, 222-230, 231-233
  eicosanoids, 223, 229
  glucagon, 223, 229
  growth hormones and testosterone, 232
  insulin. See Insulin
Hydration, 230-231

Inertial impulse, 90-91
Inertial impulse machines, 90
Injury protection, 48-49, 86-87
Insulin, 222-223, 225, 226, 227, 229-230

Leg press/body weight ratio, 10-11
Locomotor skills, 55

Mass and acceleration, 88-89
Maximum playing speed, 71
Motorvator game, 68-69
Movement, purposes of, 116
Muscle balance tests, 33-34
Muscle fiber types, 22
Muscle mass, adding, 232-233

NASE Future 40, 32-33
NASE repeated 40s, 10
Neural pathways, training, 47-48
Neuromuscular training, 191
Non-locomotor skills, 55

Olympic lifts, 91-98
On-field analysis (playing speed), 35
Overspeed training
  advanced techniques, 204
  effect on neuromuscular system, 191
  guidelines for, 192-193
  importance of, 204
  programs compared, 194
  purpose of, 191
  types of, 193-204

Parachutes, 165-166
Personal training program
  designing, 35-42, 205-220
  eating as an integral part of, 224
  in-season speed improvement, 208-209, 218-220
  maintenance programs in the practice schedule,
    218-220
  preseason speed improvement, 205-208
  sample preseason programs, 208, 209-217
  sprinting speed improvement, 206

Plyometrics
  to develop speed strength, 123-124
  exercises and drills, 131-156
  guidelines for, 125-126
  how plyometric training works, 122-126
  objectives of, 123-124
  safety precautions for, 126-127
  sample programs, 129, 130
  workout characteristics of, 128-130
Power, relationship with work, 87-88
Power exercises, Olympic lifts, 91-97
Power output, 47, 88
Power sprint, training for, 169-170
Power start, training for, 169
Proprioceptive neuromuscular facilitation, 80
Proteins, effect on hormones, 233
Pro-Think Motorvator game, 68-69

Quick feet, 23
Quick hands, 21-22

Resource thresholds, 50-51
Right and left leg hops, 24

Sand runs, 166, 168
Seven-step model
  ballistics, 116-112
  basic training, 52, 55-84
  improving biomechanics, 49-50
  introduced, 45-52
  knowing your resource thresholds, 50-51
  overspeed training, 191-204
  plyometrics, 122-156
  principles of, 47-51
  speed endurance training, 188-190
  sport loading, 157-170
  sprinting form and speed endurance, 171-190
  strength and power training, 85-115
  training with, 53-54
Speed
  assessing, 1-44
  sport-specific, 42-44
Speed endurance, 188-190
Speed improvement
  attack areas for team sports, 43
  designing your personal program, 35-42, 206-220
  improving sprinting speed, 206
  seven-step model introduced, 45-52
  training programs, practice placement of, 219
Speed strength, plyometrics improving, 123-124
Speedweek, 97, 219-220
Sport hitting power, 69-70
Sport loading
  defined, 157
  equipment for, 160-166, 168-169
  purpose of, 157-160
  and training objectives, 169-170
  when to use, 169-170
Sports nutrition
  carbohydrates menu, 225-226
  dietary balancing act, 223-228
  fat menu, 226
  game day menu, 228
  hormones influenced by diet, 221-230, 231-233

  importance of proper hydration, 230-231
  insulin and glucagon, control of, 229-230
  protein menu, 224-225
  timing of meals and exercise, 223-224
  total menu, 227-228
  weight, losing and gaining, 231-233
Sport-specific speed
  improving, 42-44
  sample programs for, 210-217
Sport-specific tasks, 60-65
Sports tasks, 116
Sprinting, biomechanics of, 53
Sprinting form and speed endurance
  drills for, 181-188
  importance of correct form, 176
  improving speed endurance, 188-189
  sharpening your 40-yard dash, 176-179
  troubleshooting sprinting mechanics, 180
Sprinting speed
  improvement, 206
  stride length and frequency, 172, 174
  tests, 2-3, 10
Sprint loading, 198
Sprint Master, 199-201
Stadium stairs, 166, 168
Standing triple jump, 20-21
Starting power, 70
Starting strength, 123, 123-124
Strength, questions about, 51
Strength and power training
  acceleration or mass?, 88-89
  exercises for, 104-115
  functional strength program, 86-87, 98-111
  inertial impulse, 90-91
  relationship of work and power, 87-88
  sample power output program, 97-98
  work fast to be fast, 89
Strength curve testing, 35
Strength tests, 10-14
Stretching, 78-81
Stride cycle, 173, 174-175
Stride length test, 14-15
Stride rate
  figuring, 29-32
  increasing with overspeed training, 191
Stride rate matrix, 30-31
Sustained power output-endurance base, 72-74

Team sports, sport-specific attack areas for, 43
Tight spots, escaping and avoiding, 120-121
Towing for overspeed training, 194, 196-201
Treadmill sprinting, 194, 202-203

Ultra Speed Pacer, 199
Uphill sprinting, 166, 167

Warm-up, 74-78
Weight, losing and gaining, 231-233
Weighted body suits, 160
Weighted sleds, 166, 168-169
Weighted vests, 160-164
Work and power relationship, 87-88
Workout drills for sprinting form, 184-188

"Zone, the", 66-67, 117, 221

ABOUT THE AUTHORS

George B. Dintiman has more than 30 years experience improving athletes' speed—from beginners to the pros. The author of 30 books and three videos on speed improvement and health and wellness, Dintiman also is an NFL speed consultant and an internationally recognized authority on speed improvement for team sports.

A Little All-American running back at Lock Haven University in 1957, Dintiman set more than 15 rushing and scoring records, four of which remained in place prior to the 1996 season. He was a draft choice of the NFL Baltimore Colts and the CFL Montreal Alouettes in 1958. He was also a star for Lock Haven's basketball and track teams.

Dintiman received an EdD from the Teachers College of Columbia University in 1964. In 1993 he was an inductee of the Pennsylvania Sports Hall of Fame, Capital Area Chapter. He is a board member of the International Sports Science Association and is president of the National Association of Speed and Explosion. His leisure activities include writing, tennis, jogging, and weight training.

Bob Ward is a sport scientist who was conditioning coach for the Dallas Cowboys from 1976 to 1990. He is currently a sports research consultant in Dallas, primarily at Mannatech, Inc.

Ward became aware of the need for sports conditioning while competing as an athlete in football and track. In 1954 he was an NAIA All-American fullback of Whitworth College in Spokane, Washington.

Ward has coached several Olympic champions and numerous championship football and track teams. During his tenure as coach at Fullerton College, athletes set national records in the high hurdle relay, the discus, and the hammer throw.

Ward has authored other books on sport speed and has lectured extensively on conditioning, track and field, and nutritional support for athletes. He developed a software program currently used in the NFL and at many colleges and along with NFL Hall-of-Famer Randy White and world-class martial artist Valentine Espiriceuta, Ward also developed a sports martial arts video, *Creating Big Plays.*

Ward received a PED from Indiana University in 1973. He is a member of the National Strength and Conditioning Association. He and his wife Joyce, a drama and dance teacher, live in Dallas.

Tom Tellez has 38 years of coaching experience as a track coach. As sprint coach for the Santa Monica Track Club, he has trained world-record holders Carl Lewis and Leroy Burrell and Olympic 200-meter winners Mike Marsh and Joe DeLoach.

Tellez is currently the head men's and women's track and field and cross-country coach at the University of Houston, where he has coached since 1976. He was an assistant track coach in field events from 1968 to 1976 at UCLA, which won consecutive NCAA championships from 1971 to 1973.

A member of United States Track and Field and the NCAA Coaches Association, Tellez was head men's coach for USA teams at the 1991 World Championships. He has also coached USA teams in Pan American competition.

Tellez's favorite leisure activities include jogging and horseback riding. He and his wife Kaye live in Houston.

More resources for a better way to train

1996 • Paper • 200 pp
Item PCHU0643
ISBN 0-87322-643-7
$15.95 ($23.95 Canadian)

(Approx 40-minute videotape)

1997 • 1/2" VHS
Item MHKV0739
ISBN 0-88011-739-7
$19.95 ($29.95 Canadian)

Prices are subject to change.

To request more information or to place your order, U.S. customers call
TOLL-FREE 1-800-747-4457. Customers outside the U.S. use
appropriate number/address shown in the front of this book.

Human Kinetics
The Premier Publisher for Sports & Fitness
http://www.humankinetics.com/